Getting Real

Kimbell R.Vincent

PRINTING HISTORY
First edition 2004
Second edition 2011

For further information contact
Tymly Books, 230 Bowlsby Street,
Nanaimo, B.C. V9R 5K1
Tel. 250-755-1118

For more information on Kim Vincent
please visit our website at tymlybooks.com

ISBN-13: 978-1468085464

ISBN-10: 1468085468

Printed in Canada

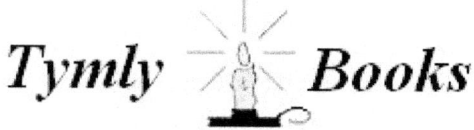

GETTING REAL

Forward

Personal reality is a form of solitary confinement from which the world is glimpsed through peepholes. This book is dedicated to those who want to see more. Like birds born in a cage, the only reason we don't fly is because we think we can't. The object of getting real is to check out our God-given wings, then discover the door that society left ajar and, finally, to explore the world in all its glory.

Getting Real has involved a lifetime of soul-searching, of wading through the hype and heavies, most of the time bogged down by personal screw-ups and preconceived ideas. Finally, I am faced with the realization that most of my presumptions were just that. Reality, it turns out, is more than I thought.

The goal of this book is twofold: To establish prerequisites for the development of expanded awareness, and to serve as a source of reference for the paranormal. Here and there, I've got my own two-cents worth in too – that's kind'a the fun part. But you'll sort it out, and in doing so maybe we'll catch an updraft together.

CHAPTER ONE
BOOTING UP

The operating system

When you were born you came equipped with the fastest computer in the world. It was packed in a shock-absorbent case and had a 100 year power supply. It weighed 390g (14 ounces) and came complete with a bio-mechanical harddrive of virtually unlimited capacity, a stereo receiving system, a syntax translator, audio capability, a graphics analyzer and the most advanced anti-virus protection in the world. All you had to do was figure out how to use it. As a result of constant upgrading, it now has over three times its original capacity; it weighs 1,315g (46oz.) and is driven by 100 billion brain neurons flashing signals across an enormously greater number of synapses. Just the neurons in the circuitry, if placed end-to-end, would reach the moon. Access to this computer is via the convoluted mantle covering the frontal lobe of your head, where neuronal centers are clustered for the processing and understanding of language, conceptualization, abstraction and judgment. You have the finest networking system ever conceived, providing, of course, that its programmed right.

Considering that you didn't have an owner's manual, you did a pretty good job of programming. You relied on instinct, observation, the examples of others and lots of help, whether qualified or not. In essence you did exactly what you were told to do, then sorted out the mish-mash through trial and error, a process called learning. The sum total of everything you learned is what you call reality. But, because your operating system is distinctly yours, and because you learn in your own unique way, you are different. In fact, what you call reality is different too. It is a virtual world entirely of your own making. In it, you see only what is real to you.

The same is true for everyone, of course. No two people see things exactly alike, because their reality is not exactly alike. But we try. Bridging the gap is called communication. Even then, the words we use mean something slightly different to each of us. They only approximate what we are trying to say.

Eventually, several problems emerge, the most glaring being that most people don't seem to know who they really are or why. That's a big statement and easily refuted, since we're programmed not to know the answers. Finding out is the Holy Grail of being, the mythical quest of all time. That's what Getting Real is all about.

Initially, every precept that went into your programming was based on the reality of others. Added to that, it was conveyed to you by the use of language. The net effect is like trying to send an encyclopedia by smoke signals. What we call understanding is the measure of how successful we are in deciphering the intended message. Unfortunately, the mode of transmission and reception leaves a great deal to be desired for both the sender and receiver. It is not merely an imperfect system, it's clumsy and fraught with errors – mine, yours, and those of everyone who has ever impressed us. The end result shows up in personality, behavior, who we think we are and our relationship to the world.

We are programmed to be what we are. We are conditioned to respond to life in a uniquely individual way, and short-term and long-term memory being as they are, we've pretty much forgotten how we did it. Compounding matters, every once in a while our self-defense mechanism makes certain we can't remember. If that's not enough, there's a creative part of us that will keep turning an experience around and around until finding something about it we can live with, at the same time denying the traumatic or the unpalatable. The system is not designed to let us unwind. It is human nature at its best. It is the essential means by which we are enabled to cope long enough to grow past an event which could destroy us. Consider how would you function if every painful experience was piled onto you at once? You couldn't. The way the system works, self-preservation is put ahead of everything – even realty.

All things considered – precepts, language and involuntary editing – it's a wonder that any of us get along as well as we do. Fortunately, the system we call self, while not entirely fail-safe, has enough back-up devices to see us through. In fact, we are survival mechanisms. Everything is contrived to ensure our well-being. Even so, sometimes glitches in the system rear their violent heads like dragons and fire-breathers and people find themselves seemingly unable to cope or out of control, acting compulsively or irrationally, or not at all. And, when least expected, the system can lock-up, rendering decisions fallible if not impossible, with all notions of right and wrong turned upside-down.

For all its marvels, the system we rely on is not perfect. Surprisingly, it wasn't intended to be. If it was, you and I wouldn't be needed. Our job, as I see it, is to fix it. Merely coping isn't good enough. We are natural-born programmers for a reason, and the best way to overcome a problem is to solve it. Then, when all is said and done, while we won't be able to take the machine with us, I'm pretty sure we get to keep the data we've collected. In the meantime, the object is to get the most out of what we've got while maintaining the system in good working order.

Getting Real is not, however, a panacea for every ill and woe, nor is it a crash course that will show you how to reformat your harddrive and start all over again; that's up to the maker of the system, whenever it gets recalled and reissued as a new and improved model. Until then, the best that can be done is to fix the programming errors in the present system.

Fortunately, the system we came with is extremely durable and tolerant of the most devastating malfunctions – which means there's still hope. But, reprogramming involves more than hitting the delete key a zillion times. I've tried. First you have to understand how the glitch was created before you know how to fix it. But, have heart, it's not all that difficult, especially now that you're past the worst of the trial and error stage – some people call it growing up.

At this point it's fair to wonder why any of this self-discovery stuff is important to our quest. If this book is about expanding one's awareness, why not cut to the chase? In reply, the rediscovery of the outer world is conditional upon one's inner state of being. If, underneath it all, you are in turmoil or at conflict with your neighbor, then a state of harmony – which is essential to this task – is not possible. It would be nice if the earth was already populated by people at peace with themselves. The fact is, however, in the past 100 years more people have died violently than in all preceding history. Meanwhile, mystics, mediums and gurus are still an oddity, especially since they don't make war. But....but....but... the mind rails, that's totally impractical. We have the right to defend ourselves and the responsibility to do so. Sure we do, unfortunately. And the greater the necessity the more symptomatic it is of universal disorder.

Uh oh, now I've done it. Let me try again. Simply put, expansion of one's personal awareness is best accomplished in a prevailing state of peace and inner happiness, because it's tough to make love and war at the same time. So, now's the time to decide what you really want out of life. You can wave the flag until you're blue in the face, but it won't make you any wiser. In the very least, while radical change may not be necessary, tolerance is. So is a certain amount of understanding and forgiveness. Nothing less will work, at least not in this scenario.

I would like to add that Getting Real is not a treatise written in technical jargon. The experts have their own reference material. The stuff I write about is down-to-earth. It is easy to understand and it works. But it doesn't come with a money back guarantee and it won't necessarily make you rich or find you a soul-mate; and when you graduate, you may not win prizes or promotions or get accolades or diplomas. All it will do is help you be yourself and to be more content with the outcome.

The bottom line is that anyone can do it. The only degree you need to fix your operating system is a degree of enthusiasm. Besides, it's what you're here for. This is the galactical school of hard knocks, bruised knees, breaking hearts and desperate souls. It's the same in every hack room. But, cheer up, you've got all the time in the world to get it right. Hopefully, it won't take that long. Likely you'll catch up to the whiz-kids and computer gurus before you know it, because you don't have to worry about binary coding, machine language or

DOS. Instead, you'll be using the language that self understands best.

Glitches

Do you like yourself? Are you afraid? There are numerous questions like these, many with onerous answers. In all probability there are lots of things in your life that you'd change if you could, but getting along and getting ahead has meant making sacrifices. It's a matter of priorities in which, very often, your personal wish list has come last. But, while your sense of responsibility is admirable, it probably isn't very satisfying. It isn't fun trying to live up to expectations, especially those of others. It's the carrot before the donkey thing and you never quite get there. In the meantime, fulfillment is put on the back-burner and you end up telling yourself that you'll be happy when such-and-such happens sometime in the future. Duty comes first. Unfortunately, someday rarely comes, because future reality is the outcome of present-day habit. Nothing changes. You'll go through a number of denial stages and then croak. Life really is too short.

You can, however, have your cake and eat it too. You can fulfill your obligations and realize your heart's desire at the same time, providing you get started now. This doesn't mean jumping the traces and marching into the sunset. There is another way.

How many times have you said: "I don't know why I did that," or "I don't know what came over me," or "That wasn't like me." Do you say things you don't mean? Do you sometimes act compulsively? Are you occasionally swept with hopelessness or dread? (That's a phobia at work.) Are you hurting inside? Have you given up trying to be understood? Are you unable to forgive yourself? Do you think you're unlovable? Do you like it that way? You'll know if any of these things apply to you; if so, then you've got a few things to sort out. The alternative, feeling futile or ineffectual, invites misery and despair into the lives of many people, although some folks hide it better than others. It's called coping. But you haven't given up or you wouldn't be here. Life is what's coming, not what was. There's a part of you that desires change and knows it's possible. It's not a matter of faith,it's a fact. You can do it, all you need is to know how.

The reason behind it all is that little thing called perception. Clear seeing, if you will, is utterly dependent on viewing the world as it really is, without blinders or the filters of preconceived ideas, bias and prejudice. Anything less and you're fooling yourself.

Manholes

Nothing is as debilitating as self-deception. If you pretend a problem will go away by itself, or that you simply have to get used to it, you are misled. Although it won't go away by itself, there really is nothing preventing you from fixing it. Others won't put up with it and you shouldn't either. You don't have to settle for less. Not really. With this in mind, it's time to go back to the beginnings.

The first step you ever took was a beaut, and everything that came after was a result of that first tentative effort. Now you can run and rock'n roll until the cows come home. Thinking is like that. One thought leads to another and another, each one a building block in the chain of experience. People are magnificent learning machines. Sometimes, however, because of seemingly impossible situations, a person may work harder at avoiding situations than solving them. It's like diving into a hole and pulling the lid after you. The trouble is, that's no fun either. Well, that can be fixed too, especially when you discover there's nothing to hide from anymore.

The new you begins with the realization that your thoughts are magnetic. This is not a mere figure of speech. Every thought is like a seed that searches out the light of day. Your thoughts determine what your environment will be. It isn't the other way around. You are not a victim of circumstance. In fact, you're not a victim at all. You are a creator of experience. If you don't like it, then change it by Getting Real.

"Winged thoughts that are loos'd in space
On planes that the eye cannot see,
Shape coming events, appoint time and place
For the things that will happen to thee."
(U.S.Anderson)

Turn left right here

What we think and how we think are functions of language, and the words we use continue to impact us long after we have taken their original meaning for granted. As Mao put it, right thoughts lead to right actions. While that may be true, the questions that remain are: What is right? And who says so? Who is it that decided what is right for you? It's for sure you didn't. It's also a certainty that you think you did. You see, that's how programming works. If you hear something often enough, especially under conditions of duress, you end up believing it without questioning and language, and the concepts it embraces, become imbedded ipso facto. The rightness of it all, however, is never an issue. It just happens. The end result is a mental-emotional program that determines how you think, how you act and how you live. When you come right down to it, you never had much of a choice at all. Until now. Getting Real will put you in the driver's seat. After all, it's your bus. Soon you'll be able to rewrite the time-table, schedule your own route, and see the things in your life that you choose.

The problem with being normal

There is an adage that says: If it ain't broke, don't fix it. That makes sense. What I take exception to is the assumption – that we all make – that each of us is relatively normal, meaning that we're pretty much the way we're supposed to be and everything is more or less peachy. Some folks appear to be wound tighter than others, but in the main we're all pretty much the same. Aren't we? What really is normal?

According to the dictionary, being normal means conforming to average patterns of behavior. That must mean it's normal to blow-up at the kids, to be overworked, to suffer in silence, to shun unacceptability, to have too many debts and live in relative fear. Is it normal to get only some of the love you'd like? Is it normal to expect not to be understood? Is it normal to be confused or uncertain? Is it normal to give up your dreams in the name of making peace or living up to your responsibilities? Do you think your only way out is to win a lottery? The same dictionary adds that being normal is being free from mental disorder. Does that mean it's normal to pop pills in order to cope? Does that mean it's normal to bury your brain in the TV set so you won't have to think about your own problems? On the other hand, is it normal to live with uncertainty and resignation? Yuck. If that's the case, who wants it?

Force-fed notions about normality are like a plague which infect us before we have sufficient discretion to decide for ourselves if we want it or not. If everyone wore a big sign declaring how normal he was, we'd all look like cans of peas. The assembly line by which personalities are developed, although more subtle, isn't much different, giving each of us normal phobias, normal needs, normal fears and normal shortcomings. In effect, if we are peas, then it was society who peeled us from our shell and graded us according to size and ability: Grade-A, Fancy or No.3. All normal, more or less.

The "less" part shows up as dysfunction, unhappiness and dis-ease, but you can fix it, and you don't need a therapist, nor penance or prayer to do it. All you need is a few minutes a day and a bit of self-guidance. That's the neat part, because when it comes right down to it nobody can do it *for* you anyway. But, don't sweat it, because personal programming is the one thing you were born to be good at. Most people don't bother about it too much though, being normal as they are.

Yet, there are those who, in their own words, would give anything to make changes, if only they could. And they live up to every word, handing out hard-earned cash to systems and shrinks by the score. Get rich! Lose weight! Make friends! And don't forget your mouthwash. But, it isn't what you pay that makes the difference: it's what you say, especially to yourself.

If you go to a counselor it's because you've told yourself that you've got a problem and you've admitted you need help. You've declared that something is haywire and you've expressed the desire to fix it. That sounds simple enough, if it works. But, all too often it doesn't. Either the problem keeps reoccurring, or it never gets straightened out in the first place, or you end up being too fed-up or boozed-up or drugged-up to care one way or another. For the most part, traditional therapy becomes a matter of learning how to cope with problems rather than fixing them. It's the ultimate bummer. Fortunately, Getting Real even works for peas, because it's a team effort. You are the captain, but you get to play too. The other half of your team is a little league player with a 100% batting average. You can't lose.

The pilot light

When you do something weird and afterward wonder why, there has to be a reason for it, even if you don't know it at the time. Even nonsense makes sense to your brain. It rationalizes everything. What comes to mind when I ask: "What would your big toes like to say to each other?" Likely, the first thing you did was to start imagining them actually talking, with nary a thought to the fact that it can't be done. That is the innermost part of you at work: *vis vitae in esse*, the living force in being. It's a kind of pilot light that never goes out. But, more than that, this is the immortal part of you, an ageless infant of spirit. We could call it one's conscience or the inner-self or whatever. For simplicity, let's call it the child part, for whom life is a fairy tale and nothing is impossible. Knowing this, you have unleashed the genie from the lamp, one so miraculous that he/she will do your bidding without reservation. All you have to do is ask. How do you ask? By simply doing it. It's called self-talk, but very little about it is childish. In this context, your inner self commands ultimate respect. It has power only dreamed of.

The skeptics will tell you it has never been scientifically proven that the child in each of us even exists. At the same time they have to admit that they have no idea how memory works either. They can tell you what it does, but not how. So, in the absence of anything more conclusive than that, and since the child thinks he exists, I'll keep on like the bumble bee which, until recently, according to the science of aerodynamics could not fly.

The secret to Getting Real is to learn how to get in touch with your core-state, your inner-self for want of another term. Without wanting to get lost in semantics, it simply means getting centered or attuning. A guru in a retreat or a holy man on a mountain do it by getting away from civilization, so that they can hear without all the background racket. But, once you know how to get in touch with your inner self, you really don't have to go that far. In fact, the child is smiling right now, watching the world through your eyes, waiting, intent upon your every thought. Self-talk is real-talk and it's almost effortless – so much so that many people pass it off as unreliable, which, unfortunately, it is unless it's done right. But there's no mystery to it. It's what comes most naturally to you. The trick, if there is one, is to simply let it flow, and for some people that's a lot easier said than done.

The reason this is so important is because the doorway through which you most clearly relate to self is the same portal through which one perceives the outer world, as in clairsentience (clear knowing), clairvoyance (clear seeing) and clairaudience (clear hearing). In each case the latter is dependent on the former. So, back to basics...

As far as communication is concerned, when you get right down to it, it's surprising how little we understand and how much we take for granted. That's why most people haven't got themselves figured out yet, at least if they're normal. So, we begin at the beginning, all the way back to the goo-goos and da-da. It was about then that the word "I" pierced your consciousness like a thunderbolt. The phrase: "I am" has remained an enigma ever since. What am I? What am you? Whatever the answer, the words "I am" are the cornerstone of the edifice you've created. Every brick and block in your make-up is modeled after this very first stone, and how you see yourself, or not, is a monument to your understanding, your development and your perception of things. You are what you think you are.

The second block that was laid was the "you" block, and the wall that extended from it included stones called "mine, yours and ours." Eventually, your mind made a giant leap in reality when the stones linked up to enclose the concept that "I am" is, to a degree, whatever I presume you are telling me that I am. This leap in consciousness gave you the ability to see yourself as others do. This was the beginning of the program that has ruled your life every day since then. Every joy you've ever had and every heartbreak is measured by the yardstick "I am," whether it's true or not, and regardless if it's justified or not.

The "I am" block is the model for everything that came after, including everything you've created. Man's greatest virtue is his ability to generate new experience. Every second of every day you've been hacking and shaping stones, new ones and old ones too, building and remodeling at the same time, and with every willful blow you have created what you consider to be reality. The difficulty, however, is that the model stone has become buried by what came after, with the result that now you have to rely on memory to get it right. Memory being what it is, you are now faced with the dilemma that the place you live in is pretty drafty at times, the roof leaks a bit and you didn't quite get the plumbing right. Still and all, it's a pretty normal place, except that sometimes it feels barely habitable. But, we can fix that by calling on the little guy. Like I said, he never strikes out.

If you could see it, your innermost self is perched right next to the very first cornerstone of being. He knows exactly what it looks like. Obviously, he's the best source of advice on how to fix things. All you have to do is figure out how to ask him, and then get where it's quiet enough to hear what he has to say.

A rose by any other name...
When addressing your inner self, it will be easier if he-she-it has a name, a name you like. This will add clarity to your dialogue and make your conversations a consciously deliberate

act. Maybe you already have a special name you call yourself, but you can pick a new one if you like. Having read this, your inner self will know when you take the first step. All you have to do is calm yourself and visualize that you are talking to him (or her), at which point you ask: "May I call you...?" You will immediately sense the answer, and when you become sufficiently attuned you can even hear the reply. There's no mystery to it, you talk to yourself all the time. What you need to learn, however, is how to listen without messing around with the message. That may take some doing, but it can be done and you'll be surprised at the results. It's like linking up with the best friend you ever had. For some people, it will be a very emotional experience. Such friends are a gift from God.

Again, when you've calmed yourself, let your friend in on your intentions. It doesn't have to be a grand statement or all encompassing. Simple is better. As before, you'll get your answer right away, but don't fish for it. Take your very first impulse. It may be as subtle as a slight feeling. A part of you will know when you've got it right.

My cousin put it most succinctly when we got skunked trying to catch salmon up north. He said: "That's why they call it fishing instead of catching." Listening to your inner-self is like that. If you go on a fishing trip you'll bomb-out. Catching, on the other hand, requires practically no effort. It isn't something you have to work at, it just happens. The danger is in trying too hard, because there is a part of your ego that is dedicated to protecting you from disappointment, and it will jump in at the first opportunity and invent something just to keep you happy. When you are working on the level of the mind, anything conceived is real, even when it is counterfeit, and sometimes it takes a great deal of experience to know the difference. This is the great chasm into which most wannabees blissfully tumble, fully convinced all the while that they're onto something special.

"Thirty spokes will converge
In the hub of a wheel,
But the use of the cart

15

Will depend on the part
of the hub that is void."
(Lao Tze)

Priming the pump

When you talk to yourself, remember to keep it simple. Be straightforward and don't embellish. It's not needed. At the same time, resist the temptation to get overwhelmingly reverent. Your inner self will not be presented in flowing robes, have a mystical name, or profess the wisdom of the ancients or be holy. If it helps to keep things in perspective, there is something like the child invested in cocker spaniels too. So don't go blowing things out of proportion and don't get carried away.

Your ego loves to be the center of attention, and will surely try to horn in if you let it, and it knows every trick in the book. So be alert, but remain calm too. Be willing to start at the beginning with a simple introduction, a choice of names and an uncluttered statement of your intention. Then don't get swept away by the gushing that quite possibly follows after. It wouldn't be too surprising if you did get a little emotional when meeting the best friend you ever had in the whole wide world. But, again, beware lest your ego use this as an opportunity to jump in with both feet.

With a little practice you'll get the hang of it and be able to maintain control without difficulty. Whenever you feel the ego surfacing, simply and gently shut the door by centering yourself before carrying on. In this context, centering yourself means quieting your thoughts. After a while you'll do it automatically and you'll know when you are properly "linked." Until then you should remain very critical if the moment you open the door you begin hearing a lengthy discourse on inner wisdom or the great role you're about to play or how you have been selected for an important mission – especially a sacrificial one. Anything like that is a sure sign that you are derailed. That one might wish it so is only the measure of the depth of the pitfall.

The Bible says something to the effect that you cannot enter the kingdom of heaven except as a child. If heaven is bliss, then learning the language of the child will surely give you the password. It is also said that from little acorns do giant oaks grow. Well, the same is true for all nuts, so keep your expectations in check and don't glob onto things that fire your imagination. When the child has something to say, listen quietly without getting in the act by embellishing. He will never lie, but, if you let it, the ego will masquerade as the child and then you're really in trouble. Your safeguard is that, once in, the ego cannot resist being a ham. You'll recognize it when it happens, at which point you have a simple decision to make: either enjoy the show or shut the projector off. Self-discipline and a little patience will serve you well, because however you handle the situation, it will be easier to do the same thing the next time, and easier still after that until, finally, your control and your awareness will be such that you can get the real goods without being interfered with. In the interim, remember that while Rome wasn't built in a day, it was destroyed in one.

The adventure begins
With a little practice you'll be surprised at how responsive your inner self is. Its entire purpose in being is to help you create reality. It's not a contest of wills. The process is so simple it's almost effortless. There's no strain and you won't feel drained after a session. If you do, that's a sure sign the ego is getting in on the act. Nor should you necessarily feel like you are on cloud nine – you may be, but the ego is good at that game too. The likelihood is that you will feel calm and be encompassed by "the peace that passes all understanding."

It should be obvious that when you talk to yourself you must not lie. You cannot live a lie and be truly happy doing it, and, indeed, your inner self doesn't know how to. The child in you is totally honest. If his precepts seem wrong, you put them there. Fix them if necessary, but do it gently and with loving intent.

It is not a contradiction to suggest that, deep down, things could be a little mixed up. You see, the child is totally innocent and without discretion. In this relationship you are the parent. The child trusts you implicitly. If you insist that black is white, he will make every effort to see things your way and won't argue about it either. But – and here's the wonder of it all – if you inform him that you suspect you're not seeing things clearly, then he'll help you fix the problem if you ask him to. Once again, that's what he's here for. The child will help you see things any way you want, hopefully the right way. What is more, he will never give up. For him, nothing is impossible, some things just take a little longer.

We'll return to the specifics of self-talk from time to time. For now it is sufficient for you to be aware of the child's power and his devotion to you. At this stage, no great exchanges are necessary. You can get to know each other merely by sensing each other out, and that, in itself, is wondrously fulfilling. The absence of dialogue also ensures that things are kept simple and at the lowest denominator possible. This is important because the first step is at the bottom of the staircase. Later, when your head is in the clouds, you'll remember you got there by keeping your feet on the ground.

The real goods
How do you know if you're catching the real goods or just fishing? If you go too far down the wrong path you never will, at least not without help, which by then usually isn't welcome. People who beguile themselves do it so magnificently that it's the last thing in the world they want to give up. Ignorance, in this case, while somewhat blissful, is horribly seductive. The only reality check that works feels like you're putting the ego on the chopping block – an oftentimes painful experience. No one wants to be told they're full of hot air (ask me) and the exhortations that follow have every built-in denial mechanism ever invented. The ego, being what it is, would sooner be mollified than rectified. And if you want a fight on your hands, just try and do it for someone else – not that you have the right. Everyone has the privilege of being however they chose, including you.

In a nutshell, if you want the real goods you have to be real honest with yourself. Anything less won't work and will only lead to pacifying regurgitations from the sub-conscious and eventually, like it or not, self-delusion. The ego is like a pair of sunglasses, rose colored ones, through which the world that is seen is all it knows and all it wants to know. But the ego isn't you, it's only the heavy armor you wear. Obviously, the instinct for survival will resist any attempt to render you defenseless. Every hurt and pain will demand it. For present purposes then, we'll leave the armor intact and deal only with why you wear it. Clunky and cumbersome as it is, it's very restrictive. Heck, you can't even run with it. All you can do is duck whenever a reality-arrow comes flying at you, from which position it's almost impossible to rise without assistance.

The why of it all involves self-esteem. People spend most of their life trying to convince the world how big they are, how right they are and how strong they are. Too many people would rather feel superior than happy. If the ego had full sway we'd all live atop beanstalks like giants, still in armor of course, hacking away at anyone climbing up the vine. It's ludicrous, but that's how it is. The problem is that the need for self-esteem becomes addictive the moment we see ourselves exalted in another person's eyes, from which time we are bound by expectation and craving for more; and the ego laps it up, glossing over reality with layer after layer until our sunglasses become more like mirrors than lenses, reflecting an image of self that is puffed-up and distorted. The ego has no problem with this, but the real you does, because it compels you to live a lie based on vanity and subterfuge. It isn't at all surprising, therefore, that so many people claim to be the reincarnation of some famous person or an object of research by spacemen. And that's the good news! There are just as many who are victims otherwise. Psychic trauma is no joke, but that is the subject of another chapter. For now, it is sufficient for you to realize that what you believe sets the stage for what happens to you. Even now, consciousness, expectation and opportunity are strutting out of the wings in full costume. The fact that's it's only a play means little when one is enrapt. It means a lot, however, if you want to get real. To do so, you have to be willing to let go of the ego as production manger, which, while bemusing, leads to utter distraction.

What you are

If your ego is one thing and the child in you is something else, then what are you? In terms of a chocolate layer cake, your ego is the yummy icing, your inner self is the platter and everything in between is you, harmonized in layers and bound together by computer-like jam.

It is said that you are what you think. While that is true, you are also a part of what you haven't thought about yet. It's because you are more than the sum of your parts. You are bigger and grander than you will ever finish imagining. To think otherwise is to presume that man made the earth.

The discovery of what you are – self-realization – is a birthright. The sun also rises for the bitter in soul, the disillusioned and the desperate, for nothing is so precious as a soul and nothing so undeniable as a soul in quest. Though the earth split asunder, you will never be abandoned. This is the grand scheme in which nothing is denied you. Everything – past, present and future – is being pulled from an endless source of treasure, spellbinding, one ornament at a time. But you need not grope blindly. You can reach for what you chose, because your sense of expectation is the most fertile ground in which to harvest the future. You are a born co-creator, just like "I am."

> "Yet man is born unto trouble
> as the sparks fly upward.
> Wherefore is light given unto him
> that is in misery,
> and life unto the bitter in soul."
> (Job)

CHAPTER TWO
PROGRAMMING
Data processing
During sensory input, a not-so discretionary part of you automatically assimilates globs of data. What you think and, ultimately, how you live and feel is based on how you absorb information; but, at best, it's a haphazard procedure. All communication is subject to generalization, distortion and deletion during the processing stage. Sometimes it's like trying to make a cake with nails in the recipe. You might get it down, but it's hard to digest and the byproduct is dysfunction.

Consider the following phrase for a moment and count the number of 'F's as you read. FINISHED FILES ARE THE RE-SULT OF YEARS OF SCIENTIF-IC STUDY COMBINED WITH THE EXPERIENCE OF YEARS.

Okay. How many did you get? Three? Count again. The first time around your brain deleted half the information. There are six.

Regardless of the way one filters information, every single word affects the programming that makes a person the way he is, especially that which was heard when young, or when under stress, or has been repeated sufficiently to allow the message to sneak in the back door while you were preoccupied with something else. Indoctrination and behavioral modification depend on this type of reiteration. Even if what you hear isn't true or doesn't make sense, if it's repeated enough times and packaged right it'll get through to you. Advertising agencies have perfected this type of subliminal seduction to the point of making it an art form, using the time-tested triggers of sex, mutilation and death. Curiously, it doesn't matter if you acquiesce or fight it, the end result is the same.

The idea of subliminal motivation got started in 1957 when James Vicary claimed to have increased Coke and popcorn sales by dubbing the words "Drink Coca-Cola" and "Hungry - Eat Popcorn" into a film strip in a New Jersey theater. Although it turned out to be a hoax, most people accept it as fact that advertisers will manipulate buyers in any way they can.

Once the trigger mechanisms are activated, input-data goes through a series of belief and prejudice filters. Whether reading the newspaper or just gossiping, these filters are at work, reinforcing what we chose to believe while rejecting anything to the contrary. For example, while some people believe that every word in the Bible is to be taken verbatim, in the writing of the King James version alone there were 22,000 edits by "helpers." To say the least it's problematical, because the assimilation of new ideas requires an open mind. Preconceived ideas, the filters of one's belief system, can be either a hindrance or a help. I wish I could say that it's simply a matter of what we choose to believe, but most of us never had the opportunity to exercise such discretion. Without wanting to seem argumentative, whether we like it or not, there is a parallel to little wind up toys that are programmed to march about waving their arms until their mind-spring gives out and they're exhausted. The objective of Getting Real is to enable you to decide for yourself what makes you tick, if you'll march to a different drum, and, since you're going to wave your arms anyway, if maybe you'd like to take up badminton.

Baby talk
When you were a kid, everything you learned was dedicated to the exploration of self. You were the most important idea in your world, and it took quite a while for you to discover that you were separate from everyone else yet connected too. The next stage was to learn how to defend yourself. Many people are still at it, trying to protect the defenseless part, the little one inside that seems to hurt the most. The phrase: "children should be seen and not heard" could never be more inappropriate than when applied to self, because it is the child who most deserves to be heard, to be understood and to be loved. All too often,

however, it is a matter of unfinished business, in which the small inner voice has been drowned out or simply ignored.

You can deny the child if you choose to. You can shove him into a corner of your mind and virtually lock the door. You can abandon the child or even try to run away from him. You can even try to kill him, but the child never dies. He may whimper and sob and be terribly alone, but he is yours forever. He's your baby, so to speak, and he's with you for life. That being the case, it truly makes sense to learn the language of the child and to get it right. The questions and issues that you need to address are the very same that have bothered you all along. Now, finally, it's time to get some answers. You do have a choice about what is right for you, and you do have the tools to make it real. After all, people are like flowers; they bloom when they are supposed to. By the way, what's your favorite color?

First words
The child within doesn't speak the same language you do. He used to, but you've changed, at least the meaning of what you say has, because the words you use reflect your expanding intellect. Not so for the child. He still sits beside the very first cornerstone of being and relates from that perspective to everything you do or say. Over the years, as you laid more and more experiential blocks in place, gradually you moved further and further away from the child, at least in terms of communication. But you never noticed, because by then you and your new companion, the ego, were intent upon building an edifice and, to say the least, you had your own ideas about things – especially about reality. Day after day you built with a frenzy, your imagination leading the way, and what you created was grand and utterly self-preoccupying. Every once in a while you'd be given cause to look back, but not often. You were, in a word, headstrong. Before long, even when you resorted to shouting, out of hurt or frustration, communication with your inner self left something to be desired. Inevitably, feelings of isolation infiltrated your consciousness and a part of you has felt disconnected ever since. All of which, by the way, is

normal. There comes a time, however, when you want to know why the roof leaks, the floor squeaks and the vagary winds of life blow so hard through your living room.

Now, at last, you've acquired the wisdom and the means to question the nagging feeling that something is missing. It isn't missing at all really, you've just forgotten where to look for it.

The meaning of words

"In the beginning was the word" – so that's where we'll start. There's an aphorism which states: "Say what you mean, and mean what you say." But, do you? Really? Some people skirt the issue by getting loud or talking too fast, as if volume or quantity could compensate.

When someone speaks to you, do you know exactly what he means, or is it exactly what you think he means? The difference may be night and day. Some people pass it off as communicating on different levels or the generation gap. In the final analysis, all too often we're left with the subtle feeling that we really aren't understood at all – and whose responsibility is that? Is it 50% you and 50% your listener? Nope: it's 100% you. If you leave 50% up to the other guy you'll never get it more than half of it right.

Consider the phrase: "The visiting old friends and relatives had a great time." Now what could be simpler than that? But, let me ask you, who is it that is old? Both the old friends and the relatives, or just the old friends? Have they been old friends for 60 years, or are they 60 year olds who just met? Were the old friends visiting the relatives, or was it the other way around? Or maybe, did the old friends have a private meeting, leaving the relatives to fend for themselves? The point is, it's almost impossible to make any sense out of anything without making broad generalizations, which may or may not have very much to do with the facts. All communication is like that, because that is how the mind works. The brain is impressed with about 2 million bits of information per second, which, in order to translate it into conscious thought, is reduced to something like a measly 7 chunks per second, a 'chunk' being a block of filtered data after it goes through the internal process of deletion, distortion and generalization. (George Miller, 1970, *The Magic Number Seven, plus or minus two)*.

Additionally, the meaning of words are dependent on personal experience and context. That is why the same word can mean different things to different people. More is communicated by what a person is, than by what he says. In fact, words alone represent only about a third of what is being communicated. The bulk of the message being conveyed by tone, body language and perception on the unconscious level.

Words without context have no meaning. What is good in one context may be bad in another. Meaning is derived only by the way in which context is processed by the brain. Getting Real involves reinstating paradigm meanings to certain word concepts, with the focus on intent rather than content. What you think you hear is the measure of what is communicated. The same applies to self-talk, in which case one needs to understand the effect that words have in order to use the language that will best create the desired outcome.

Upon landing, a U.S. Air Force pilot wrote the following comment for the maintenance crews: "Number 3 engine missing." The next day the pilot dutifully checked the work sheets to see what had been done: "Engine found on right wing after a brief search."

The stumbling block in communication is language itself. It is too vague, easily confused and subject to misinterpretation. As wonderful as the brain is, it doesn't have time to dote on every syllable and nuance. In order to make sense out of what is heard, your mind digests the message in chunks of data called presuppositions. Just as with words, presuppositions are based on personal experience. Presuppositions take globs of information and automatically reduce them to the simplest form. As concepts are generalized, detail is lost, leaving only a distorted fragment to which presumed meaning is attached. Everything you hear is subject to the same process of generalization, deletion and distortion.

Consider the following sentences:

1) John didn't know there was a blue Ford parked outside.

2) John knew there was a blue Ford parked at the curb.

3) John just realized that a blue Ford pulled away from the curb.

In each example, whether the statement was positive, negative, or time-sensitive, you made the same presupposition, specifically that of a blue car. More importantly, the notion of a blue car was accepted automatically because your attention was focused on John. Why is that important? Because the blue Ford was a truck. The fact that I didn't say so is not as important as the assumption you made.

Presuppositions carry imbedded commands which are acted upon automatically. For example, if I say: "Don't turn the page unless you have to," what happens? First, because the mind resists processing a negative, don't doesn't mean do not, it means do something conditionally – the condition being that you have to turn the page in order to keep reading. The instant you read that sentence, a part of your mind was already visualizing you turning the page, even though you really don't have to do it at all – turn the page, that is. One thing leads to the other, with the rationale behind it pretty much lost along the way. Another example: If I say: "Don't think of a blue car," that's the first thing you do think of. This is important because effective reprogramming necessitates using words in the right way. Remember, right words lead to right thoughts which lead to right actions.

If you tell yourself: "I don't want to smoke anymore," you can be sure you will; and although you may not do it any *more,* you can be sure you won't do it any less either. In effect, you have told yourself to keep doing exactly the same thing, but conditionally. You may argue that isn't what you meant, to which I agree, which only underscores the necessity to use words that will produce the desired outcome, such words as: "I chose to stop smoking," or, very simply: "I am now a non-smoker." There's is no ambiguity in that. The words are direct and precise. The rule is, when making a determination, reduce the words to their most basic form, so as to fully and adequately capture your intent. Again, say what you mean and mean exactly what you say.

Presuppositions involving cause and effect are the most powerful of all. They incorporate action words such as if, unless, then and because. For example: "Don't use two lumps of sugar unless you don't want to lose weight." This may sound like good advice, but this presupposition has a time-delay fuse that will blow-up any attempt to go on a diet. Allowing for the conditional response, this statement says: "Use two lumps of sugar you want to lose weight." The "do-nots" cancel each other out and you're left taking more sugar than necessary every time you think of losing weight. A compulsion, very often, is the result of your brain trying to do exactly what you told it to do, even if that's not what you meant.

Presuppositions always hook acceptance of something new to that which is already proven. "The fact that you're here must mean that…" The fact that you're here automatically triggers acceptance of what comes after. Words are powerful, not in themselves, but because of their trigger-effect.

A final example of a presupposition involves the famous double-bind. My grandson always acts up when it's time to go to bed. The solution is to ask him: "Do you want to go to bed at 8:30 or 9?" Or: "Because you're going to bed soon, would you like to put your pajamas on in the bedroom or in the bathroom?" Simple as it is, it works.

"I cannot stress how important your language is." How'd you like that one? Remember, the mind resists processing a negative, with but few exceptions. One such marvelous exception is the word: "Stop." It works practically every time, even if you tell someone to stop thinking. You can prevent anyone from offhandedly affecting you with negative programming by simply saying: "Stop," and he will. Then, just as casually, ask him to repeat himself in a different way. He'll do it and not wonder why. People want to be understood more than they want to avoid being told what to do.

If being understood isn't an issue, and sometimes even if it is, people naturally resist being ordered about. If you say: "Don't slam the door!" it might work, but it's not the negative that registers, it's the "slam the door" part that gets through and BANG! there it goes again. Instead, ask: "Can you close the door quietly?" (Adding please helps.) The question isn't about "if" they will close the door quietly, it's about if they know how to. The obvious answer is yes, which is proven by their mindfulness when the door closes without slamming. This is the technique of using imbedded commands to get precisely what you want, whether talking to yourself or someone else. The more precise and effective your language is, the more certain you are of getting the results you're after.

Self-talk

It is vitally important to think, talk and act in a way that is consistent with what you chose to create it your life. The creative process is thought, word, deed. The most compelling action sequence is when spoken thought is reinforced by a physical gesture, be it making the sign of the cross or taking notes. Things are thoughts on the level of thought. The way to hook a thought into physical reality is to connect it by a deliberate physical gesture. Thought is to a seed what a physical gesture is to sticking it in the ground. Any gesture will work, just so long as you know what's behind it. But, obviously, the more related the better.

The unconscious mind, through the action of its parts, is continually learning about life as we experience it consciously. But these parts do not exercise unlearned discretion. They cannot make up your conscious mind for you. That is what free will is for. They can, however, motivate you in ways that conform to how you made up your mind when faced with a similar situation in the past. It behooves you, therefore, to do your homework – meaning that it's up to you to associate correct meanings with the words you use. Remember, your inner self, like those parts, can only act on the information you provide.

My father, a high school teacher for many years, had to contend with heavy traffic every day on the way to work. In his words, it was a pain in the butt. The very act of driving completed the thought-word-deed chain and it wasn't long before he was making the rounds of medical specialists with a real problem. Then there's the case of the person who says: "I can't stand this anymore." That is a sure-fire way to get ground down. In this example there is a built-in loop that, if repeated sufficiently, will ensure a breakdown in the system. First, the statement is that he can indeed tolerate 'this' conditionally; secondly, eliminate the negative and he's left with having to withstand neither more nor less, so nothing changes. Every time he says: "I can't stand this anymore," he reinforces his inability to do anything about it, because the words he uses elicit a pre-recorded response. It's as simple as that. He gets exactly what he asks for, even if he doesn't realize it.

Free-will is like a reality sail. It catches whatever wind you set it to. Inevitably, you deny yourself what you want and attract what you fear. Nothing changes until you start saying things like: "I can," or "I chose," or "I will." Fortunately, you can chose almost anything with a reasonable chance of getting it. The words: "I am," as part of the creative process make the outcome almost undeniable. It's so simple, really. All that is required is a little self-awareness and the right words.

Perception

Everything you have ever experienced is you. You are not an abstract concept. You are not wistful energy caught up in a whirling maze – well, maybe, but everything about you is filled with grace and intention. You are a reflection of your creator, and the "I am" part of you is resplendent and holy. The thrill of being you, however, has just begun.

Part of your present realization has to include a sense of purpose as to what you are about. You're not trying to put Humpty-Dumpty back together again. Instead, you're teaching the little sucker how to get off the wall and run! There's a whole new world out there and you are an undeniable part of it. Without you the heavens would revolt and the cosmic clock would unwind. You are utterly essential to all that is. You are a vital part of everything that will ever be. You really are "I am."

Whether as a babe you grappled for a nipple, or a rubbery thing was jammed into your mouth, you were nurtured. You are not the product of chance. Everything about you is the product of thought – but not necessarily thoughtfulness. The last time somebody called you a jerk, there was a part of you that agreed. Hopefully, a tiny part. The last time anyone said they loved you, a part of you knew that it was true. In both cases, however, there were other parts with a different spin on things. This is the dichotomy of life and it is important that you understand it.

Flowers, forests and even fairies spring from dark places. Yet, the light that nourishes can be equally blinding, especially when it comes to understanding. Take the weather for example: It's a "good" day if it's sunny and a "bad" day if it's not. Well, anyone knows that's not true at all, but that doesn't stop some people from getting grouchy when it's overcast. They've heard it so many times they react without thinking. I like storms. Especially, I like the feel of mist on my cheeks. Different strokes and all that. The point is that notions of what is good and bad have become corrupted through generalization. Skinny is good. Bald is bad. Evil is black. Good guys wear white hats. Nuts. Skinny people could be bulimic. Some of the sexiest, smartest, strongest men in the world are bald. Evil has no color and the really good guys know it. All that aside, you can believe anything you want.

Do you chose to believe that evil is black and white is good? If so, how far do you take it? Do you really believe that you were born in sin? Do you believe that the supreme creation of God is an act of evil? Please understand, I'll defend your right to believe anything you choose, but doesn't it make sense to base your value system on the things *you* hold to be true, rather than accept unquestioningly what others have repeatedly told you? Surely, your world isn't still flat? The reason for harping on this is because what you believe becomes your reality. If you are a victim, guess who put you there? If you've got a phobia, guess who created it? If you're unhappy, whose unhappiness is it? Other people don't make you unhappy, they merely set the stage for you to become as unhappy as you imagine yourself to be. Now I'm not suggesting that you should be overjoyed at getting beat-up, but it is nevertheless true that you wouldn't have been in that situation unless you put yourself there.

Being happy or miserable takes the same effort. It's simply a matter of choice. Unhappy people attract unhappy circumstances to themselves. This isn't to say that happy people don't have grief too, but they certainly cope better.

Your state of being is also a result of stereotypes; but people who do apparently evil things are not necessarily evil, any more than people who do apparently good things are necessarily good. Everything must be taken in context. Nothing is fundamentally good or bad. It just is. Moreover, everyone, every time, all the time, does the best he can. Mere survival rouses us to do so. That is as true for bugs as it is for burglars. That we might question their ethics is a different matter.

The way you perceive things effects the way you create your reality. Your thoughts are magnetic, attracting to you whatever it is you assume. You are what you think, and so is your world. What you think effects what you do: what you do similarly effects the way you think. This is the law of psychosomatic response. If you make a fist, it won't be long until you're thinking about how to use it. On the other hand, smile and the world smiles with you. Either way, you're the same person, but look how your reality has changed.

Blueprints

Milton Erickson, before his death in 1980, was single-handedly responsible for taking hypnosis off the stage and putting it in the hands of the American Medical Association. He said: "The map is not the territory," meaning that the perception of an event is not the event itself. Put another way: The words we use are not the event they describe. The blueprint isn't the house you've built. There has been too much ad-hoc remodeling, too much storm damage and too many emergency repairs over the years. Added to that, you've had a host of repairmen marching around, their own code book in hand, tearing things down or adapting them while you were asleep upstairs. The present dilemma is that while you are determined to let more light in, you just might knock down a bearing wall in the process.

The solution begins with an appraisal. This means thoughtfully walking from room to room, getting to know the place you live in all over again, and taking stock of the inventory you've accumulated. In present context, it means having a fresh look at both oneself and the world. You'll be surprised at how much you've taken for granted over the years. The front door may bind a bit, so what? Does it matter if the blinds in the living room have faded? And what if the entry is a little warped, never mind the cracks in the foundation. But you must mind. A little insight will go a long way right now.

Lumber, wallpaper and bricks, as far as the house called self is concerned, are words. Words enable us to build what we imagine, thereby expressing our every idea and concept, at least up to a point. When you look at a tree you don't see a coffee table. When you look at a coffee table you don't think of a tree. Obviously, something has changed, even if the stuff they're made from hasn't. What has changed is awareness. To the extent that awareness has changed, so has your notions of reality.

Personal reality is a by-product of rationalization and specialization. According to Dr. Richard Maurice Bucke, in his book *Cosmic Consciousness*, in the ancient root language of Sanskrit there are 35 names for fire and 37 words for the sun. In Arabic there are 80 names for honey, 500 for lion, 1000 for sword and, supposedly, a staggering 5,744 words relating to a camel. The inherent difficulty is that, whether few or many, the original meaning of our words gets lost along the way, except where the inner self is concerned. The child is in no way similarly distracted, even though he is compelled to act upon the language you use when you're in a creative mode.

When you tell yourself you want something, for example, the child makes sure you do – want, that is. The action word is *want,* not *something.* Your inner self is a child of action and at your command he does his best to make certain you keep wanting and wanting. In effect, the act of wanting repels whatever it is you desire. The way to get (create) something in your world, as the Good Book says, is to act as if you already have it. The whole process of education, therefore, is to condition your mind with expectancy, based not upon wanting but upon what you really believe. The rule is: you repel want you want and attract what you fear. For this reason, the word *want* is possibly the most dangerous word in the English language. (The word *try* is a close second.) Its use presupposes a decision to move toward something when, in fact, it totally thwarts attainment of the goal by setting up a condition of merely wanting instead of attaining. You can want something forever without getting it. All you get is more wanting. For example, saying: "I want to be loved," will keep you lonely, while "I chose to be loved," will fulfill every desire. Somehow, sometime, somewhere, you got involved in setting the circumstances in motion that have led to every experience and emotion you've ever had. Oftentimes, the decision process has been more automatic than discretionary, the result of habit, programming and past decisions now forgotten.

When you acknowledge fear you empower whatever it is that makes you afraid, and set in motion the circumstances that will bring it about. The undeniable action sequence is: I-am-afraid. Well, if that's what you think I-am is, then so be it. It's your reality and you have the right to be afraid any way you decide to be. And, of course, merely wanting the outcome to be different, or wishing it was, only pushes the remedy further away from you. This is the dynamics of the words you use. Remember: "In the beginning was the word..." For the child, those first words remain explicit in meaning, even though you may have long since attributed something different to them.

You should also know that the child takes you literally and is placed in a tail-spin when you deny something that has been actualized at your command. Boldly stating that something doesn't exist is a sure-fire way to build a granddaddy of a glitch into the operating system, because then you are denying your own reality. It's like hitting the print button with no paper in the tray. You can't have it both ways without little green lights flashing and alarm messages coming onto your screen. Sometimes your system even locks up, and rebooting is a real bummer, unless, of course, you like losing data.

You can say anything

...but not if you seek positive results. Thoughts are things. They have the same energy and potential as a bomb or a birth. Moreover, the assumption that the material world is the only real world is very misleading. The fact that you can touch a chair and sit on it makes it real only in the physical world. A chair is equally real in the non-physical world. Actually, without its origins in the non-material world, the chair could not exist in the first place.

Everything is conceived in consciousness. That is where it is born, and whether it makes it into the material world or not, it is already as real as it will ever be. If you envision a particular shirt, or a way to improve your golf swing, or your next vacation, a part of you is already wearing it on the links of a resort. Whether or not you actualize it on the physical level is a matter of timing (synchronicity), effort (will) and appropriateness. This applies equally to the actualization of all things and events, which are first created in the real world of the mind before being actualized in the real world of matter. This is what is meant by the phrase: thoughts are things; conversely, it is also true that everything is a thought (not *was* a thought).

While ignorance of what is real doesn't change reality, denial of what is real leads to chaos. And, since we're stuck with the facts, we might as well get them right.

"...find the truth of your highest and inmost existence and live in it. Only by discovering your true self can your doings be perfected in a divinely authentic action. Know then yourself. Know your true self to be God and One with the self of all others."
(Sri Aurobindo, summing up the Bhagavad-Gita.)

The tiger always wins

Free will isn't: There's always a price to pay or a prize to claim. When you think about what you choose to do, you have set in motion the most undeniable force in the universe. Everything you experience and everything you've become is the result of the decisions you've made. Even the determination that sometimes you have no choice, is a decision on your part. The decision to do nothing is a decision.

But, very often, *what* you decide is not as important as *how* you decide, because the decision making process in itself effects the outcome. Here's how it works: when you make a decision – the product of thought – seeds of possibility are scattered to the wind, blowing through your world of reality to take root in myriad places. But, not all seeds bear fruit, some are thorny. The fruit-bearing variety grow from "toward decisions," while the thorny kind grow from "away from" decisions.

Whenever you decide to do something better for yourself, that is a toward-decision which creates reality of a positive nature. But, an away-from decision is based on trying to outrun your problems, in which case the tiger usually wins the race. The reason is that little thing called fear, whereby you attract whatever it is you are running from. Consider, for example, the woman who left her drunkard husband only to settle down with another drunk. You'd think she'd know better. Maybe she did, but she didn't decide better. Alternatively, she could have left her husband on the basis that she wanted more out of life, then things would surely have been different. In a nutshell: if she merely *wanted* to escape, she never could. If fear made her run, then she'd attract the same experience all over again. But, if she left in search of fulfillment, there's a good chance she'd find it.

Accidentally on purpose
Nothing just happens and nothing happens by accident. Nothing ever could. Always there is thought, then action and then the deed. This is the trinity of existence: mother, father, child. There is no exception. Everything that exists is created deliberately by the intelligent application of energy. And, as science has proven, nothing can be destroyed, it can only be

modified. How it is modified depends on toward or away-from decisions. Pause a moment, therefore, when making a decision, to question your motives in order to adapt the way you think in terms of the desired outcome. Anything less and you might as well flip a coin.

Crosswords

One of the most important decisions involves how we become convinced of something. And, believe me, it is a conscious decision process, even if you cannot remember when or how you adopted it. Somewhere, sometime, you decided everything about you. Granted, many times you were overwhelmed by others and didn't have the ability to think clearly, but the decision to accept or reject was still yours, patterned after the way you decided similar things before that. You can, of course, insist on blaming others for what you've become. That's your decision too. But, it won't help you fix it.

Studies show that most sales are made after the buyer has said no five times, one way or another, most often to himself. In other instances, most people's reassurance requires three comparisons before they can decide on something. This requirement for reassurance is called the convincer-level. No, it turns out, is often one-third of yes. It applies equally to buying a car or a bill-of-goods. A lot of irrationality stems from the process of repeated denials and then final acceptance. Unfortunately, most of the time it's the last decision that sticks. I say unfortunate because a person rarely changes his mind once it's made up. The result, in terms of ego and feelings, is not the measure of how things really are, so much as how one decides they ought to be. In the same way, most forms of self-criticism are based on criticism of self by others. The first time you laugh it off, the second time you shake your head and the third time you feel like crying. Maybe a part of you still is.

But not for long...

If self-understanding wasn't challenging enough, our ego leaps beyond self to seek identity ratification through others. If the next three people you meet say it looks like you're having a bad day, the likelihood is increased that you will. To unravel the mystery of you, therefore, necessitates understanding something about others. But, surprisingly, that will come as second nature when you know more about yourself.

Knowing self begins with the realization that hardly anyone knows you at all. They only think they do. Be that as it may, most people are bent on convincing you that their opinions about you are more valid than your own. That's how others go about including you in their reality – by attempting to make you conform to their perception of things. Somewhere along the line, however, you have to put on the brakes and catch your own ride.

Getting to know self depends on the realization that you really don't know yourself either. Most of the harsh things you believe about yourself are simply not true, or at least not as true as you make them out to be, and many of your virtues are more virtuous than you give yourself credit for. How do I know? That's easy: God don't make mistakes. Of course, that doesn't mean you're a saint. If you were perfect you wouldn't be here. Here, as I said before, is where you come to fix things and your pet project is supposed to be yourself.

"If you think something outside of yourself is the problem,
you will look outside of yourself for the answer."
(Dr. Robert Anthony)

Admitting the need for change is one thing, but getting down to cases is something else. Negative thinking is simply a bad habit, and habits are not easily altered. Consider, for example, whatever it is you are going to do after you finish reading today. In all probability you will do very much the same thing you did after the last time you finished reading. When you got out of bed this morning, or reached for your car keys, or even the way you walked to get the mail, all of it is an act of habit. Your life patterns are as much a part of you as are the lines on your palms, so much so that – accept it or not – you do most things without thinking. Once you've got the routine down, what's to think about? Not much. If you doubt it, ask yourself what you did yesterday at 10:53 AM.

In some schools of thought, people are considered to be sleeping when they think they are awake, and most awake when they are sleeping. The creative part of you is often the most active when the thinking part is at rest. This accounts for the many times when an idea seems to just pop into your head, or when you wake up in the morning with a brand new slant on things. Sleeping on it, before making an important decision, really is a good idea.

When I was just a sprout I read a book called *Pathways to Power*, by Edward L. Kramer, in which he described something called the cookie-sheet process. Each cookie, after being shaped and flattened with a fork, was placed in an oven. Then, from time to time, the cookie sheet was pulled out and the cookies were checked to see if they were done yet. The ones that were got set aside and the rest went back in the oven for a while longer. It is the same with a certain type of problem solving, in which case the problems may be as simple as how to resolve a specific situation, or as complex as inventing something. Each night, before going to sleep, spend a few minutes shaping (defining) the problems before sticking them into the oven of your subconscious mind, then let them go, as it were. The next morning, pull the cookie sheet out and check to see which of the problems are cooked enough, then stick the rest back in and forget about them until the next session. The point is to avoid trying to do the cooking yourself. Let the oven do that. All you do is shape the batter and check it periodically. And, presto! the goodies appear as if by magic. If you're cooking a large batch, it may be helpful to have a note pad at hand, just so you won't forget anything.

The effective way to address issues, then, even those that affect your personal development, involve two distinct processes: one in which you make a conscious effort to think about what you're doing, while the other involves making a conscious effort to let your subconscious do the thinking for you. This may sound contradictory, but it isn't. It simply means getting the entire team up to bat.

But, it takes some doing to break the habit of not-thinking about what you are doing. One way is to deliberately do things a different way each time. This will force you to negate habit and compel you to think about routine things in an entirely new way, which outcome is often startling indeed. It's like learning to think for yourself all over again, this time with the advantage of being an adult and having a sense of direction. Once you're firing on all cylinders, you'll be amazed at your climbing ability; and, as the hills smooth out, problems will be seen for what they are: opportunities in work clothes. Once in that state, you will find yourself in the most comfortable place in the world, smiling at the kid next to you, near a mighty cornerstone that has your initials carved on it.

Crawling back

People really are wondrously stubborn creatures. Once a person's mind is made up, his opinions are cast in stone as it were. Of course, throughout the learning process, new information is being added all the time and insight is gained along with a mature perspective. At least that is what is supposed to happen. But, as often as not, new material is either loaded aboard to be traded later, or the cargo gets left on the dock. After a while, things do tend to get lop-sided. Our job is to right the ship of soul. That means sorting through everything that bogs us down and keeping only the good stuff. And I do mean *everything,* including our notions of the world and its history, our place in both, and our belief systems too. This is part of the very necessary process of taking inventory. Change, merely for the sake of change, isn't required. Our task, rather, is to examine the melting pot of past assumptions, in the light of a new day, and remove the dross.

The problem is, way deep down in the bilge, water from the old days continues to swill back and forth with the tides of life, never totally diluted and long-since stagnant. What we are about to do now is put the vessel of self in dry-dock for a few chapters so we can remove the ballast and air the place out, scrape off the rust and barnacles, plug the leaks, and splash a bit of color around to make things ship-shape again.

Having established that a person is what he thinks, now we'll consider how he got that way. We'll examine some of the things taken for granted, the facts and the not-so-factual too. This means establishing a few new paradigms. As you will see, much of what we take for granted shouldn't be.

> "When I was a child,
> I spoke as a child,
> I thought as a child:
> but when I became a man,
> I put away childish things."
> (1 Cor. 13:11)

CHAPTER THREE

PERSPECTIVES
Living in Sin

According to the doctrines accepted by the first four ecumenical councils, held between the 4th and the 9th centuries in Constantinople, Adam and Eve were tempted by a serpent to defy God and eat of the fruit of knowledge, thereby condemning future generations to be born in sin, with Jesus Christ being their only hope of salvation.

While all major religions include sin as part of their doctrine, the meaning of sin varies greatly. In Hinduism, according to one's Karma, good and bad deeds are balanced out through reincarnation. In Western traditions, sin is viewed as a transgression of the laws of God. In Islam, the Koran (hadith) interprets those laws much in the way that the Old Testament does, including Allah's forgiveness for the repentant. The Seven Deadly Sins, according to Christian doctrine, are avarice, lust, envy, gluttony, anger, sloth and pride.

Webster's Dictionary defines sin as: "a willful violation of some religious or moral principal." Possibly, the first precept of the old Huna religion of Hawaii sums it up best with the simple injunction: "Do not do willful harm."

Be that as it may, not all harm is willful, and self-harm rarely is. More often it is a result of naiveté, foolhardiness or sheer ignorance. Other mitigations, if that is what they are, involve degree and context. A "little white lie" isn't as serious as perjury, is it? Does the Commandment: "Thou shall not kill" apply in wartime? What about swatting flies?

Another question: Can anyone truly be saved from the consequences of their actions? Does penance or absolution really get you off the hook? If not, is the responsibility for one's misdeeds accumulative? If that's the case, wouldn't we need an infinite number of lifetimes to work things out? Then there's the sociopathic point of view which states that if you are going to hang anyway, it doesn't matter how high.

Peace, reconciliation and forgiveness are not idle concepts. Neither, of course, are horror and malevolence. But, in the final analysis, all suffering is said to be an illusion – the price of self-experience – and all goodness an abstraction. Supposedly the two balance each other out. There only is. Still, when you're up to your butt in alligators, it's hard to remember you came to drain the swamp.

For those who have achieved spiritual equanimity, there is nothing abjectly evil, there is only relative goodness, the recognition of which renders forgiveness unnecessary. That's a tough one to swallow, but the bottom line is: People do not need to be excused for what they are, only for what they do. As for their victims: Suffering by itself holds little virtue, and the long suffering are not more blessed than those who get off Scott-free. And, yet, the mighty in spirit line up for this chance at self-realization. It is not rational, it just is, and judgment day, if there is one, comes not at the end of this lifetime, but upon the pondering of infinite lifetimes, when your Ultimate Self acknowledges that the only one you really ever hurt was you.

Judge not
It is human nature to frown at things not approved of. The effect, however, is insidious. Being judgmental is like a boomerang. It always comes back to whack you on the head. The difficulty with being judgmental is that things are rarely as they seem, and the truth of a matter is oftentimes juxtaposed to one's preconceived ideas. It is a matter of what I call the bug on a blanket syndrome.

Imagine a tiny bug on a blanket, going this way and that. It's more of a quilt, actually, and when the bug is in a dark spot he's depressed and sad, then comes a row of stitches – another hurdle – and he laboriously climbs over into a bright spot where he's happy until another hurdle looms in front of him. Sometimes the quilt has a ripple in it and climbing is almost impossible. At such times the dark places are overwhelming and the bright places seem glaring, forcing him, when least expected, to become lost in his own shadow. But, the bug keeps on and on, mindless to the reason behind it all. Yet, high above him is the maker of the quilt, a craftsman that is out of this world, making every stitch so perfect you'd think he's got all eternity to do it in. Like all makers of beautiful things, he wants to experience your reaction to it, and to share the glory of his handiwork which, when viewed from afar, is truly grand, the patterns breathtaking, a work of pure inspiration. Yes, there is darkness in some of the fabric, but without it the light parts would be undefined. Of course there are light areas too, for without them the darkness would have no meaning. One is necessary for the other. In fact, this magnificent creation would be unrecognizable otherwise. Are the dark areas really evil? Are the light areas the sole proof of the maker's goodness? For the bug it is, and his moods change with his opinions about a world which only appears to be in chaos.

> The truth comes into this world with two faces;
> one is sad with suffering, and the other laughs...
> but it is the same face, laughing or weeping.
> (*Black Elk Speaks* by John G. Neilhardt)

Forgiveness

To err is human, to forgive divine, and everyone makes mistakes. Whether learning to ride a bike or riding out a storm, everyone gets bruised knees. That's life. Goof-ups are inevitable. It's called learning. Sometimes the mistakes we make have catastrophic results, we are hurt and so are others. Then, there are deliberate wrong-doings of every ilk. The long and the short of it is that we all have a lot to atone for, and maybe the great Akashic record – or wherever it is they keep the score – is so lop-sided that it's nearly impossible to clean up the mess we've made.

Curiously, however, while we are totally responsible for our actions, pay-back time isn't necessarily horrific. In fact it may well be a time of jubilance. Surprise, huh? It turns out that the only way we can learn is by our mistakes and the mistakes of others. Many successful business people will tell you they learned the ropes by doing just about everything wrong at one time or another. That is what survival is all about, and that is why everyone does the best they can, every time, all of the time in terms of their perceived situation, maturity and presumed resources. In this light, no one can be blamed for doing his best. Not really. What more is there? No amount of ranting or raving can extract more than that. That's all there is. True, you can perhaps guide a person to a more productive point of view, but that is a measure of necessity and receptivity, not worthiness.

Even the innocent lamb steps all over the shepherd's feet. We all do it, and not always unintentionally. No one remains innocent for long. Naiveté, foolishness, presumptuousness, immaturity, lack of wisdom and even outright stupidity are attendant to growing up. So you learn to duck by banging your head. Clowns do it all the time. Hopefully, you have learned to laugh at yourself a little too.

One day a teenage girl – a friend of mine named Melissa – was wailing away, when her seven year old sister, Alie, who was sitting on the floor in front of the TV, turned around, exasperated and said: "Life goes on, you know. So get over it, okay?"

Well, that's one message.

Beyond bruised knees and chagrin there is willful harm, bigotry, exploitation, revenge and deeds of abject evil – like the kid who threw a rock through the windshield of a passing car. The motorist swerved to a stop, rushed out and grabbed the youngster who cried: "But, no one would stop! It's all I could think to do. Our car rolled into the ditch and my dad's hurt bad. Please, help!" That is what is meant by context. What is wrong in one context is totally right in another. Context is a function of necessity and point of view – anything goes. Well, almost.

Even so, perhaps we will never understand why people do some of the things they do, including ourselves. There are ways, however. For now, the crux of the issue is forgiveness. If you goof-up enough, it gets a lot easier to forgive the next guy. You get to know the ropes and the canvas too, as it were, because no one gets to see the knock-out punch coming. And everyone knows how easily it can happen, when something wanton or insufficiently thought out brings tragedy. From the many times you have flown off the handle, you have a good idea as to how much common sense a person is able to muster when enraged, offended or hurt. Not much. But you don't shoot the horse because it bucks. You learn to ride better. Trying again is a lot like forgiveness. It's a good start.

Very often, those who have the hardest time forgiving others are the same people who have the most difficulty forgiving themselves. Self-recrimination, beyond what enables you to learn from your mistakes, is like pouring acid down your throat. Like, maybe if you are mean enough to yourself God will let you off the hook? Don't bet on it. When the day comes that you say something like: "Beam me up, Scotty," the beam you ride up on is the same one that got you here, and the Pearly Gates are merely a figure of speech. It is you, first and last, who sits in judgment of self. No one else in heaven or earth is qualified for the job. Accordingly, you really do create your own paradise or hell, both here and in the hereafter. Ultimately, you always answer to self. How then will you judge yourself when, with greater vision, you behold your real splendor? Will you then persist in hating yourself for what you've done? Frankly, why bother? Hate, like any form of recrimination or lack of forgiveness, only inhibits your ability to see things in the real light – the love-light, if you will.

Gentleness, like forgiveness, begins with self and you have every right to make it so. Nothing is so corrupted or harder to redeem than a self-maligning soul, and no state is more unnecessary. Forgiveness is not measured by long suffering, whether self-willed or imposed. Punishment accomplishes nothing except more misery, for both you and your victim. Genuine repentance, on the other hand, is the silver lining on thunder clouds through which, given time, will beam the light of understanding. Be merciful therefore, and practice it daily – on yourself. Most of us have much to learn. The entire cosmos holds it's breath in anticipation. Forgiveness is not conditional on some future event. You have to do it now. Right now. No matter what a persons has done, or has neglected to do, what they do is not who they are. Knowing this, what you do next is more important than anything you have ever done in the past.

You've heard the saying: "There but by the Grace of God go I." Let me add: "There by the Grace of God you already are." The chances are that the behavior you most despise in another is the same behavior that you worked so hard to overcome (or deny) in yourself. But, you wouldn't do that! you protest. Maybe not now you wouldn't; but, remember, every action has an equal and opposing reaction. Somewhere, sometime, somehow, you've been on both ends of every stick, taking a beating or dishing it out. The only difference between a saint and a sinner is how sharp the pickets in the fence are.

> "Search thy own heart,
> What paineth thee in others,
> In Thyself must be."
> (John Greenleaf Whittier)

As a footnote on forgiveness, absolution by someone else is absolute nonsense. Like the song says: *You gotta do it by yourself.* It's your job. If you want a raise, work for it. For many people, absolution is like a free "get out of jail" card. They think they can do anything they want, just so long as they don't forget the collection plate. Hogwash. Such reconciliation has nothing to do with personal responsibility; it only postpones amelioration. There are no shortcuts. Life itself dictates that sooner or later all things must balance. In the meantime, if an improved outlook helps one cope better, so bet it. Getting a fresh lease on life does a lot to overcome burdens of guilt, so that one might, hopefully, pick up their socks and fix things as best able. Either way, the cosmic generator that lights countless hearts begins with the spark of a single switch. So, turn on, brother! There really is a new day coming.

> "Yet spoke yon purple mountain
> Yet said yon ancient wood
> That night or day, that love or crime

Leads all souls to the good."
(Ralph Waldo Emerson)

Damnation

One of the hardest things to overcome is the notion that a person is doomed, no matter what they do. Notions of damnation rob the individual of inertia and energy, leaving feelings of despair and hopelessness in their wake. Surely, such a state is hell on earth.

The word hell comes from Anglo-Saxon *hel*, which means to conceal or cover. Notions about hell arouse such vivid imagery that even unbelievers grudgingly accept that it might be so – just in case.

Few people recognize their innate goodness in the face of certain failings, but that is what makes us human. The denial of the worth of self, if it could be seen for what it is, is the denial of the worth of God too. Compounding matters, moral dichotomy dictates that you better be good or else!

Meanwhile, virtually all religions subscribe to a postmortem place of torture for evil-doers. For the Hebrews, Sheol was the underworld for the ever-thirsty departed. For the Greeks it was abandonment in the gloomy subterranean vaults of Hades. The Norse people believed Hel to be a place of perpetual cold and darkness. Zoroastrians believed that hell was a freezing place reeking of foul odors. It wasn't until the Christian Last Judgment that things warmed up, becoming the devil's fiery domain with a "lake that burns with fire and brimstone," (Rev. 21:8), just like Islam's *Jahannan,* where a pit of fire looms beneath the bridge to paradise. For Westerners, the most famous descriptions of hell are to be found in the *Divine Comedy* by Alighieri Dante (1321) and *Paradise Lost* by John Milton (1667). While Western religions portray hell as a place of everlasting torment, most Eastern religions see hell as a stage which evolving souls pass through on their way to another existence. In Hinduism there are 21 degrees of hell through which souls must pass to earn the right to reincarnate as the Ultimate Soul. For Buddhists, hell is a state in which the five senses are experienced through varying perceptions and bodies.

Love

Everybody loves a parade, but nobody loves a nobody. What a despairing situation! Then there are people who love ice cream. Although it's hard to believe, some people even claim to love canasta. Then there are those who love to party, who love long weekends and snazzy cars. With so many things to love, is it any wonder there isn't enough time left over for people to love each other?

So, what is love, anyway? Simply put, love is what you feel for yourself. Everything else is a substitute – something that distracts you sufficiently to enable you to ignore what's inside. This applies equally to all relationships: husbands and wives, lovers, children, relatives and friends. Obviously, I have some explaining to do. To begin, love is not passion, ardor, chemistry, hunger, need, joy, the urge to procreate or to take a holiday. Love is something else. Unfortunately, that particular something else seems to be illusive. There are hints of it, from time to time, but not very much that is substantial enough to easily identify what it is. Instead, we banter the word about, loving and hating with the same fervor. If that isn't enough, the quest for love drives people to despair, overwork, lost health and torn relationships. Fortunately, we have soap operas to help us get it right.

In the age-old barter system, it is said that women give sex in order to get love, and men give love in order to get sex, after which it is called making love. Phooey. That isn't love at all. It is instinct and self-gratification, all for very good reasons of course. Complicating matters further, there is artificial love which surfaces as aspects of vanity, greed, intemperance and self-indulgence – all attributes of an ego run amok. And, finally, there are walloping love-like pacifiers such as obedience, adoration and long-suffering.

So, back to the question: what is love anyway? Love is what is left over when everything else is taken away: No mirrors, no reflections in the eyes of others and no sports channel. Love isn't something you can extract, buy or trade for. Never mind how engrossing the substitute is – and thank goodness that it is – love is undefiled, its rays beaming through one reality to the next, illuminating all. It casts no shadow, asks no mercy, begs no forbearance. It is not demanding or compromising. Love is what exudes from the Holy Essence, and the only place you can ever find it is inside yourself.

You are what love is all about. You are it. At the core of your being, the essence of you is love. You are lovely to behold and lovable in every sense of the word. It's you that makes the world go 'round, this world and a bazillion others where your light shines through and through forever. This is the real you. You cannot get love from any thing or any other person. You can only give it. The beauty of it is, once you know how, the supply is inexhaustible.

Imagine an entire world of blind people, living in total darkness, groping for love. Now imagine that you are alone on an endless prairie, buffeted by emotional winds, your reason drenched without knowing why, and you are asking the one question which will make sense of everything. "What is love?" Then, for one split second, a flash of lightening rips at you, so brilliant and searing that it penetrates your mind, momentarily illuminating the landscape from horizon to horizon and you see for the first time. In that split second your life is changed forever, because then you know. You are love. What drives people is the need for that illumination.

> "We love too little, who live today, and fear rules more of our lives than we care to admit... Guilt, loneliness, insecurity, sadness are only symptoms of a major spiritual disorder – man's alienation from God." (*The Secret of Secrets by U.S.Anderson*)

Getting real
The Velveteen Rabbit is a wonderful little book written in 1922 by Margery Williams. It is a children's story filled with marvelous pictures and spellbinding prose. Many years ago, I was so impressed that I bought several dozen copies, which,

over the years, I have given away when I felt it was appropriate. That they turned out to be first editions is a bonus; I am ever grateful to Margery. In her book, an old, raggedy Skin Horse in a nursery is responding to a question posed by a stuffed rabbit: "What is real?"

"Real isn't how you are made," said the skin horse. "It's a thing that happens to you. When a child loves you for a long, long time, not just to play with, but REALLY loves you, then you become real... It doesn't happen all at once... It takes a long time. That's why it doesn't often happen to people who break easily, or have sharp edges, or who have to be carefully kept. Generally, by the time you are real, most of your hair has been loved off, and your eyes drop out and you get loose in the joints and very shabby. But these things don't matter at all, because once you are real you can't be ugly, except to people who don't understand."

(The Velveteen Rabbit, by Margery Williams)

Personal evolution

Memory appears seven days after birth, curiosity at 2 months, the sense of shame and the ability to use simple tools at about 6 months. By about age 3 a child demonstrates self-consciousness and a senses of the ludicrous, remorse, color perception and a more profound sense of smell.The first seven years of life are dedicated to physical control and one's faculties are primarily imitative. From age 7 to 14 growth and memory develop along with individuality and the emotions. The thymus becomes recessive with the onset of puberty and from then on the rule is guidance rather than authority. On average, by age 10 the sense of music appears, along with morality, reason and judgment. From age 14 to 21 the adrenals take over, the glands of "fight and fright," giving accelerated activity and greater acuity. By 21 to 28 years man has completed most of the development of his physical self, emotions and mental states. For most people maturity comes at age 35 and peaks at 49, the culminating age of 7 times 7. Maturity is governed by one's path, free will and perseverance. Of course, all of this will vary according to the necessities of life, bringing maturity to many at a much earlier age, and, for the increasing few, according to Dr. Richard M. Bucke, former head of the Asylum for the Insane in London, Ontario, illumination, at the average age of 39 years. His contention is that this newest faculty, like all faculties, will first appear in only a few people before eventually becoming universal. Bucke, in his landmark work entitled *Cosmic Consciousness*, puts forward 14 cases of permanent illumination and 36 cases of partial or temporary illumination, and notes the increasing frequency with which it is being observed in mankind as a whole.

The upliftment of consciousness is traced through the elementary perceptual mind of lower animals, the receptual mind of higher animals possessing simple consciousness, then the self-conscious conceptual mind. The refinement of each state is progressive, with the more recently acquired faculties being the least universally developed and the most susceptible to breakdown under conditions of stress. An example is the sense of music. Most adults are drawn to pop-music and the semi-classics, while their teenage children have yet to grow past the cacophony of thumping boom boxes and the distorted whine of electric guitars. But they'll get there... a new age is upon us. Aspects of illumination are now surfacing as enhanced sensitivity and psychic awareness. Most people have experienced something of it already, while adepts are surfacing in ever greater numbers.

> We never know how high we are,
> till we are called to rise.
> And then if we are true to plan,
> Our statures touch the skies,
> (Emily Dickinson)

In instances of illumination, it is said these individuals have generally been of good health, have strong sympathies and an exalted moral nature. According to Bucke, at the moment of breakthrough, the individual is said to experience, without warning, a sense of being immersed in light, sometimes a flame or rose colored cloud; and they are bathed in joy, which feeling, fully developed, is not that of salvation, but, rather, that salvation is irrelevant. It is such a state that caught up Buddha in the Sutras, Jesus in the Parables, Paul in the Epistles, Balzac in *Seraphita,* Whitman in his *Leaves of Grass* and Edward Carpenter in *Towards Democracy.*

According to Indian teachings, illumination is attained by the uncoiling of the Kundalini serpent as it works its way up from the base of the spine, successively stimulating the seven vortices of pranic energy known as the Chakric centers in Sanskrit, or the endocrine glands in Western culture: the gonads, adrenals, pancreas, thymus, thyroid, pituitary and pineal. At full height, the serpent arouses the male and female pineal and pituitary glands to create another child of light, as symbolized by the third eye or the lotus which opens up in response to inner light. In the words of Jesus, therefore: "Be ye wise as serpents."

Bucke added: The illumined one knows that "...the cosmos, which seems made up of dead matter...is in very truth a living presence. He sees that instead of man being, as it were, patches of life scattered through an infinite sea of non-living substance, they are in reality specs of relative death in an infinite ocean of life."

Reportedly, illumination is characterized by a subjective light, moral elevation, intellectual insight, a sense of immortality, the loss of the fear of death, the overcoming of notions of sin, increased personal magnetism and a radiant countenance. This radiance has been described by some as transhumanization, or the glow of being caught up in paradise, which, in the words of those who supposedly experienced it, defies description. Dante said: "My vision was greater than our speech." U.S. Anderson summed it up with: Someday... "All men will place their proper identification in a world of spiritual beings... they will always know their true existence is infinite, eternal, and changeless. Their consciousness will be that of Christ, and each man will have found within himself the source of all joy: the Kingdom of Heaven."

<blockquote>
Ring in the valiant man and free
The larger heart, the kindlier hand!
</blockquote>

Ring out the darkness of the land,
Ring in the Christ that is to be.
(Alfred Tennyson)

Part 2
THE OUTER WORLD

CHAPTER FOUR
NEW BEGINNINGS

Matter

That which we perceive as matter is the reaction of our senses to the vibrations given off by molecules similarly constituted as ourselves. A molecule is the smallest particle of a substance that exhibits all the chemical properties of that substance. Molecules, like miniature solar systems, contain individual galaxies in which atomic clusters of planetary electrons, protons and neutrons whirl around a sun-like nucleus.

"If we consider the nucleus as commanding the same position in an atom as the sun does in our solar system, then the relative distance the electrons are apart from one another and the protons (is) equivalent to the distance the planets are from each other and from the sun." (*On the Edge of the Etheric by Arthur Findlay.*)

How else could it be? Atoms and solar systems, like Mandelbrot patterns, are modeled the same way. The symmetry is eternal and reoccurring throughout all creation. The underlying relationship between the microcosm and the macrocosm is interdependence, in which everything coexists as a function of everything else that exists. The science of these vibratory relationships, based on the modern quantum theory of radiation, is called quantum electrodynamics.

"Life is an organizing force which can counteract
the tendency in matter to disorganize itself."
(Ibid)

Everything within the electromagnetic spectrum is essentially the same phenomena being expressed at different frequencies, rattling through space at 300 million meters per second, like ripples upon a sea of possibility. The length of sound waves is only a few centimeters up to hundreds of meters. Visible light occupies a very narrow band of vibration between about 4 trillion cycles per second (violet) to 8 trillion cycles per second (red). Wavelengths in the infrared region are 1/1,000 to 1/1,000,000 of a meter; the ultraviolet region is 3/10,000,000 to 1/10,000,000,000; X-rays at 1/100,000,000 to 1/100,000,000,000 of a meter.

The physical brain is aware of about 1/6300 of the known vibratory spectrum. It is the equivalent of seeing less than one inch of a mile. What we see is photons of light, dancing upon undulating waves of ether, like moonbeams through water. All space, whether between galaxies or protons, is permeated with ether which, although invisible, for our purposes is defined as matter in a high state of vibration. It is to creation what blood is to the body, having inertia, force of movement and elasticity in a semi-fluid state.

Jesus said, "Images are visible to people, but the light within them is hidden in the image of the Father's light."
(*The Gospel of Thomas,* translated by S. Patterson and M. Meyer)

Vibration

Everything vibrates, everything moves, whether in cycles of a millionth of a second or a single cycle over millions of years. Moreover, the interaction of various vibrations produce harmonic frequencies which appear as new forms of existence.

It is the same process of growth and evolution to which all creation is subjected. Although humans sense only a tiny part of the electromagnetic spectrum, infinite vibration binds us to this world and all other worlds as well.

> Though the mills of the gods grind slowly,
> Yet they grind exceedingly small;
> Though with patience stands He waiting
> With exactness grinds He all.
> (Elizabeth Barrett Browning)

The earliest musical instruments appeared about of 30,000 years ago. Today we have the piano, with the lowest tone vibrating at 27.5 Hz (cycles per second), the highest at 4,186 Hz, with the keyboard divided into octaves after the Latin term. Each octave corresponds to a higher pitch in vibration, which become increasingly higher as you move up the keyboard through a repeating series of seven keys designated A to G. The chromatic scale comes from the Latin word chroma, meaning steps of color. But, vibration carries more than noise. Through its organization into harmonies it also conveys thoughts and feelings. For example, a scale based on the key of C begins with a tone that vibrates at 440 Hz. This is the easiest scale for beginners to learn because it has no halftones (black notes). In this key we find simple nursery rhymes such as *Twinkle, Twinkle Little Star*, and *Mary Had a Little Lamb*. The stimulating key of C can arbitrarily be compared to the color red, the first of the seven colors in the visible spectrum, 410 to 770 nm (nanometers). Red herbs, such as cayenne, cloves or musk, similarly have a heating and stimulating effect. Music that is written in scales of higher vibration tend to portray greater sensitivity, as is found in romantic or inspirational works. Rhythm and timbre also play a part. Certain baroque music, for example, generates brain wave activity which induces relaxation and contemplation. By comparison, acid rock warps the mind.

According to ancient myth, the Egyptian god Thoth initiated the idea of healing with color. In 1810 Johann Wolfgang von Goethe published *Zur Farbenlehre* (Theory of Colors) in which he described the psychological effects of color. Then, in 1878, Dr. Edwin Babbitt wrote *Principles of Light and Color,* advocating chromotherapy, in which healing was supposed to be accomplished by passing light through colored panels. It was claimed that he dramatically increased the production of grapes, in the State of New York, by replacing every 4th white panel, in a greenhouse roof, with a blue one. He went so far as to state that distilled water, in a colored glass container, could pick up the chemical properties of that color when exposed to light. A red jar of water, for example, was supposed to take on a vivifying iron tonic. Ghadiali Dinshah (1873-1966), an American, did the most detailed research into color, based in part on the work of Goethe and Newton.

As an example of the interpretation of color, red is the color of war, ruled by the warlike red planet Mars. Similarly, red military uniforms, flags, even stop signs and fire engines all have a stimulating effect. In addition, according to Dr.R.M.Bucke, red, the first color in the spectrum, was the first color perceived by man. Some people speculate that the color red, if stepped down sufficiently through the spectrum, will emerge not as color, but as a musical tone corresponding to the musical note C. Conversely, if red were stepped up a sufficient number of times it would emerge as stimulating waves of thought. In this theory, what we sense and think, indeed our very state of being, is simultaneously expressed on many levels of vibration.

Following up on this, the second color, orange, reflects the warmth and invigoration of the golden sun. It corresponds to the musical scale of D, in which is written music of an emotional nature. As an element, gold is a purifier.

Then comes yellow which relates to the planet Mercury and quickness of the nervous system and mind, which wisdom is symbolized by the yellow robes of Buddhists. Yellow herbs are purgatives such as found in sulfur, tartar and phosphorous.

Corresponding music is in the scale of E. In its negative aspect, yellow shows up as strychnine, prussic acid and cowardice.

Green is at the mid-point of the spectrum. It's counterpart, the key of F, is halfway through the musical scale. Green is the color of balance, giving stability, calm and safe passage. Its corresponding planet is Saturn with its heavy lead, which is said to rule the spleen and harmonize the body through the white blood corpuscles. In its darkened form, one is green with envy or melancholy.

Then with the key of F, and the thoughtfully haunting strains of F-minor, we rise above the electric, hot and expansive frequencies and enter the realm of soothing, magnetic blues, inspirational indigo and spiritual violet. The influence of blue and the key of G is both narcotic and cleansing, acting as a sedative on the mind and body. Venus rules, imparting love and harmony and the true-blue of romantics or, in the negative aspect, as excessive zeal or "feeling the blues." Indigo, ruled by Uranus and represented by the key of A, imparts tranquillity to the nerves and blood, together with dignity and high aspiration. Violet denotes spiritual attainment and inspiration. From it, the scale of B gives us much religious music, as well as the color of vestments and regalia.

While science has yet to prove a correlation between such things as birth salts, colors and planetary influences (and there might not be), there is ample evidence that vibrations on different levels affect us greatly.

As an illustration of vibration, consider what happens when someone sees a falling rock and shouts a warning, causing you to jump sideways. Everything happens in about a second. It's automatic. But, think about the miracle that must take place in order to save your hide.

It begins with what your friend saw: Billions of electromagnetic streams of oscillating electrical charges, called photons, 0.0004 mm (violet) to 0.0007 mm (red), reflecting off the rock at the speed of light, 186,282 miles per second. In your friend's eye, photoreceptors translated the light waves into nerve impulses that sent images along his optic nerve to an area on the underside of his brain, the lateral geniculate, where data processing is initiated before relaying electro-chemical messages, at about 40 miles per hour, to the visual cortex at the back of the brain where it is analyzed. At this stage, nerve impulses are transmitted by millions of neurons across synapses. When sufficient incoming impulses build up, the soma (cell) flashes an urgent message from its axon to the next nerve cell and the process is repeated over and over again. Beta brain waves, at 14 Hz, now activate the speech control center in the cerebral cortex to coordinate the resonance of the pharynx, mouth, nose and nasal sinuses as the lungs and chest muscles send bursts of air into the upper part of the larynx. Membranes of the vocal cords contract and tighten to produce waves of sound which are then amplified as the lips, tongue, soft palate and facial muscles articulate the vibration into words which travel through the air at 20 to 20,000 cycles per second. It is at this stage that you get into the act. The pinna, the antenna of your outer ear, funnels the sound waves into an air chamber in your middle ear where the eardrum, the tympanic membrane, vibrates three tiny bones, called a hammer, anvil and stirrup (because of their shape), which act upon another membrane to send vibration into a snail-shaped, fluid-filled chamber called the cochlea, where specialized hair-like cells react by sending electrical impulses to the auditory nerve of your brain. This, in turn, initiates a chain reaction across the synaptic gaps between each nerve cell, which, in the case of sudden alarm, is accomplished by the release of acetylcholine, a chemical made from amino acids. Upon analysis of the signals, your brain triggers the corticospinal nerve center to send a neuro-motor message at 300 mph down 12 pairs of cranial nerves and 31 pairs of nerves in the spinal cord. In $1/200^{th}$ of a second the signals finally reach your leg muscles which produce up to 50 twitches a second, causing the muscles to contract as you jump sideways.

All this was accomplished just so you could watch a rock thump into the ground beside you. Then, upon looking up, you smile as if nothing had happened, when, in truth, in the span of one second 100 trillion individual life-support systems, called cells, sent nourishment through 60,000 miles of capillaries to provide locomotion through 700 muscles and 206 bones just to get your body to shift sideways. And, what a body it is! Mostly gas – which is more obvious in some than others – it is 95% oxygen, hydrogen, carbon, and nitrogen; 3% calcium and phosphorus; 2% potassium, magnesium, sodium, iron, copper, zinc, plus trace elements like silicon, vanadium, selenium and chromium.

If the miracle of being is at all awesome, how do you relate to the billions of equally miraculous life forms that make you what you are? Each cell is the product of deliberate and thoughtful application of universal intelligence, the sum-total of which is God.

In the world of creation you will always be at the center, united with all, one within One, eternally divisible but never more or less than what you are right now. In degree, you are godly to those subordinate to you, even as you are cell-like within that which transcends you. The only thing that changes is your awareness, the dimension of the responsibility you assume because of it, and the blessed freedom by which you exercise it.

Creation

Genesis 1:2 reads: "And the earth was without form, and void; and darkness was upon the face of the deep. And the spirit of God moved upon the face of the waters." (1:7) "And God made the firmament and divided the waters..." (1:9) "...and let the dry land appear." (1:10) "And God called the dry land earth." (1:16) "And God made two great lights; the greater light to rule the day, and the lesser light to rule the night; he made the stars also."

If the sun was only a mile in diameter, the earth would be 93 miles away from it. Our nearest neighbor, Mars, would be 20 feet across and 140 miles away. The earth, a 40 foot whirling globe, superheated internally to 300 degree centigrade, would wobble through space at 19 miles a second. The American astronomer S.C. Chandler concluded that the earth's wobble is the result of the earth being out of balance. S.Newcomb wrote: "The apparent variation in terrestrial latitude may be accounted for by supposing a revolution of the axis of rotation (every) 306 days, in a direction from West to East." The wobble described by the earth's axis is called the Eulian Circle. G.V.Schhiaparelli, an Italian astronomer, added: "This phenomena of wobbling points to a displacement of the terrestrial poles, sometime in the past."

In support of this theory, iron particles in 3,500 year old Etruscan vases, discovered undisturbed in ancient kilns, solidified like compass needles in a direction indicating a different North from that of today. Herodotus was told by Egyptian priests of Thebes: "The sun has risen four times contrary to its (present) habit, and set twice where it now rises."

Shifts in the earth's axis are the likely result of the gravitational effect from another terrestrial body passing close by, such as a meteor or an asteroid, a remnant of a gigantic prehistoric comet. Over 140 asteroids, sometimes called minor planets because they orbit the Sun, have been observed and more are being discovered, such as the Apollo asteroid which, previously unknown, streaked out of the blue in 1989 to pass within 500,000 miles of earth. It was the nearest miss since the Hermes asteroid in 1937. Relative to the size of a human head, it's like a bullet parting your hair, except these bullets are hundreds of miles across. A shot in the dark every 50 years might not be much to worry about, except that there are at least a half-million in the cosmic armament that are more than a half-mile wide. A collision with one such object, 2.3 million years ago, resulted in an ice age; but near-misses, such as occurred 4700 and 1500 years ago, can have devastating effects too.

Hubble deep-space probes indicate that the universe is 12 billion years old. Meteorites originating in space, and rocks from the moon, indicate that our solar system is only 4.65 billion years old. Radio-carbon dating indicates that the oldest rocks on earth were formed only 3.8 billion years ago, before which time the earth was in a liquid-gaseous state. The oldest life, as we know it, has been found in Cambrian rock in the Canadian Shield, which dates marine invertebrates to a mere 570 million years ago. The Cenozoic Era (Greek for "recent life") has occupied the last 65 million years. Of all life-forms created during the last 2.5 million years, called the Quaternary Period, only 1% remain to this day.

F. Rainey, of the University of Alaska, said of gold mining in the Tanana Valley near Mount McKinley, the tallest mountain in North America: "Wide cuts, often several miles in length and sometimes as much as 140 feet in depth, are now being sluiced out...This 'muck' contains enormous numbers of frozen bones of extinct animals such as the mammoth, mastodon, super-bison and horse."

In 1950, Professor P.H. Quenen, a marine biologist, and Professor R. Daly of Harvard, announced that shifts in the oceans had taken place as recently as 3500 years ago. Tectonic catastrophes that raised or lowered the ocean floor by thousands of feet have been reported by H. Petterson of the Oceanographic Institute of Goteborg, who also stated that deposits of nickel and ash in the Pacific and Indian Oceans lead to the conclusion that the shifts were accompanied by "very heavy showers of meteors and massive volcanic activity." In 1949, Professor Ewing of Columbia University said: "Either the land must have sunk two or three miles, or the sea must have been two or three miles lower than now." Other researchers have determined that sedimentation in the Alaska Delta is only 3,600 years old, and that it is only 3,000 years since the Rhone Glacier started melting. H.E. Suess, of the U.S. Geological Survey team, said that glacier ice was advancing only 3,500 years ago, not 30,000 years ago as once thought. Measurements of erosion in the Upper Great Gorge indicate that Niagara Falls didn't even exist 3,000 years ago (G.F.Wright. *The Date of the Glacial Period*). A little closer to home, in certain parts of Alabama and other Gulf States, bones of tertiary whales (Zeuglodon) were found in such numbers that farmers once used them to make fences.

Obviously, things are changing, and at a rate that ought to shake most of us out of our complacency. Even Haley's Comet, based on the measurement of its diminishing tail, could not have existed 3,500 years ago. Radio-carbon dating has established that many of the great changes in the earth are far more recent than once presumed. (All cells contain uniformly measurable radio-carbon radiation, which, after death, decreases by half every 5,568 years). It turns out that many of the greatest upheavals happened only 34 and 26 centuries ago, bringing earthquake and holocaust upon the splendor of Egypt, the Indus Valley and the jungles of Peru alike.

Darwin, from a plateau in the Uspallara Range of Argentina, wrote: "(The Atlantic ocean)…now driven back 700 miles, (once) came to the foot of the Andes. …but again the subterranean forces exerted themselves and now I beheld the bed of that ocean, forming a chain of mountains, more than 7,000 feet in height…"

The south of England and parts of Northern Europe are sinking into the North Sea, in some places at the rate of four inches per century. Meantime, Spain and southern France are rising. "Biarritz gains more than an inch in altitude every year, Cadiz nearly two inches. In France, the land is sinking in the Seine-Maritime, Somme and Pas-de-Calais regions. Rouen will be a seaport by the year 2500." (Robert Charroux from *One Hundred Thousand Years of Man's Unknown History*)

The past is but a beginning of a beginning,
and all that has been is but the twilight of the dawn.
(H.G.Wells)

The emergence of man

If the history of the earth was compressed into a single year, there would be no life for the first 8 months. Primitive life would appear by the end of October and mammals would appear mid-December. Man would emerge on the last day of the year, about 15 minutes before midnight, and only the very last minute would be recorded history.

According to Robert Charroux, until recently, the only proof that ancient man existed fifteen minutes before midnight was the Grossetto shinbones, an Atlanthropus jawbone, a little pile of ash for Zinjanthropus, a plaster cast for Australopithecus and a few scraps of Plesianthropus, of which nothing compares to modern man's cranial capacity of 1,350 cubic centimeters. But, all that changed in 1975 when Mary Leakey, excavating in the Olduvai Gorge of northern Tanzania, found hominid remains that were more than 2.4-million-years-old. Her son, Richard, digging in East Turkana, Kenya, uncovered hominid fossils that were 3 million years old. But, most astounding of all, in 1978 Mary Leaky unearthed two short parallel trails of hominid prints that extended more than 80 feet in rock that dated from 3.6 million years ago.

It was during the Miocene Epoch, 20 million years ago, that genetic mutations began to differentiate hominids from our nearest relative, the pongid (ape), and only 4 million years ago that we emerged as a separate specie. All creatures on the tree of life are related however, those on different branches as well as those on branches that have broken off. Out of 2 billion species that evolved over the course of the last 600 million years, 99.9 percent are now extinct, leaving you and I to be among the select 2 million species that survive to this day. Even so, we are not far removed from our ancestors. Great apes and humans still have similar skeletons, the musculature is the same, as are the physiological processes, serological reactions and chromosomal patterns. Even our blood is similar. In the hemoglobin molecule, which makes blood red, all 141 amino acids are the same except one. The most noticeable differences are in the way we walk and way we think, the result of our brains having evolved to a cranial capacity that is 2 ¼ times larger than our distant cousin's.

Evolution is the accumulative process whereby new structural and functional traits are encoded in the genetic material that is passed from one generation to the next, thereby inducing the changes necessary to ensure survival. Deoxyribonucleic acid (DNA) in the genes, modifies enzymes to produce change through mutation. DNA is like a spiraling ladder, the rails are sugar-phosphate and the rungs are nucleotide bases. There are so many genes in a gamete (sex cell) that mutation is practically inevitable. Yet, because of the vast number of genes, apparent mutation is a slow process, during which time the combinations of genes is so distinct that nature will never ever create another you. You are the original one and only.

Marching through time
Thousands of years ago the solar year was recorded by placing giant stones according to the movement of the sun along the horizon; months were determined by observing the moon, while Easter rites were celebrated at the time of the spring equinox. Ancient calendars were usually numbered according to a particular ruler's reign. It wasn't until 525 that a monk named Dionysius Exiguus proposed the years be counted both ways from the birth of Jesus, with AD (Anno Domini: "the year of the Lord") being the current era, and anything "before Christ" being designated as BC. Unfortunately, chronology being what it is, they got the starting point wrong. It now appears that the actual birth of Jesus might have been around 4 BC., but nobody dares change the calendar again.

The Babylonians, and then the Jews and Romans, divided the year into weeks of seven days, keeping the last day as the Sabbath, naming it *dies solis* or the Sun's day. The rest of the days were named after the moon, the planets, and various Norse deities, giving us Monday, the Moon's day; Tuesday for Tiw, the pagan god of war; Wednesday for Woden, the chief Norse god; Thursday for Thor, the god of work; Friday for Freya, the goddess of love; and Saturday, for Saturni or Saturn's day, the Jewish Sabbath.

In the 1600's, an Irish clergyman, by the name of Bishop James Ussher, added up the years of the biblical genealogies and announced that the Earth was created in 4004 BC. Be that as it may, Genesis 2:7 states: "...the Lord God formed man of the dust of the ground and breathed into his nostrils the breath of life; and man became a living soul." Later on things get more complicated: "And all the days that Adam lived were 930 years, Seth 912, Enos 905, Cainan 910, Mahalaleel 895, Jared 962, Enoch 365, Methuselah 969, Lamech, and Noah 777 years. (Gen. 5:3-31) Wow, that'd take some birthday cake! One wonders if such longevity is possible, or perhaps, if their years were shorter than ours. The News Service out of Pasadena, California, reported: "Scientists say they've learned how much the Earth's rotation is slowing by studying ancient Chinese records of solar eclipses. Just as a spinning skater slows down by extending her arms, the Earth's rotation on its axis slows as tidal interaction makes the moon orbit the Earth more quickly." Kevin Pang, an astronomer at NASA's Jet Propulsion Laboratory said: "Four billion years ago, the moon was only one-third as far away as it is now, and the day was only eight hours long at the time." If that's true, the average age of the reported Genesis life span works out to 282 years. That's still pushing it. But, things get straightened out in Genesis 6:3: "...for that he also is flesh, yet his days shall be an hundred and twenty years."

Humankind has not only survived, but has continued to evolve, reaching a population of perhaps 10 million by the time of the New Stone Age, 10,000 years ago. As agriculture and animal husbandry eclipsed hunting and gathering and permanent settlements became cities, the population increased to 250 million by the year 1 AD, 340 million by the year 1000, a half-billion by the year 1650, 3.6 billion by 1970 and then it nearly doubled in only 30 years to reach 6 billion by the year

2000, of which nearly 1% have Aids. Nevertheless, projections are that the world population will reach 8 billion by 2028, and 12 billion within 50 years.

"The Universal mind is the central self that inhabits all beings, that incarnates endlessly in manifold expression of its infinite nature."
(U.S. Anderson in The Secret of Secrets.)

Twilight

The Renaissance, from the 14th to the 16th century, was heralded as a time of freedom of thought. It owes its name to the French word for rebirth. During the Reformation, freedom for scientific investigation came to the fore while Christendom attempted to purge itself of medieval atrocities and restore the church in conformance with the New Testament. It was during this time of enlightened, in 1415, that the church burned John Huss, a priest who criticized the church for its corruption and propensity for wealth. The most noted philosopher of the Italian Renaissance, Giordano Bruno, a Dominican priest, was accused of heresy, then imprisoned by the Inquisition and burned at the stake in 1600 because he worshipped God as part of the infinite cosmos. Then, in 1633, the church condemned Galileo for suggesting that the earth, rather than being stationary, moved around the sun. Two hundred and fifty years later the church made a giant leap forward when Pope Pious XII declared it was up to the individual to determine if he would believe Darwin's 1858 Theory of Evolution or the creation story in Genesis.

The Hebrew texts, upon which the Old Testament is based, place the creation of the world at about 3761BC. Well, maybe. U.S. Anderson, in *The Secret of Secrets*, describes creation this way: "Form is the shaping out of matter of an idea called forth from Universal Mind...The process of creation involves juxtaposition of finite mind with Universal Mind, so that the former pours into the later as a lake might pour into a river."

A New Day

If you had been caught reading this book five-hundred years ago you would be considered apostate, having forsaken God's laws. With two accusers you would be brought before a tribunal of Dominican or Franciscan friars and would face the wrath of the inquisition. Then, according to Saint Augustine's interpretation of Luke 14:23, in which force is endorsed for use against heretics, you would be tortured and put to death. One can only wonder what would happen if they caught you reading a Superman comic. The times are a-changing. Only 400 years after the inquisition, by the start of the 20th century, the world was in a tizzy over psychic phenomenon and Spiritualism, then touted as being the fastest growing religion in the world. Table-tapping and seances were vogue. Books on the subject appeared in droves, on everything from fairies to communication with those who died in the Great War. Then, about fifty years ago, horoscopes went from being practically non-existent to becoming syndicated in 70% of U.S. newspapers. Today, there are hundreds of self-help spiritual sites on the internet. Things are indeed changing, not just fast, but faster all the time.

How fast? The first airplane, the Wright Flyer, lifted off the ground in 1903. Only 66 years later, in 1969, Neil Armstrong, commander of the Apollo 11 project, landed in the Sea of Tranquility and walked on the moon, proclaiming: "That's one small step for man, one giant leap for mankind." But, there were other leaps for mankind too. Consider, for instance, the ancient Greeks, Aristotle and Xenophanes, who knew of only three colors. Democritus knew only black, white, red and yellow. Moreover, in the primitive Indo-European language there is not a single word describing color – at a time when there were supposedly 5,744 words describing a camel! Even in the bible, in which the sky is mentioned more than 430 times, the color blue is not mentioned once. How come? The same is true in the 48 volumes of the *Iliad and Odyssey* by Homer, the 10,000 lines of the *Zend Avesta* and the *Rig Veda*. All names for blue were merged in words that described black. English blue and German blau descend from a word meaning black. The Chinese hi-u-an, which now means sky-blue, used to mean black. Nil, in Persian and Arabic, which means blue, is derived from the name of the Nile, the black river, of which Niger is the Latin form. Totems of Western Canada, dating to 6,000 years ago, were painted only red and black, and no wonder: The astonishing reason is that, not so very long ago, our ancestors could not see the seven colors and the thousands of shades that we do. That is another great leap.

An expanded sense of color, like the rest of our senses, first appeared in only a few individuals. Gradually, over time, the ability has been acquired by more and more people until, now, one is considered deficient without it. In the same way, simple consciousness of millions of years ago has evolved to become self-consciousness of about 300,000 years ago. Color started coming to us about 20,000 years ago, and music about 10,000 years ago. Morality – of which love is a hallmark – may have appeared as recently as 5,000 years ago. It seems that the Vikings spent a heck of a lot more time making war than making love.

Forty years ago the amount of information in the world was doubling every twenty years or so. Now it's down to less than five years. Meanwhile, the capacity of computer chips is doubling every 18 months. Everything is being accelerated. Growth on every level and in every sense is being increased exponentially. In keeping with this, the newest faculty to be acquired is intuition, that of heightened perception and awareness, the forerunner of illumination. Call it ESP, cosmic consciousness or whatever, we're all in the stream of it, getting wet and swimming for all we're worth.

One day, in the near future, one's greater reality will be far less speculative. Gone will be the days when man perceives things but not himself, and the notion of death will be seen as the absurdity that it is.

There never was a time that never was. There never was a beginning or an end. There was, in its place, murmurings and gestations of myriad sorts and wonders, all sublime, all of divine origin. The use of the word origin does not connote a beginning, at least not as we define it in physical terms.

Beginnings, in this sense, are the appearance of a new means of expression of that which has existed all along. The central player is the same, only his costume has changed. It is a difficult concept for the finite mind to grasp, but for those less limited it is as natural as the scent of fresh flowers upon the cosmic air.

It is out of such beginnings that man and spirit find themselves, often interchanging places, oftentimes bemused and set upon with distraction. But our purpose has always been the same, that we might grow in the light of the One who placed us here. People, as has been said, are truly like flowers, blooming exactly when they are supposed to, and of ineffable beauty.

But we're not the only ones in the dark. Even on the spirit side of things, the mystery often remains. Those who are closest to us don't necessarily have all the answers, but, then, they don't necessarily ask the same questions either. They do comprehend our motivation, however, having walked the proverbial mile in our shoes. That they understand, or that we think they do, is attested to by the hundreds of books on the subject.

In the twilight of realization, each of us peers into the gloom, necessarily asking about life itself. What is it? Where does it come from? And why bother? To answer the first question: life is. That's all there is to it. To answer the second question: it always was. To answer the third question: life is what you make it.

You cannot kill life – not any in any form. You may have the illusion of having done so, but that is contrary to the facts. Life is God. All life is. There is no single aspect of life which is otherwise. Can you kill God? My friend, you cannot even kill yourself, though at times you might presume to try. Life is the one thing that cannot be destroyed, and from it extends everything else, equally indestructible. What is, is.

Doomsday

"For nation shall rise against nation…and there shall be famines, pestilences and earthquakes in diverse places…and then shall the end come... for then shall be great tribulation, such as was not since the beginning of the world to this time, no, nor ever shall be. The sun shall be darkened, and the moon shall not give her light, and the stars shall fall from heaven, and the powers of the heavens shall be shaken."(Mat. 24: 7-29).

Oh, goody.

Of the great Hindu epic poems of 500BC (the *Ramayana* and the *Drona Parva)* the *Deeds of Rama* recount in Sanskrit the wars of Rama (an incarnation of Vishnu):

"The hero Rama destroyed whole cities; hurtling fire at them, that produced a light brighter than a thousand suns. A high wind arose, and the fire of the terrible weapon burned elephants, soldiers, chariots and horses. Yet no one saw the fire, it was not visible. It made man's hair fall out and bleached the feathers of birds. To escape the effect of the invisible fire, the soldiers leapt into rivers to wash themselves and all objects that they would have to touch."

To anyone who knows, the forgoing is about as accurate a description as you can get of nuclear war – in ancient times! almost 3,000 years before the common era. Whether it actually happened, or is prophetic, is a moot point. Since WWI, the war that was to end all wars, there has been another global war, about 20 limited wars, easily 50 political assassinations, 100 rebellions for independence and about the same number of revolutions – either political, economic or religious – of which many are still continuing, together with guerrilla activity and terrorism of every kind. The body count for the last century is the highest in the history of mankind. That's progress for you.

In 1945, the United States was the first country to acquire nuclear weapons, the USSR got them in 1949, Britain in 1952, France in 1960, the People's Republic of China in 1964 and India in 1974. Obviously, the likelihood of a nuclear holocaust is proportional to the distribution of such weapons. By 1960 the American nuclear arsenal was capable of destroying about one-third of the Soviet population and 75% of their industry, even after a first-strike. The USSR had the same retaliatory capability, thereby locking both sides in the stalemate of Mutually Assured Destruction (MAD). Although 130 countries signed the Non-Proliferation Treaty of 1968, it isn't much of a safeguard because it has become increasingly less difficult to obtain nuclear technology and fuel. On the internet you can get instructions on how to build a nuclear bomb that will fit inside a suitcase. Today, at least 7 countries possess nuclear weapons and another 13 either have them or are working on them. With the breakdown of the Soviet Union and attendant loss of control over parts of its nuclear inventory, together with China's continued willingness to sell fissionable material, it is likely only a matter of time until nuclear weapons are in the hands of terrorist groups as well.

After 5 limited test bans and various treaties, it was the far-sighted Mikhail Gorbachev who made a serious effort to limit USSR-US confrontation through the Intermediate-Range Nuclear Forces Treaty of 1987 (INF), which eliminated all land-based missiles having a range of between 500 and 5,000 km (310 and 3,100 mi.). The cold war finally ended in 1990 when the USSR agreed to reduce its conventional weapons systems to match that of NATO and the Warsaw Pact forces, specifically 20,000 artillery pieces and 50,000 tanks and armored vehicles. Immediately following, in 1991, under the START-II treaty, each side agreed to reduce its nuclear arsenal by a further 30%. By 2003, America and Russia will have reduced their current nuclear arsenals from 15,000 and 24,000 respectively, to 10,000 each, thereby fractionally reducing their global overkill capacity. In addition, there will be at least another 1,000 nuclear devices in the hands of others.

"God is our refuge and strength,
A very present help in trouble.
Therefore will not we fear"
(Psalm 46)

A little bird told me
Michael Nostradamus (1504-1566), a famous French physician and astrologer, prophesied the rise of Napoleon and Hitler as

the 1st and 2nd Antichrist. He went on to say that the 3rd Antichrist, Mabus, will first appear in the 1980's in the east. Then, some say, Nostradamus predicted that in July 1999 a great King of Terror will come from the skies, following which there will be 30 days of darkness, a return of the Mongols and 27 years of war in which Dalmatia plays a key role. Dalmatia, of course, is the old name for Yugoslavia, where NATO troops defended Kosovar Albanians in March 1999.

> The year 1999, seventh month,
> From the sky will come a King of Terror.
> To bring back the great King of the Mongols,
> Before and after Mars rules happily.
> (Nostradamus. *Century 10, Quatrain 72*)

Mars is the god of war and spiritual transformation.

Before the 2001 terrorist attack on the World Trade Center, the name of the 3rd antichrist, Mabus (C2,Q62), was frequently interpreted as Sadam Hussein of Iran, or as a North African terrorist (C2,Q30) from the land of Hannibal, or as someone like Genghis Khan, who led the Mongolians of the Central Asian steppes to conquer Iraq, Iran, Pakistan and parts of the former Soviet Union. After the 9/11 attack on New York and the Pentagon, likely the name Osama bin Laden has been added to the list, along with his al-Qaida network.

All of this paints an extraordinary picture which is very frightening for some people. But, prophesy and its interpretation being what they are, July 1999 passed without the skies darkening for 30 days after all. In fact, nothing has happened before. Edgar Cayce, the famed American "sleeping prophet," said that a polar shift would sink Northern Europe into the sea in 1998. At the same time, Japan was supposed to be destroyed by earthquakes and the west coast of America slide into the sea. Well, judging by the Seattle broadcasts of classical music that I listen to, they're still there. Obviously, one shouldn't despair, even if all the planets are in alignment on 5 May 2000; even if Malachy, an Irish archbishop, was credited with an 1138 prediction that after Pope John, the very last Pope, named Peter the Roman, would leave office out of a burning city. Nostradamus also prophesied that the last pope would leave over the bodies of his priests, and added that after Pope John there will be two more popes until the "great change" in the year 2012. And, then, there's the Mayans whose wonderful calendar stops in 2012 when the world is supposed to end, coincidentally with the return of asteroid 1989FC, which gave us a close call in 1989 and is supposed to return in 11 year cycles around 2000 and 2012. Some astronomers predict it will hit either Mars, our moon or the Earth.

What to believe? Many experts claim that Nostradamus' quatrains are simply too vague and cryptic to mean much of anything. He frequently uses puzzling anagrams, several different languages and nothing is in chronological order. Other experts claim the verses foretold everything from the Great Fire of London in 1666 to the assassination of President Kennedy in 1963.

Either way, the believers of Millenarianism expect the worst – or the best, depending on how you look at it – the imminent second coming of Christ and the establishment of a new world order. According to the renowned preaching of William Miller (1782-1849) and his interpretations of Daniel and Revelations, the second coming was supposed to happen no later than October 1844. The fact that it didn't has not, however, dampened the enthusiasm of the remaining 1,000,000 or so Millerites, who have since formed the Seventh-Day Adventists and the Advent Christian Church.

Fundamentalists believe in the inerrancy of the Bible, meaning that it has no errors whatsoever. They, therefore, interpret the Bible as the literal words of God. They accept the divinity of Jesus, the virgin birth, his death for our sins, the resurrection, and his second coming to judge the living and the dead upon establishing a millennium of peace, all of which was affirmed in the 1878 creed of the Niagara Bible Conference and the Presbyterian General Assembly of 1910. This belief is widespread, with American fundamentalism and evangelism thriving on religious broadcasting, while organizations like the

Moral Majority oppose just about everything else just for good measure.

The judgment day scenario and the second coming is, however, thinly supported by the Bible. In the New Testament there is a hint about the second coming in Hebrews 9:28: "So Christ was once offered to bear the sins of many; and unto them that look for him shall he appear the second time without sin unto salvation." Considering the importance this event has assumed in modern Christianity, this isn't much to go on.

The early Christians expected the second coming would take place right away, but no such luck. Since then, at the turn of every century, there has been renewed fervor and watchfulness. The advent of the present millennium, however, did pass without much fanfare, even though for many people it was fraught with personal trauma. For anyone who believes in the miraculous, and even those who don't believe but fear it anyway, the prospect of doomsday is hard to ignore. For the stoic, if it happens they will have the privilege of witnessing mother nature's birth pains of a new era.

The new world
At the other end of the scale, millions of people are now embracing what can aptly be called The New World Order. The new world is a wondrous place in which you are a wizard of all-time. But it is not heavily populated. Few people will see your world as you do. Other wizards may, since it takes one to know one. Being a wizard is like being a master painter. The one who will most appreciate your work will be another master, not those who merely dabble and have yet to learn how to get magic out of their medium. Still, it is not a lonely place. Far from it. Loneliness stems from isolation, the result of not understanding and not being understood. In this new state you will be able to say what you mean and mean what you say. With comprehension comes acceptance, by self and others, and peace.

This is a place of transformation. Like the butterfly, you will rise and see things differently. In a sense, as you are lifted on gossamer wings, flashing brilliantly, your feet will no longer touch the ground.   I am reminded of the words of Walt Whitman:

"We too take ship O soul,
with laugh and many a kiss;
O soul thou pleasest me, I thee."

This is your right of passage.

CHAPTER FIVE
BELIEF SYSTEMS

The right path

Everybody likes to believe they are on the right path. Why else bother? But, these paths have a way of converging and separating again, always leading higher and higher, the vision at each plateau being shared by all who pass that way. But, human nature being what it is, there is a tendency to think that one particular view is better than another. No doubt, for the one that is enthralled, it is – at least for the time being.

All paths share the same mountain, however, sometimes bringing us within shouting distance of each other, even if we can't quite see eye-to-eye. At other times we hear people whispering, as if they were just around the next corner, egging us on. Whether murmuring or yelling, do you believe what they're saying? How much credulity do you give Herodotus, Diodorus, Pliny or Virgil, who speak of the legendary lands of the Hyperboreans, supposedly somewhere in the Arctic of long ago? Babylonian and Greek sailors claimed to have seen them. Is it possible?

In 1957, old maps were discovered that date back to the time of Alexander the Great, presumably from the secret archives of Egyptian and Moslem priests. The maps contain details of the earth before being covered over by the last glacial period 10,000 years ago. The maps, found in the Topkapu palace in Istanbul, once belonged to a Turkish sea captain named Piri Reis, the commander of the Ottoman fleet in 1550. The maps showed the coastal outlines of North and South America and Antarctica, including the topography and mountain ranges, and showed Greenland as being three islands, not one – all of which was not confirmed until 1952, by seismic probes, when Paul-Emile Victor led the American Task Force

43 on behalf of the International Geophysical Year. If that's not enough, the old maps had to be aerial.

And, what about the mystery of the Himalayas in Northern India, where shrouded peaks rise 29,000 feat above sea level, yet the rocks bear evidence of fish fossils, mollusks and under-sea vegetation. Is this proof of Noah's flood? Even in the Swiss Alps, in the Drachenlock cavern, bones and man-made artifacts have been found at the 8,000 foot level in the center of massive glaciers that date to the Pleistocene age. Life, apparently, has existed where it ought not to be possible. Does this not add at least a hint of plausibility to Plato's Atlantis or the Hyperboreans? Are the secrets of the ages to be found at the end of the Bimini Road, or in the slime covered vaults of Poseida? What do you believe?

Believe it or not
All belief, when it comes right down to it, is personal, regardless of what church or philosophy is endorsed. It is one's heart and mind at its best. Inspiration comes to house painters as well as artists; to auctioneers as well as biblical scholars; to bus drivers as well as disciples.

The dictionary defines religion as a set of beliefs concerning cause, nature and purpose. On the personal level, cause is based on what you think; your nature is conditioned by how you apply it, and your purpose is its validation. Yet the religion of self, if I can put it that way, is an unavoidable consequence of what you believe about the greater world. At the same time, your view of the world is a reflection of what you believe about yourself. One is conditioned by the other and both are reciprocal. What you believe infiltrates every aspect of your life, even if you claim not to believe anything. You may be judgmental, skeptical, or tolerant, it makes no difference. If you so choose, you can see yourself as an unforgivable product of evil, or as a spark of the divine. However you decide, the end product is you.

In this light, and to begin to exercise your expanded learning abilities, now is a good time to shake up the system a little by reevaluating some of the assumptions that have been carried forward since childhood. The object is not to suggest that any given belief system is better than another, but, rather, to create a sense of worth and unity in all pursuits. We all desire the same things in life, to fulfill the intention by which we were created. Our mandate is to create reality that is based on the best information available to us and to seek the enlightenment to apply it well.

Religion, in all its varied forms and tenets, is utterly fascinating. It is the sum total of the endeavor of generations upon generations, in every clime and culture. Our quest is to see the grander vision, the reason behind it all and the glory. Bowing to Mecca, supplicating before an icon, or seeing one's ancestors in the stars, it's all the same: people doing the best they can to perceive the best that is.

Long ago, it all began with fetishism, the worship of the sun and earthly objects, together with considerable preoccupation with fertility and death. Gradually, this evolved into polytheism, the worship of many personal gods and various sacred idols, which are still used in religions such as Buddhism and Hinduism. The Jews continued to have many Gods long after the acceptance of the Ten Commandments. The prophet Jeremiah said, in the 6th century: "According to the number of cities are thy Gods." Then came monotheism and the worship of one God, at which time Judaism, Islam and Christianity banned the making and worship of idols. (Exod. 20:4-6; 34:17) Finally, with pantheism, God is identified with the universe and everything in it.

Jesus said, "If your leaders say to you, 'Look, the (Father's) kingdom is in the sky,' then the birds of the sky will precede you. If they say to you, 'It is in the sea,' then the fish will precede you. Rather, the kingdom is within you and it is outside you."

The Gospel of Thomas,
(Translated by Stephen Patterson and Marvin Meyer)

Revelations

It is said that Abraham, Isaac and Jacob received the first revelation of the one, true God, who promised special protection to the twelve Israelite tribes. This is affirmed daily in the opening words of the Shema: "Hear O Israel, the Lord our God, the Lord is One" (Deut.6:4). The basic source of Jewish belief is in the first five books of the Old Testament, called the Torah or the Pentateuch, from which springs both Christianity and Islam, now the dominant religions in the world. In Judaism, many of the ideas surrounding angels, Satan, doomsday, the last judgment and resurrection of the dead were borrowed from the early Persian religion of Zoroastrianism, which is based on the teachings of the prophet Zarathusthra, also known as Zoroaster.

Zoroaster profoundly influenced Greek, Jewish, Christian, and Muslim thought. The earliest Zoroastrian writings and mythology parallel the Indian Vedas. Two groups of opposing gods were worshipped, the ahuras and the daevas, of which Ahura Mazda was the wise creator of the world who delegated his authority through seven Amesha Spentas, or Bountiful Immortals, the first of which was Spenta Mainyu whose twin, Angra Mainyu, (Hostile Spirit) is bent on turning all of creation into a battleground until Ahura Mazda destroys the world and creates anew. Following persecution in the 10th century, most followers of Zoroaster migrated to India to become known as the Parsis of today's Bombay.

Mithraism arose out of the declining ranks of Zoroastrianism, once dominating the Roman Legions, making its appearance in connection with the sun, water and fertility. Ahura Mazda became Ormazd and is identified with Spenta Mainyu, while Angra Mainyu, now Ahriman, remains his evil antagonist. Ahura Mazda, meanwhile, having lost some of his power, now needs the help of Mithra, who acts as mediator and protector of the world. This typical dualist view eventually became the orthodox position from which the Greco-Romans adopted much of today's religion as expounded in the apocalypses, a series of books which were omitted from the Hebrew Bible, with the exception of the Book of Daniel.

It is said the Hebrew tribes, later called Jews, were rescued from Egyptian slavery by Moses. Much of our information of the period comes from Josephus, a Jewish historian, Philo the philosopher and Pliny the Elder, a Roman historian. By 1200 BC the Jews had settled in Palestine, only to be captured again, this time by neighboring Babylonians and Assyrians. Over a thousand years were to pass before the tolerant Persians allowed the Jews to return to Palestine, only to be ousted once more by the Romans in the 2d century AD. All the while, the pharisaic leaders, later known as Rabbi, laboriously recorded hundreds of years of history in the *Mishnah*, the *Talmud* and the many works of *Midrash*, in which they maintained the concept of one God who created the universe and rules with divine purpose. At the same time, other Jews, the early Christians, chose to believe that Jesus was the messiah. Following leaders such as Saint Paul, the Christians split apart from Judaism and, within 400 years, gentile Christianity became dominant, with the message being spread to the Mediterranean and Western Europe by the Greeks and Romans.

The Old Testament refers to God as YHWH, which translates as "He who is," which is written as Yahweh or Adonai, meaning Lord. The combination of the two became Jehovah in English Bibles. Allah means the same thing in the Islamic religion. But, there are other views as well. According to Tao, "the way" of Taoism, the hymns to Indra in Hinduism, the concept of the Logos in Stoicism, and the devotion to Ahura Mazda, the Zoroastrian god of light, the notion of a personal God is replaced with that of divine harmony. Some religions even claim that God is quite beyond ordinary speech or comprehension, such as in Mahayana Buddhism, in which the ultimate principle is Nothingness or Voidness, and the idea of a personal God is considered both unbefitting and derogatory.

Around 1500 BC, Hinduism surfaced after the Aryan invasion of India and a subsequent merger of beliefs. The Vedas, which are early Aryan hymns, give the account of an amazing number of deities, including Brahma the creator, Vishnu the preserver, and Shiva the destroyer. A thousand years later, Siddhartha Gautama (560 to 480 BC) became the Buddha, the enlightened one, while, at the same time, the prophet Mahavira founded Jainism. Both Buddha and Mahavira repudiated the luxurious surroundings in which they were raised, Mahavira to become an ascetic, while Gautama taught about karma, the overcoming of physical and material desires and union with the infinite through the loss of personal identity. Although Buddhism eventually disappeared from India, it is now widely practiced in Asia.

Elsewhere, the countries of Eastern Asia share an ancient Chinese culture from the Shang dynasty of 1500 BC which, by AD400, had spread to Vietnam, Korea and Japan. Ancient concepts of familial duty and ancestor worship are still practiced according to the teachings of Confucius (*K'ung-fu T'zu*), as found in Japanese Shintoism (the way of the spirits), Taoism Tao – *the way* which embraces reincarnation and Karma – and Chinese Buddhism. Confucius, born 551BC, a contemporary of Buddha, was greatly influenced by Lao-Tze, the Jesus of China who was born of a virgin mother and conceived under a falling star. He preached a high moral code as the way of attainment.

Confucius believed in one God and three types of subsidiary spirits as recorded in the *Digested Conversations*, a large part of which was destroyed in the *Ts'in* dynasty.

Finally, there is Japan's Zen Yoga, which originated in China. The Zen classic is a poem entitled *The Taming of the Bull,* the bull being the animal lure to materialism. As an aside, it was the Zen monks who invented Ju Jitsu as practiced by Samurai warriors.

In more recent times, the Islamic prophet Muhammad Ibn Abdullah (570-632 AD) was born in Mecca, the center of power under the Abbasid caliphate. Muslims believe that God sent Muhammad as an apostle with the message in the Koran. Meanwhile, in Western culture, present day ideas about God were shaped by Greco-Roman philosophy in the period 200 to 1400 AD, as well as Platonic and Aristotelian philosophy, with a bias toward a transcendent being about whom there has been endless debate ever since. Is God to be known by reason or by experience? And, if all else fails, should he be known by faith alone? In the final analysis, it is abvious that God is as personal as individual belief makes Him out to be.

The Bible

The word Bible is derived from the Greek word *biblia*, meaning books, and refers to the sacred writings of Judaism and Christianity as translated from Hebrew and Aramaic into Greek during the Diaspora, the scattering of the Jews out of Babylonian captivity. The Bible consists of two parts: the Old Testament, the sacred writings of the Jewish people between 950BC and 550BC, and the New Testament, the stories of Jesus and the early Christians.

The Old Testament gives the revelations of the prophets, the nature of sin and worship, and details of the covenants that God (Yahweh) made with Abraham and his descendants, thereby making them his chosen people so long as they obeyed his laws. The Ten Commandments, supposedly revealed to Moses, are a literal translation of earlier Mesopotamian laws, which are preserved in their unique type of cuneiform writing on a diorite column found at Susa, likely dating from the time of Hammurabi, who reigned about 1800 years prior to the Christian era.

Genesis, as told in the Bible, is borrowed from the Israeli creation stories, in which six different groups of deities had their own day of creation, after which they rested. The Bible merely leaves out their names in order to support the one-God premise. The word Moses, in Egyptian, simply means birth. The story of the Exodus and the flight of the Jews from Egypt is a complete myth that lacks any archeological proof that 600,000 people (a third of Egypt's population at the time) lived in the desert and rocky barrens for 40 years. Moreover, the timing: "In the fourth year of Solomon's reign over Israel," does not match known Egyptian history, nor even other biblical texts. Equally untrue is the notion that the Egyptians persecuted the Israelites: They welcomed all religions and nationalities. Egyptians accepted religion as a natural aspect of day to day life, in which the simple routine of everyday affairs was raised to an act of worship. They saw God in all things. Records from the old Hermaic books are few, but writings on the mummy-cases about rituals for the dead are excerpts.

The canon of New Testament literature originated in the 2d century, 200 years after the time of Jesus, and is likely based on ten letters from Paul. But, for almost 400 years after the time of Jesus, there were a great many gospels having the names of various apostles attached to them, such as The Book of Thomas, written 130AD, which, like the Book of Josephus, is omitted from the modern Bible.

Athanasius, the bishop of Alexandria, and Jerome, included 27 books in their official Latin version of the Bible called the Vulgate. It was only in 367AD that those 27 books were accepted as the New Testament that we have today. Official or otherwise, the Bible as we know it propagates gross contradictions of truth and reason, such as in John 8, in which the Jews were labeled as children of Satan, quite ignoring the fact that Jesus was a Jew as well.

Just for fun, here is an open letter that was posted on the internet in response to comments made by Laura Schlessinger, a US radio personality who dispenses advice to people who call in to her radio show. Apparently, she said that, as an observant Orthodox Jew, homosexuality is an abomination according to Leviticus 18:22 and cannot be condoned in any circumstance. Here is the reply she got:

"Dear Dr. Laura: Thank you for doing so much to educate people regarding God's Law. I have learned a great deal from your show, and I try to share that knowledge with as many people as I can. When someone tries to defend the homosexual lifestyle, for example, I simply remind them that Leviticus 18:22 clearly states it to be an abomination. End of debate. I do need some advice from you, however, regarding some of the specific laws and how to follow them. a) When I burn a bull on the altar as a sacrifice, I know it creates a pleasing odor for the Lord (Lev. 1:9). The problem is my neighbors. They claim the odor is not pleasing to them. Should I smite them? b) I would like to sell my daughter into slavery, as sanctioned in Exodus 21:7. In this day and age, what do you think would be a fair price for her? c) I know that I am allowed no contact with a woman while she is in her period of menstrual uncleanliness (Lev. 15:19-24). The problem is, how do I tell? I have tried asking, but most women take offence. d) Lev. 25:44 states that I may indeed possess slaves, both male and female, provided they are purchased from neighboring nations. A friend of mine claims that this applies to Mexicans, but not Canadians. Can you clarify? Why can't I own Canadians? e) I have a neighbor who insists on working on the Sabbath. Exodus 35:2 clearly states he should be put to death. Am I morally obligated to kill him myself? f) A friend of mine feels that even though eating shellfish is an abomination (Lev. 11:10), it is a lesser abomination than homosexuality. I don't agree. Can you settle this? g) Lev. 21:20 states that I may not approach the altar of God if I have a defect in my sight. I have to admit that I wear reading glasses. Does my vision have to be 20/20, or is there some wiggle room here? h) Most of my male friends get their hair trimmed, including the hair around their temples, even though this is expressly forbidden by Lev.19:27. How should they die? i) I know from Lev. 11:6-8 that touching the skin of a dead pig makes me unclean, but may I still play football if I wear gloves? j) My uncle has a farm. He violates Lev. 19:19 by planting two different crops in the same field, as does his wife by wearing garments made of two different kinds of thread (cotton/polyester blend). He also tends to curse and blaspheme a lot. Is it really necessary that we go to all the trouble of getting the whole town together to stone them? (Lev.24:10-16) Couldn't we just burn them to death at a private family affair like we do with people who sleep with their in-laws? (Lev. 20:14) I know you have studied these things extensively, so I am confident you can help. Thank you again for reminding us that God's word is eternal and unchanging. Your devoted disciple and adoring fan."

The oldest Old Testament exists as Aramaic targums, or free translations, some of which are thought to predate the Christian Era. The Greek Septuagint was produced in the last

300 years before Jesus and ancient versions still exist in Coptic, Armenian, Syriac and other languages.

In 170 AD, Martin, a Gnostic, took part of the Gospel of Luke and some of Paul's letters and used them to make the first Italian Bible. It wasn't until the Middle Ages that parts of the Bible were translated from Latin into English by John Wycliffe (1328 -1384). However, he rejected papal authority and was condemned by the Council of Constance in 1415, with the result that 31 years after his death his remains were ordered exhumed and burned. Did he know that nearly half of the Popes, after their death, would be labeled false Popes by the very institution they led?

William Tyndale wrote the first full version of the English Bible in 1526. The church denounced him for heresy too, and executed him for his troubles ten years later. Subsequent versions include Martin Luther's Book of Concord in German (1580), Miles Coverdale's Bible (1535), Matthew's Bible (1537), the Great Bible (1539), the Geneva Bible (1560), the Rheims-Douai Bible (1582 and 1609), the King James, or Authorized, Version (1611), the English Revised Version (1881-85), the American Standard Version (1946-57), the New English Bible (1961-70), the Jerusalem Bible (1966), the New American Bible (1970), Today's English Version (1966-76), and the Revised Standard Version (1946-1971).

Looking back, the modern Bible was written over a period of about 3000 years by 400 contributing authors who produced dozens of different versions in over 1500 languages. In the aftermath, entire segments have been left out, while the remainder has undergone hundreds of thousands of edits and corrections.

Although theologians have known this all along, it was the 1947 discovery of the Qumran scrolls which focused attention on Biblical omissions by establishing a direct link between the Essenes and the early Christians, through their treasured *Book of Enoch*, which was judged non-canonical and dropped from the Bible in the third century AD. But, it resurfaced when a British explorer discovered a copy in Ethiopia in 1773. Distinctly Messianic in content, the Book of

Enoch seems to have been written over a two hundred year period by four different authors. The church also banned the *Book of the Secrets of Enoch,* written about 30BC to 70AD, which only surfaced 1500 years later in Russia and Serbia, in which account Enoch talks about his visit to the seven heavens and how God explained creation and the idea of fallen angels.

The official version and the Holy Trinity
Quite naturally, the pagan Romans did everything they could to overcome the threat of Christianity. Yet, within 400 years, a rag-tag bunch of radicals had succeeded in making Christianity the official state religion. That they managed to do so at all is proof enough for some people that it was God's will all along. Be that as it may, it wasn't long before the Christians imposed their belief on the entire Roman Empire, by making it illegal to worship otherwise.

The turn-around began with Constantine the Great, the first Roman emperor to adopt Christianity. He was born Flavius Valerius Constantinus, in Naissus, Yugoslavia, about AD 280. Apparently, Constantine had a vision on the Millveian Bridge which, fortunately for the Christians, was interpreted by a nearby bishop whose church had both the Old and New Testaments as part of its canon. Constantine converted, and upon becoming Emperor he convened the First Council of Nicaea, in 325AD, to settle Arian disputes as to the divinity of Jesus. Led by the bishop of Alexandria, Athanasius, the upshot was the Nicene Creed, the official and, from then on, the only acceptable version of Christianity in which God and the Son of God were proclaimed consubstantial and coeternal. As a footnote, they also settled on an official date for the celebration of Easter. Thereafter, all dissenters were persecuted, including other non-conforming Christians such as the Gnostics and the Dualists, who still didn't consider the Old Testament canonical. While the bishops on the right side of the fence rubbed their hands with glee, they set up factories to turn out hand-written copies of the Bible and began erecting huge basilicas.

But, even after Constantine's death in 337, the battles raged on. Radical Arianism asserted that the Son of God was dissimilar to God; the homoeanist view argued that the Son was indeed similar, while semi-Arianism sought the middle ground by claiming that the Son was both similar and distinct at the same time. When the dust settled, the semi-Arians won out by joining the ranks of the orthodox. From then on the Logos, the official Word of God, postulated that Jesus Christ was united in human nature and that his crucifixion and resurrection overcame sin with the promise of immortality. The argument was that if Christ were not fully man, then human nature could not be saved. On the other hand, Salvation would be impossible if Christ was not one in being with God as well. Over the next 500 years, more ecumenical Councils in Constantinople were attended by hundreds of bishops from the Eastern empire, who further affirmed the existence of a Trinity as well, in which the Holy Spirit also proceeded from God and was coequal and consubstantial with him. Naturally, dissenters were excommunicated and a pope was condemned in the process.

Metaphysical trinities

It is said that Dionysius the Areopagite divided the higher realms into 3 groups of 3: Angels, Archangels and Archai. The Angels, being the closest to man, were accessed during sleep, the 4th dimension, in which time and distance have no reality and souls of like-state are drawn together. These angels, the *Fehoher* of the Persians, the *Genii* of the Latins, are called the sons of life and their element is air. Archangels, such as the *Asuras* of Hinduism have fire as their element.

The Fire Principal was first formulated by the Rishis of India, in an ancient doctrine in which fire is the essence of the universe and the instrument of the Gods. *Agni* is the fire hidden in all things, of which smoke, flame and light are external manifestations. Spirit descends on the road of flame and rises on the road of light. The early doctrine of the fire principal, as found in the Vedas, was later formulated by the Greek philosopher Heraclitus, of the Ionian school, as the generative element.

Virtues, Dominions and Principalities, the second triad, are the spiritual spheres of expansion and concentration within the 5th and 6th dimensions, which compares to the *Devas* of the Hindus. Within this sphere are the planners of the planetary system, whose role is ordaining and balancing the powers as they act upon the whole.

Thrones, Cherubim and Seraphim are the highest triad. They relate to the infinite and eternal and transcend space and time. The Seraphim, in Chaldean, means love. The Cherubim stand for wisdom and infinite force. These of the third triad are considered to be the thoughts of God embodied in spiritual essence. They do not toil, they radiate. They do not create, they vivify.

In religious and metaphysical philosophies through the ages, the trinities reoccur as father-mother-son, positive-negative-action; in the harmonies of blue-yellow-red, the numbers 1-3-5 and the water-earth-fire of alchemy. For the Egyptians of 5,000 years ago it was Osiris the Supreme, the god of the underworld; Isis (or Typhon) the All-mother, and Horus the child. Also in Egypt was Ptah the father, Ra the Sun-God and Amun the unknown god. The prophet Ra lived at On, the city of light, which the Greeks called Heliopolis or the city of the sun. In Persia we find Ormuzd, Ahriman and Mithra the reconciler, while the Hindus have Brahma, Vishnu and Shiva.

Bible story parallels

India, the cradle of religion, sponsored many of the religious concepts that eventually flourished elsewhere. Some of the earliest records of Aryan thought, of about 5000 BC, are recorded in the Indian *Veda* and the *Upanishads.* Their central deity was *Dyans-Pitar* and various spirits in control of the elements. Hinduism, which evolved over 4,000 years and is now the dominant religion in India, teaches an ideal way of life known as Dharma, in which one's karma is progressively resolved through the transmigration of the soul and successive reincarnations. About 3,000 years before Jesus, Manou appeared on the scene as a great Indian reformer. In the *Laws of Manou* he taught moral striving and spiritual rebirth. His systematized teachings about God and creation are enshrined in Brahminical lore which, in turn, greatly influenced Zoroaster and then Mithra. The most popular Hindu god is the Messiah called Krishna, who was born a thousand years before Jesus as the miraculous son of the virgin Devakl. Sometimes depicted playing a blue flute, his story, in the *Bhagavata Purana,* combines erotic love, the quest for salvation, folk legends and ancient Sanskrit traditions.

While giving consideration to other religions, one cannot help but notice frequent parallels with Christianity. The story of Jesus being tempted on the mountain, for example, originated with the mythical story of Jupiter being taken up the mountain to be tempted with an offer of the surrounding countryside. Hindus, Greeks, Egyptians and Romans used holy water long before Christianity was even thought of. Similarly, baptism came from the Romans, as does the confession of sins. Holy communion originated with the worship of Dionysius and Mithra, being celebrated on what was called the Lords Day, once a week. Egyptians and Africans practiced circumcision hundreds of years before the Jews did. Jay Leno once said the only reason the Jews do it is because Jewish women won't touch anything that isn't 20% off.

Christianity absorbed Mithraism and all it stood for. The worship of the sun-god Mithra came from Persia and was the most widespread middle-east religion when Jesus made his appearance. Hundreds of years prior to the advent of Christianity it was believed that Mithra was created by, but equal to, God. They believed in the trinity and Sun-day was kept holy as the Lord's day. Mithra died at Easter and his birth was celebrated on December 25th. Lent was observed. They practiced the sign of the cross on the forehead. They believed the soul of man was reunited with God through the sacrifices of Mithra.

The Lord's Prayer originated in Babylon, as proven by the 1882 discovery of a tablet containing similar inscriptions, now in the British Museum in London. The text is also similar to an old Jewish prayer which was repeated in the Chaldaic tongue, having been learned by the Jews when they were captives in Babylon.

So it is that the star in the heavens, as it appeared above the cradle in Bethlehem, was the same sign in the vision of Osiris, which told of the coming of the promised one, for whom Zoroaster himself waited thousands of years later, already knowing of the anticipated the arrival of the three Babylonian Magi. In a sense, nothing changes, yet everything does.

Syria and Chaldea bequeathed to us the science of the arts, cement, set squares and massive temples. Babylonian art was colossal, as evidenced by giant men wrestling with lions. Although the kings of Babylon and the Assyrian armies of Nineveh were the scourge of the Jewish people, out of this struggle rose the prophets Issiah, Ezekiel and Daniel. At the same time, the priests of Chaldea, strongly influenced by Zoroastrian traditions and a knowledge of celestial mythology, greatly affected the unwritten precepts which were handed down generation after generation through the early Hebrew religion. As a result, the Jesus story is the propagation of Persian, Chaldean and Egyptian teachings which can easily be traced through the Aryan influence to the western world of today.

Two-thousand years ago there were about 100 Gods of various importance. Today we're down to a tenth that number. In another 2,000 years, will future generations be as disdainful of our present-day gods as we are of the many so-called pagan gods? Today, every religion claims exclusivity to the one and only true god. Millions of people are currently opposed to each other as a result. Is it not curious that, over the many centuries, perhaps as many as a billion people have died fighting holy wars and jihads, through ethnic cleansing and religious persecution? Obviously, the struggle to believe leaves something to be desired, not the least, of which, is love for our fellow man.

Abraham Lincoln said that people get the politicians they deserve. Perhaps that is true of our deities as well. Primitive though the barbarity of the pagan era may seem, the biggest difference nowadays is our ability to kill off non-believers on a grander scale. Holy wars are still considered virtuous. But, isn't there an important phrase that begins: *"For God so loved the world..."* Do we love the world less? Is the Will of God merely a matter of politics?

In the pagan era, mercy was considered a weakness. The very notion of getting unearned assistance was ridiculous and unjust. Pity was an indication of weakness and the strong and the wise new better. Fortunately, modern Christians tend to be somewhat more benevolent. Although, when considering the role of the Vatican during the World Wars, which went unscathed, and their blind eye to the persecution of the Jews and their duplicity with the German Reich, it is difficult to credit the Catholic church for much more than fine diplomacy. The original Aryan meaning of the word church is "the mind of God." Sometimes, one wonders if the church minds at all, when priests and parsons on both sides of the battle-lines pray for victory with the same veneration, and never mind the injunction: "Thou shall not kill."

Saviors

In the final analysis, all religion is personal and subjective. Everyone has the right to believe as he chooses. Does it really matter if all of the savior gods have a story similar to that of Jesus? The cross was used 7,000 years ago in Egypt to represent the power that upholds the human soul in death. The Annunciation, virgin birth, baptism, temptation, teachings, miracles, the disciples, the last supper and the resurrection all existed for hundreds if not thousands of years before Christianity was even thought of. Is that really so surprising? Xenophanes, 600 years before Jesus, said: "If the ox could paint a picture, his god would look like an ox." Men and women of every age have sought to personify that which they hold most dear. Some of the savior gods include: Osiris of Egypt in 1700BC, Baal of Babylon in 1200BC, Attis of Theria in 1170BC, Tammuz of Syria in 1160BC, Dionysius of Greece in 1100BC, Krishna of India in 1000BC, Hersus of Europe in 834BC, Indra of Tibet in 725BC, Io of Nepal in 622BC, Alsestus of Paria in 600BC, Quexcoatl of Mexico in 587BC,

Promithius of Greece in 547BC, Querilius of Rome in 506BC and Mithra of Persia in 400BC.

When all is said and done, surely it matters not if one prays to Vishnu or makes an appeal to the Virgin Mother. What does matter is that each of us is true to our highest ideals and that we are moral and tolerant of those who, although not exactly on the same path, most certainly share the same mountain.

It saddens me greatly that people of conviction feel justified in making war against those who believe differently than they do. This applies equally to both Western and Eastern cultures. Surely, nothing is as abhorrent as making war in God's name, while ignoring the timeless injunction: "Love thy neighbor."

God is my champion,
Riding a steed called time.
Armed with light,
He charges the rampant dark,
And rouses heavenly seas:
The waves of infinite experience.

Part 3
THE WORLD OF SPIRIT
CHAPTER SIX

PARTS

Other states

There's no point in welcoming you to the etheric world or the astral zone, or whatever you chose to call it, since you've always been there; or, to put it another way: you've always been here. Where we exist, contrary to material logic, isn't over here or over there. Real life isn't lineal and it doesn't have a beginning or an end. Moreover, each state is integrated within every other state. In some metaphysical circles the idea is that these states are built up in layers around a core, like an onion, each stratum being of increasingly finer vibration as you progress outward. That description fits easily into earthly notions of here and there, or up and down. But, it's not the case. Everywhere is here, strange as it may seem.

The human mind, accustomed to dealing with finite reality, has difficulty coming to grips with ideas about the infinite. Our concepts of place or state automatically involve time, distance, beginnings and endings, and it is confounding to relate to physical reality as other than what it appears to be. Our limitations, however, do not alter the facts – they merely become harder to quantify. The scientist cannot poke or pinch greater-reality, nor stick it in a bottle with formaldehyde. It defies logic, at least human logic. But it exists nevertheless, so wondrous and grand that when it is glimpsed it defies explanation. In Walt Whitman's words, in *Leaves of Grass*: "When I undertake to tell the best I find I cannot, My tongue is ineffectual on its pivots. My breath will not be obedient to its organs, I become a dumb man."

What proof do we have that these other states co-exist with ours? That's easy. Everyone has experienced the so-called paranormal in one fashion or another. The fact that it isn't sufficiently understood does not make it less normal, however. Moreover, our ability to sense these subtle levels at all indicates that we are indeed a part of them already or, conversely, that they are a part of us. You don't have to buy a ticket in order to have an experiential dream or a presentiment about the future, a part of you is already there, or stated another way, you are already a part of it – at the very center of it all. You always have been and you always will be. You are a part of everything, reaching outward from your present point of realization, extending infinitely in all directions at the same time.

You are an universal, immortal being. You are as I am. I say that because, if you could know it, we are the same. I am as much a part of you as you are part of me, even if my ego and a whole bunch of inner parts might like to differ – and have all-time to do it in. The ultimate quest is to define ourselves through creativeness, diversity and introspection. No matter how long the road may be, through whatever realities, somewhere along the way each one of us will come to the conclusion that we are truly aspects of the same Oneness.

> For I am the first and the last.
> I am the honored one and the scorned one.
> I am the whore and the holy one.
> I am the wife and the virgin....
> I am the barren one, and many are her sons....
> I am the silence that is incomprehensible....
> I am the utterance of my name.
> (Nag Hammadi, *The Thunder of Perfect Mind*)

Because we are more than mere physical beings, it follows that we will experience more than physical reality alone. It's all a part of life. Our life. Accordingly, everyone is a spiritual being and everyone is more or less psychically aware of it. But, like weightlifting, while everyone can lift something, not everyone is an Olympic contender, at least not yet.

The larger part of what we are, and what we are about, falls into the realm of the unknown, the imagined and the inspirational. Hope, horror and healing are pages in the same book, thinly separated, eternally bound. Yet, human nature is so plagued with presumption and ignorance that nearly everything invokes fear. Judgments, it seems, must come first: the facts later. Nevertheless, like it or not, and informed or otherwise, we are constantly being bombarded with the inexplicable and the wondrous, instilling panic or promise, depending on how it strikes us.

The age of enlightenment

Regardless of what you believe, it is impossible to be unaware of the mass of material surrounding mysticism, the occult and New Age wonders. People are talking about intuition, second sight, deja vu, faith healing and past life experiences, and the TV psychics are (regrettably, for the most part) having a field day. It's all around us, pervasive and sometimes unsettling. Everybody's doing it, even the hucksters and con-artists who eagerly exploit anyone they can get their hooks into. For many people it's just a lark— nothing to take seriously, or so they say, although sometimes not convincingly. For the majority it is a real dilemma, because if you listen long enough you can hear just about anything, from half-baked courses on spontaneous enlightenment to pay-as-you-go cults and, if all else fails, you can telephone your spirit guide for $5.99 a minute. Fascinating or otherwise, the age of enlightenment is upon us.

For those who jump into things with both feet, discretion is more important than ever. Considering the overwhelm in the name of entertainment and religion, and the plethora of wild claims made by those serving the Human Potential market, it is difficult to avoid being affected one way or another. How do you sort the wheat from the chaff? How do you know if you're not being led down a garden path? Do you know enough to protect yourself? Half of the solution is to know when your suspicions are justified, the other half is to know what to do about it.

People fear the unknown, but, as often as not, the reaction to what is feared is worse than the thing that caused it. Consider the case of King James I, who was paranoid about witchcraft. In 1611, when he authorized 40 scholars to rewrite the Bible as the Tindale version, he inserted the words: "suffer not a witch to live." As a result, 40,000 innocent people were tortured and burned to death, despite the section in I Corinthians which states: "The manifestation of the Spirit is given to *every* man to profit withal (12:7) ...to one the working of miracles; to another prophecy; to another discerning of spirits. (12:10).

In future chapters we will touch again upon the subject of discretion. It is sufficient for now that your alertness be roused, because the next stage in our quest takes us into the realm of parts. Not car parts: your parts.

The hierarchy of being

"A part of me wanted to, but another part didn't." How often have you said or thought something like that? At least once in a while, no doubt. These words elucidate the exquisite truth: you are made up of parts – different parts, parts that are not always in agreement. Indecision is symptomatic of parts in conflict. But, there is more to it than that: you are the product of rivers of power, streaming parts and droplet-like particles. In the hierarchy of being there are powers, parts and particles, in that order, quite aside from the child within and your connection with universal consciousness.

The powers are any name or force you wish to identify them by: Seraphim, Cherubim, guiding angels, or maybe the Holy Spirit. This river of power, by whatever name, flows from the source. It is what animates and empowers you.

Parts are divisions within the human unconscious mind that are responsible for the maintenance of the filters that control memory, morals, decisions, conceptualization and state of being. Input from any source, including self, when passed through these filters, causes internal representations which govern our behavior and attendant physiology. Parts, therefore, govern particles through departmentalization.

Particles include every cell in your body, but they are much more than that. Each cell and particle is a being unto itself and unto you. It has memory, volition, hunger, reproductive instincts, it knows how to communicate and create and it knows how to defend itself and you too. Moreover, particles know how to live in harmony. The particles in your body compare to the world's population: different entities in different places with a social structure dedicated to mutual survival.

All in all, powers, parts and particles comprise but a tiny fraction of the total you. Understanding this places your feet in two worlds at the same time: the corporeal world of physical existence and the transcendent world of the greater self. In a metaphysical sense all worlds are one, but, being practical, we seldom relate to more than one at a time. Yet, the wheels do turn and life goes on.

"The Great Spirit has set his hand upon the earth, that man should share in his glory; not through denial and materialistic opportunism, but through the raising of mass consciousness and the realignment of purpose to that of peace, harmony and unrestricted growth within the natural laws. The era is now being heralded; the time of gestation is nearly over; and out of the agonies of birth will come spirit-babes whose shadows shall cover the land, the faces of each one turned to the light." (Author unknown)

The "other" world is the world of spirit. You are already a part of it. You don't have to die to get there. In fact, the only prerequisite for eternal life is already being alive. Let me ask you: what is more miraculous, being born again or having being born at all? Nothing dies. Everything is. You are the essence of *I am*, forever and ever, a living soul. If that's not enough – fasten your seat belt – there's more than one of you. Oops. You see, the spirit part of you creates manifest selves in order to experience and grow with all that is and with every possibility by which you may be expressed. You are always you, however. You never ever lose that. The idea of manifest selves is what is behind ideas about reincarnation, judgment and karma. It may seem far-fetched, but everything you do is balanced by an equal and opposing reaction. Whenever you make a decision to take the road to the right, an aspect of self has already set foot upon the path to the left. How else do you suppose that an *infinite* God would express himself?

What you think you are is a reflection of wherever you happen to be in the course of creating your reality. The blueprint that enables you to grow from small to big, from child to adult, is conceived in the mind of spirit and then actualized in simultaneous aspects. I say simultaneous because there are no ticking clocks in all-time. Everything you are exists independent of time. Time, as we know it, is merely the measure of this reality, which is why, in a spiritual sense, it is said to be an illusion. There are other realities. In fact, there are endless, limitless other realities. The universal you is boundless. You are an endless and eternal being in quest of self – only some of which is your present undertakings in a material state.

Transcendence

Recognizing that our consciousness relates to the physical world by way of compartmentalization, or parts, it must be added that infiltration from other selves is also possible, although somewhat rare. On a very subtle level, our other selves can sometimes influence present reality and disposition, such as happened with Chopin, who composed breathtaking music and gave his first concert when only eight years old. In another light, it is possible to identify with one's other selves as past-life experiences or such. It must be said, however, that such identification is usually more fanciful than fact. Were it otherwise we'd be in a constant tizzy. Nevertheless, it does sometimes happen that the most inexplicable things on this level make sense only when taken in context with the influences generated by our other selves. We will touch upon this issue again, but for now it suffices that you have a notion of how marvelously unique, complex and enduring you are.

Parts

Now comes a fun part – no pun intended – that will drive the skeptics up the wall. As far as traditional approaches are concerned, anything that presupposes the existence of personal parts is a pseudoscience at best and quackery at worst. So, what else is new? Parts, in this context, are components of the unconscious mind and nervous system. That the nervous system is part of the unconscious mind is proven by the fact that we are not conscious of it. The unconscious and the nervous system function as an integrated but compartmentalized unit, in which each part is capable of independent thought. Parts are created in response to highly associated, negative or positive emotions and non-integrated language. (Alfred Korzipsky in *Science and Sanity*, 1933). The three contributing factors in emotional states are peak intensity, the rate of change, and repetition, in which a repeated experience may have the same effect as a single peak experience. When a traumatized person says: "I can't handle this," another part is bound, sooner or later, to try.

Parts, by the nature of their organization, can sometimes be in conflict with one another, as in the case of this offhand admission: "A part of me wanted to, but another part didn't." More profound than "split decisions" are multiple personalities, which result when a part has become sufficiently isolated that it is incapable of integration within the whole.

For all their complexity, parts may be worked with in a very effective manner. Fortunately, our parts are usually very cooperative, since they are always motivated by our best interests. Moreover, they will respond when you talk to them and you don't have to be a psychic or a guru to do it. Upon inquiry, you will discover that most parts have a personal history. They know when they were created and they know why, and they have their own belief systems and goals. When a person says: "That wasn't like me," it is likely he was acting under the influence of a non-associated part.

A non-integrated or non-associated part is, by its very nature, in conflict with itself and the whole. It is the action of these independent parts that is most often responsible for disharmony and conflict in people. Part of the process of Getting Real is the process of atonement (at-one-ment), in which independent parts are enabled to reintegrate. But parts do not necessarily integrate willingly. If a part believes its highest purpose is being frustrated by integration, it will bounce back and become independent again within a short time. This accounts for both the immediate successes and the eventual back-sliding that may occur. If that's not confusing enough, sometimes a part will flip back and forth between being integrated and non-integrated.

Working with parts

Parts are neat. In fact they are wonderful. Each one is a precious aspect of you that enables you to cope with the world, based upon your past experience and present determinations. The goal of every part is to protect you. Ideally, parts become most effective when they work in harmony with your whole being, the unconscious "core-state," which is not to be confused with the child within. As a curious adjunct, it is the child who is the doorway through which transcendent parts migrate into your present reality. Having said this, I must add that, while the child does not have any problems with parts integration, there is such a thing as overwhelm, which can effectively bring things to a standstill.

Death compares to throwing off a physical overcoat, at which point all that you have learned is preserved in the child as bliss is reclaimed. You see, it is true, you cannot enter the kingdom of heaven except as a child. Now you understand.

Every part has a counterpart to maintain functional balance within your psyche. Usually, they are easily accessed and, upon questioning, will reveal that they share the same highest intention. Realizing this, you have a wonderful opportunity for integration of parts and the resolution of conflict between them.

Taking a page from NLP (*Neuro Linguistic Programming*), the following process may be used to resolve some conflicts. In this example, let us presume that a person, named Joe, is having difficulty with money and freedom, in that he is so determined to get ahead that his work deprives him of enjoying life. Neither state is a negative condition in itself, but there is nevertheless conflict between the two. Fortunately, Joe is able to fix things, and although the following method may seem simplistic or presumptuous, there are many claims as to its efficacy.

Joe is sitting calmly with his eyes open or closed. In his own way and in his own words, he sends out the thought that he desires protection and guidance for his present undertaking. Thusly assured, he extends his arms, palms up, a comfortable distance separating them, and he begins: "I desire to speak to the part of me that is in charge of money. When you are ready, will you please step onto my left hand." (I warned you.) Not surprisingly, Joe senses when the part is in place – one of the wee folk, if you will, beautiful in its own right. Joe then asks: "Is there another part that you are most in conflict with?"

Joe senses the Money part's answer as: "Yes."

Joe: "Would it be all right if I ask that part to come out and step onto my right hand?"

Money part: "Yes."

Another part takes its place. Joe asks the new part: "What is your highest intention for me?"

New part: "Freedom."

Joe: "For what purpose?"

New part: "So you will be happy."

Joe: "For what purpose?"

New part: "So you will be healthy."

Joe: "For what purpose?"

New part: "To ensure your survival."

Joe thinks about this and then addresses the money part again: "What is your highest intention for me?"

Money part: "To make you secure."

Joe: "For what purpose?"

Money part: "To ensure your survival."

Joe: "Since both of you share the same highest intention, and because each of you has important resources that would assist the other in being more effective, would you like to combine resources?"

Because each part is determined to use every means to achieve its highest purpose, the appeal of additional resources is undeniable. Joe senses when the parts agree, whereupon he slowly brings his hands together thus forming a super-part and the integration is complete. Joe then blesses the new super-part and acknowledges its assimilation, and it is done. For Joe, the attendant feeling is one of peaceful acceptance. No longer is the pursuit of money in conflict with its purpose. The process of integration may sound like gobbledygook, but before you remonstrate too loudly, it really does work, and gracefully too. In the technical jargon of experts, there may be exquisite names for what integration is and isn't – some of them likely not too kind – but, frankly, who cares? It's the results that count.

Loggerheads

Sometimes, parts are so much in conflict that they refuse to merge. If that happens, after asking for each part's permission, you can imagine a third part in the center of the two, then, as you bring your hands together, imagine them combining so that only the center part remains. Then close with thanks to your guiding force and an affirmation of completeness.

The key to ascertaining a reluctant part's highest intention is to find out what it was that made it react so strongly in the first place. When you seek such understanding, never ask a part: "Why?" because the very answer reinforces it. The questions to ask are: "How?" or "For what purpose?" You will probably get an immediate answer; if not, ask again, explaining to the part that your state of being depends on such understanding so that you can cope better. Then, when you remember the event in question, don't get swallowed up in it. Simply be aware. Then ask the part, based upon your need for understanding and happiness, if it will be okay for you to extract all the beneficial learning from the experience and let the negative stuff go. Having approval, visualize leaving the trauma behind and taking all the goodness and learning forward into the present, unplugging all negative reactions from old memory as you do so. It's like unraveling knitting, just keep pulling on the thread of original experience until everything is resolved. But don't get bogged down in the process; do it smoothly, steadily, and without becoming overly involved in any of the events along the way. When back to the present, in which state you are calm and in control, allow yourself a moment to let go of the thread, whereupon like elastic, it too will disappear, effortlessly. Now you are ready to work with the part that was formerly distressed beyond integration. But, if you sense that you have to repeat the unraveling process again, even a number of times, simply bear in mind that when integration of the part is complete you will know it, and the effort will have been worthwhile.

I realize this is a real grabber for the skeptics, but I can't help that. Remember, it wasn't so long ago that the Wright brothers were crazy for trying to fly. The union of parts is effective and often dramatic. That it is so simple is what confounds the experts who – in the name of specialization – try to complicate everything. Relief is sweet, and the creation of self is a very deliberate, thoughtful and liberating experience. The integration of parts resolves personal conflict and empowers you greatly. There is no substitute for harmony, and the attendant peace is the hallmark of Getting Real.

"It is better to light a small candle than to curse the darkness."
(Confucius)

Transient parts

As a preface to what follows, I want to make it easy for anyone to discredit me. The reason is simple: none of it may be pertinent to you. If that's not reason enough, none of it may be true either. There's no need for you to fit into my notions of reality. There is a need for me, however, to at least give you the opportunity to fit into mine. That's why I wrote this book. So, bearing that in mind, here we go again…

The shortness of human life makes it transitory by nature. Equally, the parts that make up a person's being are in transition, passing from one stage to another while subject to the influence of yet other states. At the time of migration, most parts migrate willingly and intact, as a bundle so to speak. Even non-integrated parts usually graduate being attached to the whole. But, the complexity of our parts is such that upon migration – birth or death – not all parts are capable of an easy passage. Indeed, some radically fragmented parts may not migrate at all.

Physical death does not necessarily happen all at once. It can be a progressive thing in which some of the parts are drawn away hours or months prior to final depletion of the body. The same is true in some instances of aberration, in which it is casually stated that a part of the person is missing. Truer words…

It is not so much that parts resist integration as it is that they are attracted to the state which most affords them functionality.

The over-self, or spirit body, can cause the integration of parts as a result of balancing between levels or between diverse life-states. To understand this it must be remembered that we are expressed on simultaneous levels, independent of the rationality of time. When viewed from physical reality alone, these lives appear to be in the past, present or future, but that is merely a present illusion. Eternal life transcends corporeal time. For the real self, time is neither a boundary or a limitation. The same is true for parts.

It is the quest of the Overself to seek harmony through the integration of its parts, wherever and however they may be. In this light, parts from different life experiences may become integrated in the present, thereby crossing reality borders. Sometimes, this accounts for abrupt changes in people, as if they had turned a new leaf overnight. Meanwhile, non-integrated or fragmented parts pose the greatest challenge for growth and expansion. Although often cumbersome and unmanageable, these so-called stray parts put a new spin on reality, generating both horror and hope.

Upon death, a part that fails to migrate remains somewhat animated, but without the benefit of the host body it is spectral in nature, a part of present reality, but not fully actualized. Such a transient part retains a degree of free will, but left to its own resources it is less enterprising than before. At some point, however, every transient part becomes integrated with a counterpart and, eventually, balance is restored. Until then, the transient part has a foot in both worlds at the same time, but is not totally real in either.

Sticky parts

If you believe something is true, then it is, at least for you. It may not be an aspect of other people's reality, that depends on the nature of the power generated, how it is directed and it's conformance to patterns of possibility, which in this instance includes both free-will and, for want of a better word, destiny or karma. Life, after all, isn't a random shooting match; there is order even in chaos. Belief, expectancy, power – these are the ingredients of magic and the miraculous, both of which strain our definitions of what is possible and what is not.

In old Huna lore, there is a ritual of murmuring, whereby one appeals to, and thereby empowers, ancestral parts. Max Freedom Long, in his many books, mentions the power of such appeals as having a kind of stickiness to which parts are drawn as they transit through different experiences. Repeated appeals, through ritual incantation, can enable certain parts to affect specific outcomes. The action of some parts may also be the result of unmindfulness, in which case vagrant parts are stimulated by superfluous energy and opportunity. In any case, the words used in ritual incantation or prayer are empowered by belief, expectancy and a physically reinforcing gesture. Power begins with a thought, is complimented by words and then given the wing of expectation. Expectancy is not the same as hopefulness or merely wishing for something; it is a form of unquestioning, in which the process of actualization is unhindered by doubt. This power can, it is said, move mountains. It is called faith.

Sticky parts know no limitation. What gives them mobility, as it were, are persistent appeals, mutterings and incantations (malevolent or otherwise), unmindfulness and 'puddles' of superfluous energy. Unmindfulness, simply put, is a source of neglected energy that is pliable unto any purpose. It arises out of the negated potential for actualization. Once in motion, however, power must do something, eventually. Energy from unmindfulness is that which is thrown off during frenzy, violent agitation or delirium. Mutterings, whether malevolent or mere disgruntlement, together with superfluous energy – often exuded by teenagers – are prime sources for such things as poltergeist activity, which invariably abate with maturity. More about that later.

Parts are not created equal, some have more potency that others. It depends on why they were created, what set them in motion, their intensity and purpose. Parts strive to remain existent. They have a reason to be and are determined to fulfill it, drawing the energy to do so at any given opportunity. The great disadvantage for sticky parts is that business of having a foot in both worlds at the same time. Although unbound by time, they are restricted in mobility. They can be somewhat as they please, but rarely can they come and go as they please. The exception is when they attach themselves to another person, or a place or a thing that has "soaked up" high-impacting emotional energy, which accounts for a host of paranormal activities: phantoms, ghosts, ghouls and so forth. It also accounts for a lot of erratic behavior, bearing in mind that people attract what they fear. At this juncture it must be added that merely witnessing or sensing a transient part does not mean that the part has attached itself to the viewer. It simply means that the part was in the vicinity and for a brief moment there was a breakthrough of sorts.

Transient parts and sticky parts are not necessarily evil, although more often than not they arise out of urgency and trauma. Theirs is the nature of both unfinished business and desperation to get the job done. Some parts simply refuse to die, and remain behind after unexpected or violent death of the host body. Nevertheless, sooner or later the transient part will be reunited with the whole, either by hitching a new ride or by integration with a balancing counterpart.

During their independent sojourn, transient parts may try to form symbiotic relationships with other people. It is their nature to seek the means to fulfill their highest intention. Suppose, for example, a drug addict left a part behind that was created as a result of addiction, and that part attached itself to a new parent body, specifically someone who has yet to overcome his own addiction. Is the transient part evil? Not likely, since it's highest purpose is to learn how to overcome addiction. For what purpose? To help the addict survive, of course.

There are numerous cases of possession, and certain types of schizophrenia, which tend to sensationalize the facts. But, if possession were as easy as the movie-makers suggest, then we all would be. In reality, our own defense system protects us, even from our foolishness. Even so, mortals do indeed go where angels fear to tread. Too many people think that ESP in any context is fun to dabble with, an amusement or merely an engrossing pastime, and they play with the mind as if it were a toy. The Ouija Board, for example, is not a game at all.

CHAPTER SEVEN
LIFE IN SPIRIT

Death

What follows now is a summation of the many sources I've studied on the subject. Death, they say, is like falling asleep on a train, when, upon awakening, the traveler rubs his eyes and asks: "Where am I?" Death is the disassociation of the mind from the mortal body. It is merely the non-physical body slipping away from the moorings of matter; severing the mystical silver cord as if an anchor chain, thereby enabling the ship of soul to drift in the company of like kind. God is the pilot. In the world in which one awakens, loved ones are eager to greet the "newborn" and take him on a guided tour, throughout which the new arrival is wondrously vibrant and more alive than ever. Death is an awakening, not a mindless state of perpetual slumber, nor purgatory. The next life will be just as real to us as this life is: personality, mind and free-will remain intact; the adventure of living being before us without, quite possibly, the faintest notion of how we got there. Indeed, many do not even know they have passed over until they meet someone who has preceded them.

Ut supra, ut infra.

(As above, so below)

When your physical body dies, you take your mind with you as part of a more rarefied body of vibration. Without wanting to get lost in metaphysical semantics, there may be a distinction between the new body – which isn't new at all – the spirit body, the astral body, the mental body, the etheric body and what have you. For present purposes, however, I will use the term spirit body, which encompasses, if you will, a host of lesser bodies. Either way, you are still you.

Sometimes it happens that the spirit body has lost some of its vitality through having to energize an increasingly debilitated physical body, or perhaps the shock of passing-over has caused severe trauma. As a result, it is not unusual for the *graduate* to be taken to a place of rest and recuperation. A dear friend, who long mourned the passing of her epileptic son, had a dream in which the young man said: "Mom, just relax okay? I'm in rehab right now, but I'll be out soon."

If immortality is the ultimate reality, then death is the ultimate illusion. Even what we perceive to be inanimate is forever alive; it is transmutable, but remains indestructible. A lifeless rock, as seen by a materialist, is vital and nourishing to the cosmic body of God, even as protein is to the body of man. Everything, from pebbles to mountains, from hamsters to humans, lives within the Infinite Being and exists forever. That it may not seem so is only the measure of one's preoccupation with his present state. The valley of death is indeed in shadow. It is only from the summit that the everlasting seems to shine so brightly upon all of creation. To know it is to know it undeniably: anything less denies everything.

The realization of one's immortality, as any skeptic will tell you, has little to do with common sense. But the audacity to insist otherwise is like a barnacle trying to sit in judgment of the British Navy. That it defies logic is the measure by which the human intellect cannot feel beyond the limits of the brush, to see the Master at work. So, how do you know? the skeptics ask. Without wanting to be trite: perhaps such a one should ponder marine life for a while, crustaceans in particular.

> "And (God) will wipe out every tear from their eyes,
> And death will be no more,
> Neither will mourning nor outcry
> nor pain be anymore…
> Look! I (really) am making all things new."
> (Rev. 21:4-5)

It's all in the mind

When I was young (hard to believe, but true) I was fascinated by the prospect of another world after this one. Well, not a world in the sense of another globe, but, rather, that of another state. By the time I was in my 40's I had read hundreds of books on the subject. Some of them seemed pretty far out, but not all. The common thread, once you overlook the semantics, is that life does indeed go on, even though the facts of it are not easily discerned from this side. In what follows, I will recount, in summary fashion, what I gleaned. I have no interest in proselytizing, nor do I presume that my findings are the final word on the subject. But, for those who haven't got 20 years to spare for research, here is what I discovered:

To begin, when the mind is freed of the body, it is something like a water-logged cork, floating within a sea of consciousness – not on the surface, but deep inside where everything around it is of similar "specific gravity," for want of another word. The law is: "Like attracts like." In this mode, dominant thoughts determine an individual's environment. Overriding fear and notions of damnation invite mental torture that is as real as anything perceived can be. Expectations of happy reunions lead to just that. Anticipation of sitting at the feet of a master will surely accomplish it. All of this, however, is tempered by what you are, which is the product of how you have evolved while continuing to create your reality.

While much effort is put into self-creation within physical reality, the process of growth is not limited to that which you can touch or remember best. It happens on all levels and it happens simultaneously. As a consequence, your continuing life-state, following the present one, is not necessarily a linear expression of your present expectations. It could never be. Future life is not squeezed through the eye-of-the-needle of earthly experience. Life is grander than that.

If one could see self in its entirety, one would have eyes with which to see everything. But, we do not. Our vision is limited to that which is closest at hand, and our conclusions about ourselves are a reflection of our immediate reality. We see what we think we are. That is as true for the present as it is for what comes after. Accordingly, when leaving the world of the physical, you will find yourself immersed in a realm that is coincidental with how you are, how you think and how you relate. That is your next state of reality, but it is not all that is real.

No matter how evolved your perspective and state of being, you migrate through every life-death-life experience as a child – a child of God, if you will. As such, although the opportunity to *be* is endlessly expansive, invariably you will always discover yourself as only a tiny part, seeing but little and hoping otherwise. No matter how mature you think you are, you are a child of experience and an infant in terms of self-realization. Through every transition it is the same, never ending. What changes is perspective through the accumulation of realities, by which process you knowingly infiltrate an increasingly greater number of life states. If it were possible, which it is not, ultimately you would omnisciently experience yourself as Allness. The reason it is not possible is because you have so ordered your existence that it cannot be. You are infinitely expansive. That is your joy. Your bliss is the endless pursuit of self-discovery.

On a more mundane level, which it isn't, your next reality will likely overtake you without you having any idea as to how it was accomplished. This also is a part of the scheme of things. To know otherwise would circumvent self-realization. In other words, knowing the entry and exit points in reality would take the meaning out of what lies in between. Do you think you'd like to know everything there is? Think about it. What fun would there be in that? Now let me ask you this: do you think God knows? Do you think he wants to? or do you presume to equate eternal bliss with eternal boredom?

Golly, I'd better back off a bit.

Anyway, getting back to cases, your next reality is already laid out for you, waiting for you to explore it, by which process your enthrallment will be the progressive realization of self. Being is the absolute adventure.

So, where will you be next? Shucks, how would I know? But I can tell you something about where many of our friends have gone and what, supposedly in their own words, they have experienced as their next reality.

I have not heard of anyone who landed on their feet without wobbly legs. Apparently it takes some getting used to, and, as with all children, one's perception is clouded over as the new state of learning unfolds. The best yardstick for what happens "over there" is to compare it to what happens over here. Dimly, at first perceived, reality seeps into the consciousness as if from a great well-spring, calling us forward, egging us on and sometimes dragging us by the heels kicking and screaming. The lessons of life are not always learned willingly. Then, there are the brats who prefer to sit in a corner, pouting. For them the new world is a gloomy place indeed, and their only friends are just like themselves. Exploitation, deprivation and meanness are the rules they play by, and they are only more-or-less content when making others as miserable as they are. They can, however, snap out of it any time they chose to. Thank goodness.

The school of life is such that everyone graduates with honors, sooner or later. There are no spiritual illiterates. But that doesn't mean that everyone learns gracefully. Some folks simply don't want to know any better. For whatever reason their minds are made up and preclude anything else. Well, that's reality too. Theirs. If someone believes they must forever wait to hear a trumpet before they can rise again, so bit it. But, that being the case, don't be surprised if they are greeted by an entire brass band wearing Gabriel name tags. Those who tremble before a glowering figure in robes as he turns pages in a great Book of Judgment, will be relieved to know that, just in back, there are ranks of smiling editors (believe me, editors can smile too) busily scratching out any entries that might prejudice your case. Resurrection, if that is what you call it, really doesn't apply. You cannot be raised from the dead because you never ever died. You are immortal. You changed, that's all, like water that becomes invisible as vapor, but it's still the same water and you are still you. So, welcome aboard, and for heaven's sake quit fussing about it.

There are others who arrive in their new reality being quite unfit to cope because of overriding debilities brought forward from a previous sojourn. That's what hospitals are for, and other places of recuperation where loving souls repair damaged bodies and bent minds. All heal, however; all wounds are bound and all perceptions made clear. Eventually.

For most migrants the new land is all they hoped it would be, even though some of the rules are different. It seems that everything that is real is a construct of mind, even ourselves – nay, especially ourselves. For those in spirit, the chair they sit upon is as real as the chair that you are sitting on now. There's no difference. In fact, many of the locals are quick to point out that their world is less illusory than our own, and that they are more alive than ever. Be that as it may, the mental world takes some getting used to. For example, you don't have to go to work to earn a living, unless you think you have to. When you pluck an orange from a tree, another one pops into its place. When you peel the orange the rind just disappears without ever hitting the ground. There is no garbage to collect. Weird, huh? While the rules of cause and effect are still apparent, nothing is wasted. The world of the mind knows no such limitation. Everything is as it is seen to be, or, better stated, as it is thought to be, including self. It is for this reason that people – let me call them that – grow in both directions, and I don't mean vertically and horizontally. Just as the young grow into their most perfect state of maturity, so do the elderly. As they come to accept that they are what they think, it pleases them most to think about themselves in the most pleasing way, when they were at their best. Accordingly, as the habit of looking at self evolves, the wrinkles melt away, the walking sticks are left by the wayside and one's step quickens even as does the mind. Everyone becomes as beautiful as they know themselves to be.

With a quickening mind comes the momentum of new possibility. If a person wants to learn, there is nothing stopping him, be it in the vaulted Temples of Light, in the company of Masters, or at the used-used bookstore down the street. Home, by the same process, is similar, yet unlike any other. For some it is a quaint, thatched cottage with a profusion of flowers, and winding paths through shade trees beside perpetually bubbling brooks. For others it is a place of vine covered pedestals and marble columns, where the wine of sunset pervades the cloisters of like-minded souls. It is all a matter of envisioning and acceptance. You can create your reality however and wherever you believe you can. Best of all, because you are always in the company of like-kind, there is no dissension, nobody heaves milk bottles from the second story and nobody gets killed. Big surprise, huh? There is no war... unless, of course, you haven't outgrown it yet, in which case you may find yourself in the ranks of Trojans, hacking away endlessly, or sweating it out in a Sherman tank, blasting away with an infinite arsenal of shells. Sooner or later, however, your mind gets tired of it, even if your sword arm doesn't, and you'd just as soon tie the barrel of your gun in a knot as have to shoot it anymore.

It turns out that reality is a matter of persistent thinking. If you want to change something, all you have to do is learn to think about it differently. But, that is not as easy as it sounds, because they way we think is ingrained habit. Making changes therefore, that is creating new reality, necessitates breaking old thought patterns, and you should know how arduous that can be. Remember the last time you went on a diet, or tried to quit smoking? Well, it's like that. Apparently some folks never quite get the hang of it, in which case changes have to be virtually forced upon them. When that happens, the big booking agent in the sky looks for a suitable vacancy and scoots them back to repeat grade three. Who knows, the next student might be one of your grandchildren.

For those who do get to hang around a while there are endless fascinations, one being the endeavor to help those who are still in school down here, working their way through for the first time or repeating a grade. But communicating, it seems, is more involved than picking up a cosmic telephone or wishful thinking. By some accounts it is a group effort, but not always. In one marvelous old tome that I came across, human consciousness was compared to soft wax into which an impression was made by those on the other side. Geraldine

Cummins in *The Road to Immortality*, when controlled by the spirit of F.W.H Myers said: "The inner mind is very difficult to deal with from this side. We impress it with our message. We never impress the brain of the medium directly. That is out of the question. But the inner mind receives our message and sends it on to the brain. The brain is a mere mechanism. The inner mind is like soft wax; it receives our thoughts, their whole content, but it must produce the words that clothe it." These impressions then filter through as inspiration or, sometimes, even as audible messages. But, it is a primitive process that is fraught with difficulty, not the least being that whatever is "received" is subject to all the machinations of the recipient's mind, including his beliefs, prejudices and state of receptivity. The conscious mind, it seems, is oftentimes more of a hindrance than a help, necessitating conveyance of the message during the sleep state, sometimes even during hallucinations, but rarely, unfortunately, when a person asks for it. It seems that the same process of distortion, deletion and generalization that affects human communication, also affects communication between the here and the hereafter.

The problems with communicating are not less profound when the call is initiated from this side of things. More often than not it is a one-way affair: our thoughts may go up the ladder, only to have the response, if there is one, come crashing down to our feet in fragments. Two-way communication is possible however, although I suspect it is more rare than many presume. As often as not it is a fleeting thing. There are those, however, who seem better "linked," for whatever reason. Maybe it's because they work at it, or maybe it's because they presume too much. Maybe both. There is a great body of evidence that supports either point of view. Out of the mountain of chaff, however, the illusive kernels for which we search have nourished mankind as nothing else ever has.

Of paramount importance are the questions relating to the reunion of friends and family. Some of the greatest attempts at spirit communication have been generated by those who so desperately seek confirmation of the afterlife and the continued existence of loved ones. Indeed, there seems to have been quite a number of successes in this. Equally true, however, there has been a lot of – what shall I call it? – other stuff. Unfortunately, if you listen long enough you can hear just about anything. Still, while all that litters is not literature, it is the aggregate of group effort that provides the forward momentum which, in the final analysis, is of benefit to us all.

How many people have lived out their lives longing to be reunited with loved ones who have preceded them? I would be surprised if there was even one person who didn't. It is a burning issue. The good news is that we got here together, and it is reasonable to expect that we will get *there* together. We couldn't have been in the same place at the same time without being of like kind. Souls, like birds or bees, migrate together, streaming through realities. As to whether or not joining loved ones is possible, it appears to be inevitable. Love is the thread by which all realities are connected, which thread, veritably, is a life line. So, do not pine or waste yourself in mourning. Instead, dress your spirit in happiness in anticipation of the best family reunion you've ever had. By the way, the invitations were sent out a long, long time ago, and this is one shindig that won't be called off because of bad weather.

As an adjunct, there are a few people who would just as soon not attend such a reunion, life being as complicated as it is. For example, if you have been married three times down here, and if everyone lives forever, does that make you a bigamist in the hereafter? Perish the thought. You have been, like practically everyone else, married at least a million times. Nifty, huh? So much for wallflowers...

Before leaving this segment, the subject of intervention comes up. The question is, other than intervention by God, can those in the other realms have a direct influence upon earthly matters? In answer: they do and they don't. For the most part, things go on here without them giving it the slightest nod. They've got other fish to fry. But, for the few determined anglers, it's open fishing season and there's no limit to the catch. They can do it if they can do it. But, usually they cannot and must settle for coming back personally to take a more active part. The law of possibility is congruent with the law of probability. It's simply a matter of opportunity, appropriateness and necessity. Even if it has never been done before, the Big Guy doesn't back away from an opportunity to create something new. In fact, he thrives on it.

Joel

Islam and traditional Judaism, like most religions, foster the idea of life after death, but Christianity, in particular, seems preoccupied with resurrection of the dead as exemplified by Jesus. Upon leaving the physical body, it is said that one is "shining like the stars in heaven" (Dan. 12:3) or has become "like the angels" (Mark 12:25). Saint Paul said that the resurrected body will be new and spiritual (1 Cor. 15:35-54). Frankly, I like the idea of bobbing around in a spirit body, au naturale, as it were. Long hair is in, no clothes and – Yeek! Are spirits naked?

Oh, dear. Maybe I'll have to think this over a bit. In the meantime, here's what happened to a friend of mine, named Joel.

If you were to ask him, Joel had no idea how he got here. Never mind that it was the most important event in his life, he simply couldn't remember, possibly because he was child-like in so many ways. When he arrived, loved ones gathered around and made a great fuss over him. But, for Joel, other than being reassured, it meant very little. His ability to perceive things was clouded over and he had much to learn before he would be able to get around on his own.

In the early stages, someone was always nearby, coaching him, caring for him and encouraging him. Little by little, Joel developed the ability to relate, discovering that while he could do many things, there were other things over which he seemed to have no control at all. It was as if circumstances were being thrust upon him, forcing him to grow. And, grow he did.

Eventually, as Joel was drawn into ever expanding relationships, he saw less and less of the people he grew up with, but he never forgot them. Life had become totally engrossing and he reveled in the opportunity to discover all that he could. He made some terrible blunders from time to time, but the wise ones around him understood how confusing things could be. Growth, it seemed, was a process of trial and error, such that no matter how well-intentioned he was, screw-ups were inevitable. Although Joel didn't know it at the time, that was the whole purpose of his being here. Inevitable growth, enforced growth, if you will, is the name of the game.

After what seemed like twenty years, Joel developed a strong, loving relationship with another spirit person and, to their delight, two spirit-babes were placed in their care, to nurture as had been done for them. By the time Joel had matured, however, he was on his own once more, and quite alone. It was the natural way of things, in which relationships and close ties wax and wane in the pursuit of new experience.

While Joel had developed considerable understanding by then, it was also true that there was still very much to learn – too much, in fact, to accomplish in only one spin around the wheel, so to speak. But, to Joel's credit, he did persist, becoming ever more wise. As he did so, he saw himself differently; indeed, others saw him differently too. Before long, so much had happened that, even when he tried, Joel couldn't remember back to the time of his arrival in the new world, and the comings and goings of life remained pretty much a mystery.

Then, unexpectedly, everything changed.

"Hey, I'm up here," Joel shouted, but the people below paid no attention.

When someone shouted "Code blue," the emergency ward became bedlam, with nurses and orderlies scurrying about as hard-pressed doctors left one screened enclosure for another.

It all began when Joel lost his breath, dancing of all things. He had been on the surgery waiting list for a year by then, something like when you have to take a number and line up at the deli counter. Joel's number was in five digits – not very reassuring. In the meantime, he took his pills and tried not to think about his demise too much. That was why he went dancing.

When he collapsed, I felt sorry for his partner. Like everyone, she was just out for a good time, no strings attached

– at least that's what they say. But it didn't work out like that at all, at least not for her. Her name was Ethyl, a nice girl who was merely trying to piece her life back together.

Joel should have known that he was pushing it, but Ethyl was a real charmer and he was determined to make an impression, which he did. By the time the guys from the ambulance got there, she was almost in shock.

The attendant pulled on Joel's tongue, then covered his face with a plastic gadget and started mouth-to-mouth on him. At the same time, another attendant attached a bunch of wires to monitor Joel's pulse and such.

Joel never knew that Ethyl rode in the ambulance with him. Later, she couldn't explain why she felt she had to. After all, she hardly knew the guy. It was just one of those things that, later, she frequently wondered about.

"Hey, you guys!" Joel shouted again, to no avail. Puzzled still, Joel watched as one of the doctors injected a thrombolytic drug right into the heart of the guy below him. "Bummer!" thought Joel, enrapt, noticing the flat line on the nearby screen.

The minutes ticked by in slow motion, the man's brain cells dying due to lack of oxygenated blood. The doctor put his finger to the carotid artery on the man's neck, watching the screen while a monotone whine filled the room.

"That's it, I'm afraid," the cardiologist said, whereupon the nurses started pulling plugs and tubes and what not. It was just routine. Some made it and some didn't. That was life.

Joel understood. But death was a curious thing just then. He hadn't seen too many fellows give up the ghost, as it were. In the minutes following the departure of the medical staff, Joel studied the guy anew. "Hmph, he looks just like me. I'll be darned. He's even got my tattoo! Sumbitch, the guy told me that—" Joel blinked hard, trying to comprehend. "Is that me?" he asked, panicked. "Hey!" he shouted, but no one paid any attention. It was as if they couldn't hear him. After a time, Joel swallowed hard and looked at the guy anew. He shook his head sadly, his voice low: "Bummer. Is that really me? But I'm not dead! Hey, somebody! Don't you see? I…"

Joel couldn't go on. It had happened too quickly and he wasn't ready for it.

Then, as he watched, the body below him released its fluids. In disdain, Joel looked away, embarrassed and perplexed too. It was then that he saw the shadows on the ward curtain. They were indistinct at first, but coming closer in a way—not getting bigger, just clearer maybe. Joel wanted to call out again, but his voice failed him. He felt terribly alone. "Please?" he whispered, looking up.

Nothing.

Then, as he looked at the curtain again, the shadows were stronger, inside this time, with a kind of light around them, drawing his attention. One had close curls, just like... "Ma?" Joel blurted, unbelieving. The image reconciled itself, smiling now. That smile was the last he had hoped to see in this world or the first in the next, and it was so. She was reaching for him.

Shortly, the shadows faded from the curtain, even that of Joel's, and he was gone, taken to a new place with a new way of life and a new way of looking at things. But it didn't come easy. He was confused at first. In time, however, Joel accepted his newfound state, any dissension quickly put aside by the fact that he was just glad to be alive. Still, though, the pain in his chest lingered, and his left arm didn't work too good. He thought about it. "It'll pass," his mom said, simply, "...as soon as you stop thinking about it." Which, after a while, he did.

Then, gradually, Joel came to realize that he was getting special treatment. It began when he was introduced to Micah, a fellow with a great white beard and a knobby walking stick. Joel was surprised.

"Were you expecting someone else?" the old guy inquired.

"Well, no." Joel stammered.

"All right, then, let's get down to cases."

"Cases," it turned out, had more to do with the way things really were, as compared to Joel's opinion of how they ought to be. One day, sitting on a garden bench, Joel looked up with shock: "I've got to tell her!" he blustered.

The old guy nodded. "Figured you might," he said. "How do you propose to do it?"

"Hell, I don't know!"

Chagrined, the old man replied: "Watch your language, son. You never know what part of you is listening."

Joel was puzzled.

The old man shook his head. "Never mind, I'll explain later. So, what about this Ethyl person – that's her name isn't it?"

Joel nodded dumbly.

Ethyl tossed in her sleep, visions of faces known and others forgotten flipping upon the screen on her unconscious. Then, there was Joel. She regarded him uncertainly, resisting the mixed feelings that he roused in her.

"Ethyl" he began, tentatively, "this is Joel."

The screen of Ethyl's mind blinked.

"Really!" Joel added. Then he calmed down. "I want to thank you for the last dance. It... it was the best one of all. I didn't know it was you who'd be there, but I know now, and I want to thank you for that. I couldn't have chosen better."

Ethyl awoke, strange visions and recollections floating through her mind. Then, surprising, even to herself, she said, aloud: "Thank you, Joel." And it was done.

In the years after, Ethyl rarely thought of Joel, but when she did she smiled, glad to have been there when it counted most. "That's life," she told herself, knowing that somehow, even if beyond reason, it was so.

Joel, meantime, was cruisin'. The old guy turned out to be a travel agent of sorts and he was determined to take Joel to all the sites on some kind of excursion pass. Apparently the old guy had pull. So it was that Joel went from place to place, as if on a magic carpet. All he had to do was think about it and he was there. Casually, one day he commented to his guide: "You know, it's just like dreaming. Only now I can chose what I dream about."

"True," the old gent replied, "but there are things you haven't yet dreamed of."

So it began again, the adventures of Joel in Wonderland, in pursuit of that which, in the fullness of reality, would somehow loom larger than life itself.

"There is a natural body and there is a spiritual body."
"And as we have borne the image of the earthly,
we shall also bear the image of the heavenly."
(1 Cor 15: 44 and 49)

Migration

Physical death does not automatically resolve conflict between non-integrated parts. For some parts, the prospect of change – birth or death – may be filled with dread, rendering it anything but a voluntary experience. Sometimes a part will resists with such tenacity that the passage between realities is aborted. Yet the part continues to exist, in limbo as it were, waiting for the return of the host vehicle.

Be that as it may, nothing happens by accident. For those who cannot believe in anything greater than themselves, the world is a fearful place indeed. But, the higher-self of such an individual knew beforehand the rigors to be encountered, and either chose to experience what lay ahead or was compelled by the necessities of growth and amelioration to do so. Anyone who is desperately afraid of dying is, in one way or another, equally afraid of living, which in some cases accounts for still-birth and crib death. As I said, not all venture willingly, and this equally applies to entry into every reality – this one and the next.

Within the great scheme of things, however, there is always balance. For a being to have set certain elements in motion, there must always be an opposite and equal reaction. Sometimes the opportunity to strike that balance undeniably draws an aspect of transcendent-self back into the vortex of earthly reality, to pick up the pieces and attend to unfinished business. Some parts migrate joyfully, while others are overcome with horror, the transition through death and rebirth invoking stages of fear, resentment and resignation. Graduation day is not something everyone celebrates. The prospect of having to "make a living" can be fretful. Most often, though, the passage is uneventful. It just happens. It's one of the things we were born to be good at.

Migration, in this context, refers to both the coming and the going from the physical state. In the beginning, assimilation with a fetus can arise at any time or hardly at all. Now, there's a can of worms for you. Let me explain: gestation may last nine months on earth, but may eclipse generations when viewed from spirit. The difference is that spiritual beings exist in all-time and are not regulated by linear reality, ticking clocks, accumulated phases of the moon or trimesters. There is a moment, however, when the migrating one is irresistibly attached to the fetus, at which time life-identity is imparted. It may happen anytime during pregnancy or, in rare cases, not until a short time after physical birth. Prior to attachment, every attempt is made to insure that the path ahead is the most appropriate for the newcomer, his parents, and every other person with whom the new arrival will interact in this reality. For all the planning and preparation, there is nevertheless an element of divine unpredictability. Although a conundrum at times, it is vital. To suggest there is unpredictability in life does not imply that it is merely happenstance however. Nothing is an accident, surely not one's path. Compare it, if you will, to setting sail for a new land. You know the route, you know how to navigate and you have with you all the provisions necessary to make the journey. What you don't know is if you'll weather the unexpected hurricanes. Like the storms of life, there's a whole bunch of people out there in a frenzy of creativity, changing things all the time. Everything is in a state of flux, constantly evolving. That is why nothing happens twice in exactly the same way, not in nature, not in man and not in the transcendent world either. Fractal geometry gives us a clue to this, whereby not all perfect numbers divide perfectly. At the end of a long line of decimal places a single digit will change and, subtle though it is, it is the wheel from which all that is spirals upward and outward through infinite growth.

As to ethical matters surrounding migration, there is the question of assistance and interference. Is abortion wrong? Is suicide? Is assisted death? While it would be ever so convenient to have a clear answer, there isn't one. Moreover, there isn't a man-made law that can rationalize it. While governments must generalize in order to protect the masses, the circumstance and context of such events is entirely personal. There is no right or wrong. There only is. Notwithstanding, a little love goes a long way.

While we're on such a happy topic, what about murder? What about murder on a mass scale? War, for example? In answer, every organism struggles for life and will defend itself if necessary. This applies equally to amoebae as it does to nations. It is nature's way of self-preservation. What cannot be sanctioned, however, is doing willful harm and, regardless of the financial burden to society, this applies to correctional institutions as well.

Free-will is not intended to be a license to commit mayhem, yet mayhem exists. A lot has been said about the scales of justice, righting wrongs and retribution. What hasn't been said is that the life you take is your own. Every life is invested in every other life. That may seem strange, but consider what it is that makes you real. Where it not for them, you wouldn't even know you were. It is not enough to say that you are your brother's keeper when, on the highest level, if you could but know it, you are your brother. Everything is divisible (and actualized) by one. We are one. The body politic of souls is one. Guess who the One is? Guess who you are?

Group souls

If birds of a feather flock together, then we are all winged. Like a school of fish or a herd of wildebeest, we track the same track and rise on the same updrafts. We have more than nationality in common, we are spirit in very essence. Yet, remarkably, the sum total of all that is created is invested in every single individual. It is something like a Mandelbrot pattern, repeating itself endlessly within itself, but variegated by shades of color and definition, always emerging more beautiful and more compelling. Yes, we belong, each and every one of us, to each other. There is no depth so great, nor despair so distant that it is not imparted to every other living thing as well. We are what we are, and what we are is glorious, the reminder of which is in the eyes of every stranger who will, but for a moment, stand still, wherein we behold the eyes of God.

Part 4
PERCEPTION

CHAPTER EIGHT
PSYCHIC DEVELOPMENT

Mediumship

According to Webster's Dictionary, a medium is: "A person through whom the spirits of the dead are supposedly able to contact the living." The problem with that definition is that only the living contact each other. The very connotation of "spirits of the dead" dredges up impressions of ghouls and such, which no medium in their right mind would have anything to do with. Still, it's a starting point.

A book known as *"The Teaching of the Twelve Apostles,"* written in 140AD, gives instructions about psychic gifts and advice to mediums. A similar book, *The Shepherd of Hermas*, also 140AD, was ranked with other scriptural books of the time and held to be divinely inspired. It was read in church by Bishops Eusebius and Athenasius, and described the difference between true and false mediums, claiming that it was the Holy Spirit that spoke through the true medium. Tertullian, 60-230AD, in his book *De Anima*, describes church services which are led by spiritual mediums.

In this context, a medium is a person who, being sensitive to spirit, is able to act as an intermediary between this world and the next. The same could be said for someone who is psychic, the distinction being that mediums are professionals in their own right. Contrary to popular opinion, mediums are not necessarily born as such. The development of spiritual gifts invariably involves considerable dedication and refinement of both character and ability. Admittedly, however, as with any profession, there are degrees of competence and natural ability.

At the start of the 20th century there was a concerted effort to pursue spiritual and psychic matters as a legitimate science. Numerous doctors, scientists and prominent people got together and formed groups such as the (1882) Society for Psychical Research in London, which continues to this day. At the same time, the American Society for Psychical Research was founded in 1885. There is the New York Parapsychology Foundation, founded in 1951 by Mrs. Eileen Garrett, who became a subject for Dr. J.B. Rhine and Prof. William McDougall at the Parapsychology Laboratory of Duke University. The Parapsychological Foundation of 1953 organized the First International Conference of Parapsychological Studies at the University of Utrecht, in Holland. Typical of many other efforts is the work done by Gardner Murphy, the director of Creativity and ESP research at the Menninger Foundation in Topeka, Kansas. Dr. Iam Steveson, head of the Department of Neurology and Psychiatry at the University of Virginia Medical School, did original research into reincarnation. Also of note is Dr. Karlis Osis, the Director of Research for the American Society for Psychical Research. Mediums and other interested persons have, meanwhile, formed collectives the world over, such as the Spiritualist's National Union, the International Spiritualist Federation and the Spiritual Alliance of Great Britain. The objective of these societies is to provide research and investigative facilities, together with training, examination and certification of working mediums. As a case in point, through the efforts of the world-famed spiritual healer, Harry Edwards, a healing sanctuary has been operating in Burrows Lea, Shere, England, for over a half-century. Beside the long, curving driveway, Queen Elizabeth planted an oak tree beside a commemorative plaque in bronze. Another example, also in England, is the Arthur Findlay College at Stanstead Hall, Essex. It is a magnificent structure, laced in vines, with chimney turrets, galleries, and lecture halls. In back, in the center of a great expanse of lawn there is a solitary tulip tree. You can see it from the crystal chapel, a retreat so fine and aged that one would think it could speak if the mediums present did not.

Certification of a professional medium usually follows a three to five year period in which the fledgling medium serves as an understudy to the accrediting society, after which, during demonstrations, the medium is subject to periodic, unannounced testing by society officials. Generally, the major societies take their work very seriously and have earned a good reputation over the course of many years.

Few people, however, realize the tribulation that is faced by those who seek to serve through the development of mediumship. Aside from the fact that most mediums live in borderline poverty, the quest for development involves much more than a five year stint in college. For most it is a lifelong undertaking in which, while psychic gifts may be developed, so is the person. The phrase: "Many are called but few are chosen," (Matt. 22:14) is apt, since so many drop out along the way. To those who heed the calling, 1 Corinthians 12 is as if a banner binding the heart: "And the manifestation of the Spirit is given to every man to profit withal. For to one is given by the Spirit the word of wisdom; to another the word of knowledge by the same Spirit; to another faith by the same Spirit; to another the gifts of healing by the same Spirit; to another the working of miracles; to another prophecy; to another discerning of Spirits; to another divers kinds of tongues; to another the interpretation of tongues; but all these worketh that one and selfsame Spirit, dividing to every man severally as he will."

James Hervey Hyslop (1854-1920), Professor of Logic and Ethics at Columbia University in New York, stated, in his uniquely bombastic way: "I regard the existence of discarnate spirits as scientifically proved and I no longer refer to the skeptic as having any right to speak on the subject. Any man who does not accept the existence of discarnate spirits and the proof of it is either ignorant or a moral coward. I give him short shrift, and do not propose any longer to argue with him on the supposition that he knows anything about the subject." Hyslop James Hervey, *Borderland of Psychical Research*, Published by H.B. Turner, Boston, MA..1906.

The quest

There is as much reverence in a true spiritual séance as there is in any monastery or church ceremony. The invocation and benediction are the same; the deep desire for personal worthiness and truth are the same. What is different are the rules: there aren't any. A person is free to believe whatever he chooses, so long as it is consistent with high moral integrity and elevated purpose. A medium, in the truest sense, is there to be of service to others.

It is through attunement that the medium comes into his or her own. But it is not a casual once-a-week affair; it is a constant, daily exercise in the quest for self-perfection, during the prolonged course of which one's patience and faith are tested over and over again. Attunement necessitates living up to one's highest ideals in every aspect. Being an instrument of spirit requires living it, even through the dry spells when: "high are the hurdles." It is not, however, a crash course in personal sacrifice; that is not required at all. The world already has enough martyrs. What it requires is people whose very nature is sensitive to more than the mundane; who, with genuine humility, seek the means to be of service to others.

"We pray always for you,
that our God would count you worthy of this calling,
and fulfill all the good pleasure of His goodness,
and the work of faith with power."
(Thess. 1:11)

Meditation

The word *dhyana* comes to us out of antiquity; it is at least 4,000 years old and is Sanskrit for meditation, the process of involuted non-reasoning in which truth becomes self-apparent. Meditation, although not necessarily a religious practice, is prevalent in Buddhism, Hinduism, Christianity and Islam, and was popularized in the West in the 1960's by Maharishi Mahesh Yogi, under the name Transcendental Meditation – a good title since all meditation is intended to be transcendental.

In practice, meditation leads to a type of contemplation in which merely thinking is a distraction. The final stage is the *prayer of simplicity*, in which pure thought is without the clutter of language precepts.

For some people the requirements of meditation are quite overwhelming; for them, doing nothing is the hardest thing of all to do. For the novice, blanking the mind seems like an impossibility, minor distractions become major incidents, with successive scratching and irritations preoccupying the mind. Fortunately, one does not have to become a Zen monk in order to open the inner door, and the initial developmental exercises are not very demanding. To begin, one cannot really think of nothing. The trick is simply to slow the rate of perception so that the mind focuses inward, rather than outward.

Start by assuming a comfortable position, sitting in the lotus position – Indian style, if you will, with the palms up – or you may sit upon a straight-backed chair, with your hands resting on your lap. One's posture must be erect, however, because correct breathing is important. To set the tone, soft music of an appropriate nature may be played in the background for a while at the start. Some people like nature recordings of rolling surf or inspirational music such as Jules Massenet's *Thais Meditation*. For some people, the mood may be enhanced by burning incense, a candle in a colored holder, or flowers. Other folks find such things distracting. Nevertheless, use whatever it is that gives you a sense of calm upliftment. Upon opening, an invocation is appropriate: state your quest, ask for guidance, then relax with surety. Avoid anything that causes strain, including staring into a candle flame or crystals. Subdued lighting, or no light at all, is often preferred, because it lessens sensory distractions. For the same reason, most people close their eyes. The next step involves controlled breathing with the mouth closed. Breathe slowly and deeply from the bottom of the diaphragm. Some call it belly breathing.

Everything thus far has served to set the stage whereby your thoughts may be released from daily preoccupation. There is no effort in meditating, nor strain or discomfort. It isn't something you have to work at. It comes naturally, together, initially, with a host of jumbled thoughts. The mind is used to being busy and it takes practice to learn how to calm it; and, just about the time you think you're getting the hang of it you'll catch yourself having spent several minutes thinking about work or the grocery list. Sometimes you get derailed without even knowing it. Again, gentle persistence is the key. Learning to meditate isn't accomplished overnight; it takes more than, say, three months of schooling – the equivalent, of which, is meditating once a week for nine years.

Ideally, three times a week is adequate, for about an hour at the same time each day, early morning or early evening being preferred, in the same place if possible. If not, a shady bench, a park or a quiet beach will do. Do not sit when overly full or when the stomach is grinding on emptiness. Before long you will find that you are able to access the meditative state without difficulty, and often in spite of what at one time would have been quite distracting.

To get in the groove, some people find that it helps to visualize being in a peaceful setting, beside a bubbling brook, for example. When you do this, involve yourself totally. Hear the ripples, the buzzing bees and distant whippoorwills; feel the gentle breeze on your cheeks and the coolness of the grass; notice the wafting scent of buttercups and mown hayfields. Feel the arms of the overhead trees protecting you, the winking sun amid the rustling leaves. Be there, soak it up and drift with it. Another technique involves repeating, as slowly as possible, a simple word like home. Hold the long syllable as long as you can, then when you detect a stray thought entering your mind, complete the word and start over again. Another exercise, somewhat more demanding, is to mentally tune into inspirational music, something that possibly you've never heard before, in which you hear more than one distinct voice in harmony. It's like hearing two songs at once. Don't be surprised if it takes some doing. It does. But, as you get better at it you will notice that something quite unexpected happens, which compares to "reading between the lines." When one is able to enter into such a state without effort, there are few words to describe it – touching the Essence, perhaps.

All of this is not intended to put you to sleep or induce drowsiness, although that may certainly happen, especially for beginners. After the tensions of the day, it's like the body says: "Oh, goody," and tries to hunker down. If you find yourself repeatedly drifting off, end the sit, improve your sleep habits and try again another day. Eventually, things will come together for you. In the meantime enjoy the inner peace that you are discovering.

Meditation can lead to a very unique form of inspiration: the ability to think without words. In this contemplative state, pure thought is indeed transcendent, and quite beyond the constructs of language. It is in this state that one, rather than loosing self, discovers self.

> Upon the sea of seeing
> I am
> A part of all that is
> Infinite being.

Sitting in circle

"We made these little gray houses of logs, and they are square. It is a bad way to live, for there can be no power in a square. Birds make their nests in circles, for theirs is the same religion as ours." (*Black Elk Speaks* by J.G.Neilhardt)

Having learned to meditate, which is essentially focusing inward, the development circle offers the opportunity to learn how to focus outward as well. In either case, sensory deprivation is a key factor, so that the "screen" of the mind will not be impacted by outside stimuli. It is for this reason alone that many development circles are held in relative darkness, or, at least, with a low intensity 15W bulb, blue in a metal circle and red in a physical circle (more about physical circles later).

The development circle is not an ad hoc affair. "Sits" are held regularly, certainly not less frequent than once a week, at the same appointed time and, preferably, in the same place. Ideally, the sit room should not be used for any other purpose and will be kept clean and aired out between sessions. Equipment includes recording devices and something on which to play taped music, activated by a silent switch, with only the speaker inside the room. Another innovation includes a tape recorder placed outside the room, with a remote on-off switch to a high-sensitivity, directional microphone inside the room.

Other equipment may include a camera using infrared flash bulbs, with the infrared film stored in a refrigerator between sits.

The number of sitters usually ranges from two to a dozen people, in comfortable clothing. Regular sitters often supply their own chairs and leave them in the sit room between sessions. Chairs are placed so that sitters may hold hands if desired. Of course, circle etiquette requires personal cleanliness, and the avoidance of perfumed soap or cosmetics beforehand. Menstruation is of no consequence. Avoid coughing and exaggerated breathing that will distract other sitters. Punctuality and preparedness are important, bearing in mind that your companions include more than those physically present.

"You do not know the difficulty which changes in conditions make for us. Sitting down immediately after a meal is not good. The bodily conditions which we seek are passivity and quickness of receptivity; but not passivity which comes from sluggishness and torpor. No worse condition can be than the state of somnolence…it opens the door for the advent of the more material spirits, and stops our power. You would do well to think of this and guard yourselves against any excess in any way when you are about to seek communion with us. …One such member in a circle, even as one ailing or suffering, will create conditions which we cannot overcome." (*Spirit Teachings* by W.Stainton Moses)

A circle leader will be appointed, someone supposedly rational and, hopefully, experienced with the routine, but not necessarily a medium or someone with demonstrable psychic gifts. A small collection is usually made to cover the cost of light snacks and beverage after the sit. A secretary looks after the various records that might be kept (please, not a scribe) and a technician the electronic equipment.

The majority of circles start off with an opening prayer, affirming purpose and protection. The group may sing uplifting songs or hymns to "raise the vibrations," or listen to a few minutes of inspirational music. A circle, although a place of reverence, is not a somber affair. Light hearts and laughter win the day. As a matter of choice, sitters may join hands during the invocation and singing, but, thereafter, usually sit quietly with their hands comfortably in their laps. Avoid "closing up" by crossing the arms and legs. In some circles men and women are seated alternately. Children are rarely invited to a circle, except, perhaps, when a special circle is held at Christmas or such, when messages are given as a seasonal blessing. Development circles usually sit for one to two hours, but not more, up to three times a week.

For the beginner, the harder one tries the more jumbled things become. As the mind seeks to focus, minor discomforts become major events and normally overlooked sensations become a serious distraction. The ticking of a wristwatch can end up sounding like cannon, the faintest perfume overwhelming. At first, it is as if the sitter has no control over his thoughts while the engine of the mind keeps huffing along from one item to the next. Regular, deep breathing helps greatly to quell such distractions. Soon, one's body is at rest and thought processes are slowed down as quietude prevails. Then the mind, like a calm sea, reflects that which is beyond self, while any disturbance sends ripples across the surface, distorting the images reflected there.

Psychic perception is a wonderful thing. It is uplifting in its own right. Always, however, one must guard against the ego getting in the act. It is ever so easy to be misled and self-beguiled. For that reason, do not be in a hurry, do not embellish what you get or inflate your position in the scheme of things; especially, resist the temptation to presume that just because you get something you are special, that you rank among the chosen and are destined to spearhead a great cause. An ounce of humility is worth a bucket of leavening. At the same time, don't believe everything you hear from others. Use your common sense: that's what it's for.

"Forasmuch as ye are zealous of spiritual gifts,
seek that ye may excel."
(II Cor14:12)

Discernment
There is a difference between a psychic forced-march and rational endeavor, just as there is a difference between open-mindedness and hobbling skepticism. While you owe it to yourself to maintain a healthy perspective, nothing is as frustrating to psychic development as overriding negativity, scientific prejudice included. It is the role of inquiring minds to exercise both expectancy and objectivity, not in terms of preconceived ideas, but with a view to discovering that which adds to the bulk of present understanding. It is utterly unreasonable to insist that new experiences be packaged in the same old way.

"He did not many works that night because of their unbelief."
(Matthew 13:54-58)

Psychic phenomena, when it comes, is differentiated as either subjective or objective, or a combination of the two. Subjective phenomena is based on internal representations, whereas objective experiences seem to initiate outside of the mind. In truth, all perception is the same, whether viewed as an internal or external event. What changes is the way the impressions are rationalized, or processed, by one's consciousness. Most people, for instance, place more credence in what seems to originate outside of themselves, rather than what impresses them internally. But, either way, it is the same vision, the same message. In practice, subjective experiences are far more common than objective ones. The difference is like hearing words inside your head, as compared to hearing someone talk to you from across the room. Obviously, the latter seems to be more convincing, as it is easy for the screen of the mind to be dominated by regurgitations from the subconscious, which, in itself, is the greatest barrier to getting the real goods. Most people, unfortunately, are too impatient, or have the silly notion that they are special for some reason and have been "chosen" by the other side as a channel or such. While such notions lead to engrossing evenings, oftentimes there is more worth in the message on a box of Corn Flakes.

One of the most common forms of phenomenon is called stepping-in. The theory is that spirit, when drawing near, causes a tingling or shuddering sensation about the sitter's head, shoulders or spinal system, which is often passed off with the phrase: "Someone just walked over my grave." For the psychic, this is an opportunity to tune-in and go with the flow. Granted, stepping-in may be a purely physiological function, but not necessarily. Indeed, for many psychics it is a prerequisite to believing that they are *linked*, and it is not uncommon for them to differentiate between visitors according to the sensations imparted. While some people claim that it makes a great difference as to whether stepping-in is on the left side or the right, others claim that it makes no difference at all.

When in circle, a common routine is to push power. Imagine, if you will, each person sitting around a great wheel which rotates from right to left. The energy to get the wheel turning comes from the solar plexus and can be felt as a pulling or pushing sensation. This wheel of power is often seen and is certainly felt, causing nausea in some, for which the remedy is to lift the heels for a few minutes. Whether this action really has anything to do with the actual power is beside the point, because it does seem to work.

If a sitter is not contributing to the circuit, as it were, the power can sometimes be seen to loop around them, effectively excluding them from the circle. Of course, the power in a circle is not always a visual thing, nor is the success of the circle dependent upon it being so. It's just one of the things that happens.

During the sit, it is not uncommon to feel wafts of air or to notice a host of things such as flashing or streaking lights, various odors and what have you. It usually takes considerable practice, however, before impressions become more profound. When sitting in dim light, a thing called transfiguration often happens, in which case the features of a person sitting opposite you seem to change. Some claim that it is proof of spirit stepping-in, but very often it is the result of eye strain and an over-active imagination. That spirit can be seen, however, is without doubt. Too numerous to mention are the instances where psychic impressions have been corroborated by subsequent investigation. As well, it is always a high point when two or more sitters experience the same phenomenon at the same time. That kind of confirmation goes a long way to ameliorate one's uncertainties during the inevitable dry spells.

Novices, especially, are quite thrilled when they get something in circle, and tend to let their enthusiasm carry them away with the urge to share everything. While this is quite understandable, it is a good idea to keep something back in hope of getting outside corroboration. It is one thing to sense a *guide* standing beside you and to get an impression of what he looks like, and quite another for someone else to describe him to you after the fact.

Sometimes a link is so strong that it feels overpowering. If uncomfortable, tell your visitor to back up a bit. This isn't as ludicrous as it sounds. Spirit, oftentimes, is learning the ropes too. As to possession and involuntary control, forget it. Like attracts like, and if you sit with good intention and have anything near reasonable control and expectations, you are as safe as a babe in a cradle. Safer, actually. If possession was at all like the movie hacks make it out to be, then we'd all be possessed, and think it was normal! In fact, as spiritual beings, we are as naturally isolated from unwanted spiritual influence as, being physical beings, we are protected from unwanted physical intrusion. At the same time, it behooves the sitter to be selective. You have the right, indeed the obligation, to determine what you will or will not be a party to. Your free will is free only if you exercise it. If you don't like what you're getting, tell it to take off. Having done so, don't sit and fret about it. Simply, let it go.

It may come as a surprise, but spirit can lie or, at least, seem to. Just because someone sprouts wings doesn't mean he suddenly acquires the wisdom of the ages. Be assured, however, that "by their works ye shall know them." Be aware, that's all; keep an open mind and don't jump to conclusions. Additionally, as you may or may not discover, there are many on both sides of the veil who play at this. Again, like attracts like and frivolousness has its own reward. Simply put, if you are determined to play with your mind, be prepared to share your toys.

Sitting in development circle is not intended to be an amusing pastime, nor should it be confused with parlor games or commercial opportunism. If you don't know the difference, take up bowling instead. The rule is to assume nothing and test everything, even yourself. The world is full of people who are full of themselves.

Need it be said that guides and spirit helpers are not trophies? Nor do they come bearing great titles. After all, just because humans are impressed by such nonsense, that doesn't mean that spirit has to be. Invariably, those who come to you have long since outgrown such infatuation. Yet, what about the quest to contact, say, Aunt Emma, one of the dearly departed? The truth is that it happens all the time, frequently quite independently of the development circle. When it does happen, remember to maintain control of yourself and seek out that which is uncontrovertibly evidential. Would you want to settle for less?

Finally, under the heading of mediumship and psychic development, I reiterate that like attracts like. If you expect to be nurtured and guided by the highest and most evolved, it is incumbent upon you to govern yourself accordingly. This means practicing what you preach. It is unreasonable to expect help from the unseen when you deny giving help to the seen. You get as you give, notwithstanding that spirit is far more tolerant and understanding of our shortcomings than we are of each other's. The quest for spirituality is not a hobby. You cannot tune in once a week like a TV series. You have to live it, not for its sake, but yours.

CHAPTER NINE
MENTAL MEDIUMSHIP

Altered states

For the skeptic, there never has been, nor will there ever be, sufficient proof that an altered state of conscious (ASC) is other than some sort of electro-chemical stimulation or delusion. For them it is as real as unicorns are. Some scientists have been able to simulate many supposedly psychic happenings by stimulating the brain with electric probes and such. Others, perhaps not quite so scientific, have done it with LSD or mescaline. But, unlike the picture on your TV screen, fine-tuning one's sensitivities involves more than a sharp whack on the side of the head. Presuming that there are other ways, and since people who can't face drugs turn to reality, we push on.

The price of free will

Free will is surely a remarkable thing. In view of karma and what appears to be the ordination of events, how free is it really? In reply, free will is indeed just that, but may only be exercised within certain bounds. Imagine you are on top of a skyscraper, peering down at an intersection below. A red car is coming from one direction and a blue car from another. Accordingly, you may correctly make a number of assumptions: they may collide, pass safely, or both be held up by pedestrians. Upon closer scrutiny, you could predict that the blue car is certain to be held up by the lights and the red car will likely catch enough of the green to make it through. In effect, you are seeing the future. All the facts are in place, the outcome more or less obvious. The lesser part depends on the unpredictable element: will the driver of the red car speed up or slow down? That's up to him and his free will. Will the scurrying pedestrian make it across, or will he get knocked down when the guy in the red car floors it? That is free will too. In effect, anything can happen. Heck, the guy in the blue car just might run the light. Still, from a given perspective, you could reasonably infer an outcome, even though nothing is cast in stone. While everything that is already is, it is also true that everything is constantly changing, including, to a degree, one's path.

Sign posts

Every once in a while you may get a flash of something, usually triggered by an incidental or trivial event. It is a peculiar kind of knowing, without knowing how you know, or even what you know. It's just a weird feeling. It might be a deja-vu thing, like something re-experienced, or it may be as subtle as an inexplicable presentiment. However it comes and for whatever reason, you are left with the feeling that it's important, even if you don't quite know why. It isn't like a hunch that you can pin down, it's something different. It is, simply put, a sign post, indicating that you are where you are supposed to be, when you are supposed to be. It is, if you like, a psychic cairn on your path. Take it as reassurance, that's what it is for.

Time and space

Psychic phenomenon is based on information that transcends the limitations of our physical senses. Yet all psychic perception, in order to be received, must filter through the construct of physical mind. To a degree, it is like trying to put a square peg in a round hole. That it works at all is a wonder. One of the wonders is time.

Time is the measurement of what happens between beginnings and endings. But time is not constant: it may be mathematical, like the ticking of a clock, or it may be emotional, when an hours seems to last forever or a lifetime flashes by in the twinkling of an eye. If that isn't enough, time is an illusory aspect of one's current reality. For humans, time is measured in galactic cycles. But, because we are spirit too, we are subject to the reality of all-time. All-time is spirit time.

To understand time, one must look at it in a different way, as if akin to a reel of film of infinite possibility, that plays through our consciousness one frame at a time. All-time encompasses beginnings and endings, causes and effects, all of which exist simultaneously, even if not yet actualized one frame at a time on the personal level of reality. Put another way, what is is. It is not so much that a thing changes, as does our perception of it.

Another way to look at it is from the center of the reel when, upon illumination, one is able to look through frame after layered frame, with the notion of beginnings and endings becoming no longer relevant. From this perspective, time jumps ahead and back without any tangible connection between the two. Yet, all of the beginnings and all of the endings remain connected, even as does the viewer.

Then there is the curious thing that happens when the reel is put on fast forward. To the viewer, the faster the images then the more encompassing is his perception of reality. As the frames continue to speed up, it is as if more and more time is being compressed into the same space. At maximum velocity, time and space merge as one. Indeed, all worlds exist as such, in one-ness, in the same place and time.

In one sense, time passes as one proceeds from the cradle to the grave. Yet, upon our demise, we do not go way down to hell or way up to heaven. As spirit, in an infinite world of all-time and all-space, we remain right where we are. We are always at the center of being. I know it's hard to accept, but there it is.

Clairvoyance

Mental phenomenon is divided into three broad categories: clairvoyance, French for clear seeing; clairaudience for clear hearing, and clairsentience for clear knowing. There are a number of additional terms, such as psychometry, but they are all aspects of, or combinations of, the above.

Clairvoyance is symbolized by an eye inside a triangle, such as is on the American Dollar. Clairvoyance is often used as a catch-all phrase that includes everything except the movement of objects. That is, however, much too great a generalization. Clairvoyance is quite specific in that it refers to extra-sensory impressions of a visual nature, generated subjectively in the mind, or objectively at a distance. Seeing into the past (postcognition or retrocognition) or seeing into the future (presentiment or precognition) are offshoots.

Some people claim never to have had a clairvoyant experience, even as there are many people who do not dream in color. At the same time, much of what passes for clairvoyance is put down to other things – just the mind at work, busy doing its thing. For those who do see clairvoyantly, it is a remarkable experience. It is as if the whole mind becomes absorbed in visual impressions, something like a movie screen. The trick, it seems, is to differentiate between what is imagined, or regurgitated, and what is real. The real goods, in this instance, are not the product of conscious thought. The impressions simply appear spontaneously. Not only does the viewer not have control over the images, but the instant he tries to get involved the images become distorted or disappear altogether. To maintain the state of mind suitable for clairvoyance, one has to "go with the flow." There is no other way. It is possible, however, to notice details without affecting what is seen, providing the viewer can remain both passive and objective at the same time.

Some people never get the hang of it though, or are simply unwilling to learn how to get their conscious mind out of the clairvoyant process. Either they don't know what they are missing, don't care, or presume that whatever it is they are getting is the real thing in any case. The ego, together with the subconscious, or perhaps it is the action of parts, can have a field day masquerading in this way. This form of self-deception, being as rampant as it is, not only invites others to follow suit, but provides endless fuel for the deluded and skeptics alike – and little wonder.

The only way you can tell if you are getting the real thing is to ask yourself: "Who put it there?" If you did, own up to the fact. If you didn't, well golly gee, who or what did? The wonder of second sight is not so much that it exists, but that it is not more prevalent. In time, no doubt, it will be. Until then, those so gifted must run the gauntlet of cynics, which is a very small price to pay under the circumstances.

According to the definitions provided by spirit, clairvoyance is an inflection of the mind, something like a spiritual FM radio signal that modulates a physical AM carrier wave. In another instance it was explained that spirit makes impressions upon the subconscious much as might be done in wax, at which point the mind of the recipient translates the impression into a visual image. For the most part, these images are fleeting and often without clarity. At other times, faces, for example, can flash by in vivid detail, much as if walking down a crowded street. Very frequently, myriad patterns are seen, colorful and exquisitely detailed. It is rare, however, that a scene will be played out like a clip from a movie. Dreams do that, but clairvoyance rarely does. Usually it is more like a series of still shots, or of seeing everything all at once. Sometimes the images will be tiny, like a penny on a TV screen, sometimes many. This will evolve with development, in which case the beginner simply makes a mental note of what he's getting, which thought is picked up by spirit, who then sets about making adjustments.

Does it sound strange that one should interact with spirit in such a direct way? No doubt to some folks it sounds pretty haywire. Shucks, they may be right. But, in the absence of any better methodology, and since this system seems to work, we'll just have to keep plugging along. Someday, hopefully soon, science will be able to provide the technical explanations that have been wanting for so very long. Many people see spontaneously and have done so since childhood. They know what they get and they know what, for them, is real. Clairvoyance, in itself, is nothing new, but, obviously, the understanding of it still is.

Clairaudience

The development of clairvoyance usually precedes the development of clairaudience, and yet there is an aspect of clear-hearing that has been with us always. For some it is the small voice of conscience, while for others the problem isn't how to tune in, it's how to tune out. For such persons it is like standing in a mall and listening to a dozen conversations at the same time. Is such a thing a symptom of mental disorder? I doubt it. I suspect it is an indication of something else, something so new that control over it has yet to become as automatic as it is with the other senses. Either way, it happens, sometimes with the most startling consequences.

For the most part, clairaudience seems to parallel one's innate thinking processes, making it very difficult to discern what is of self and what is not. While it is marvelous to get outside confirmation that what you are hearing is accurate, there is a simple way to test it yourself. After having considered a question for some time, one for which you have no satisfactory answer, put yourself in a calm state and ask for assistance. Then, inside your head, state the question and wait for the answer, without any further effort on your part. If you are linked, and if the answer can be given, the words will stream through your mind, already formulated. All you have to do is remain passive and take it all in. Afterward, when you consider "what you got," it is surprising how gracefully, and with what erudition, the problem was solved. Obviously, an intelligent solution requires an intelligent source, and if you didn't do the work then who did?

Now that's the granddaddy question of all time. Could a part have provided the answer? Maybe. But, what about questions and answers that involve situations that are beyond one's scope of experience or knowledge, such as problems having to do with other people? If you know nothing of the details, the implication is that maybe spirit got involved after all. At the same time there is a plausible argument that we are all linked to universal intelligence and we get our answers that way. Maybe it's both.

Whatever the answer, we are spiritual beings. Is there any doubt about it? The activities of our subconscious minds far outstrips anything we do consciously – like patting your head and rubbing your stomach at the same time is supposed to be a big deal, while your unconscious simultaneously directs and coordinates a hundred billion cellular life states within your body, and does so without strain or diversion. Like an iceberg, our consciousness is only a fraction of what we really are. And, deep down in the sea of universal being, we really are connected, and in more ways than can possibly be imagined.

Does your right hand know what your left hand is doing? Or, being the intermediary, is it something that only you know? The subtle difference is that their only connection is via your mind. Does the neighbor living on the right of you know what the neighbor on your left side is up to? No, but you do, at least in part, and perhaps your unbound spirit knew it even before you moved in. Anyway, back to cases: Is clear-hearing really such an enigma? For the time being it is. The challenge is to render it ever more reliable so that, one day, we will understand it sufficiently to described it within the norms of natural science.

Objective clairaudience, that is hearing words as if they originate outside of one's head, is rather rare. Subjective clairaudience, hearing internally, is far more commonplace, but its subtleties are such that it is easily passed off as stray thoughts or such. Oftentimes, it is as if incoming material is on the same wavelength as self-generated thought and you can hardly tell which is which. But, the difference is not so much in the way that the thoughts are processed, as to how they are generated. Clear-hearing depends on being able to differentiate between what you do and what, seemingly, an outside agency does for you. When you get "stuff," ask yourself: "Did I put it there?" If you didn't, then maybe you're on the right track. Barely. The next step is to analyze what you're getting in terms of reliability and appropriateness. At this point, it may seem to you that the message is, shall we say, foreign? But what's the point if it turns out to be from little green men on a space ship who speak a different language? The fact that you can convince yourself that it's real doesn't make it so. Content, in this case, is as important as context.

Compounding the problem, hard facts are rarely given. That is why mediums have such a hard time with names or dates. The problem, apparently, arises out of the difficulty to create a feeling or visual impression of something that is abstract. For the most part, messages are philosophical in nature and deal with soft issues, rather than picky details which defy broad conceptualizations. In spite of this, everyone wants proof of some sort, including the message-giver.

While some mediums have apparently developed rapport with a trusted spirit entity, most of us are left dangling – on to something, albeit usually not very conclusive. It would be nice if there was an easy way around this dilemma, but there isn't one. The process of development is one of trial and error, abiding persistence and critical discernment. It's not an easy thing by any means. Discernment means being willing and able to distinguish between what is real and what is fanciful, in which case it's better to throw the proverbial baby out with the bath water than let an overeager part, or the imagination, jump in to satisfy the cravings of ego. Unfortunately, all too often it is a case of the blind leading the blind. Is that harsh? No, that's reality. But that doesn't mean we should give up. Time and time again real clairaudience has lifted the hearts of mankind. It is our inspirational nature at its best, but, in fairness, it demands the best of us too.

Clairsentience

Clairsentience, clear knowing, is the ability to "pick up" feelings. In platform addresses, a medium may be heard to say: "I feel like…" But, clairsentience isn't limited to public demonstrations. When was the last time you met someone who made you feel uncomfortable even before they had uttered the first word? Or, how about the time when you walked into a room and, for whatever reason, you said to yourself: "It doesn't feel right in here." Then there is the time you went to a movie theater: The seats weren't all that bad, but you still couldn't get comfortable.

People are psychic sponges, picking up everything indiscriminately, both good feelings and "bad vibes." We live in an ocean of feelings, and it is impossible not to get wet. Feelings, any strong emotion for that matter, permeate the space in which they are generated. If you're sensitive enough, and if you want to have a lulu of a trip, sit quietly by yourself in the back of an ambulance, a paddy wagon or even a taxi. You won't want to do it twice. Then there are those who go to relax at a bar, imbibing sufficiently to drag home with them half of the world's dismay. By contrast, one can sit beside the ocean and get nothing. It is the absence of clairsentient stimulation that leaves one with a calm feeling. It's not just the ozone or the waves. A walk through a field or a forest may do the same thing.

There's no doubt that some people have the remarkable ability to tune-in to what others are feeling. At such times it isn't something that is in doubt, for a part of them knows with certainty what is being picked-up, even if it defies explanation. How about the person in mourning who is confronted with the comment: "I know how you're feeling." Rationality dictates that the sympathizer hasn't got a clue, but sometimes they do. And, every once in a while the consoling one knew, three months in advance, what was going to happen.

Clairsentience is peculiar in that, oft times, it is more spontaneous than controlled, as in the case of the woman who said: "I don't know why I feel like I do. I just do, that's all." Then there's the strange comment: "I don't feel like myself at all." For the person who recognizes what is happening, the remedy is as simple as thinking: "Please take it away, it's not mine." Any thought that is given the impetus of emotion is like a dart. Any powerful thought that is wrapped in intense emotion is like a spear. For the unwary, it is as if one's nerves are turned inside out. For the unfeeling it's merely life as usual, but not necessarily their own.

Empathy is a fine thing, but mass hysteria and religious mania operate on the same wavelength. It's only a matter of degree. Excitement, like tragedy, is infectious, and few people are immune to it. The only difference between ordinary folk (I mean it kindly) and a clairsentient person is that the latter has learned how to dig deeper. It is very much like clairaudience, except that this time the words are replaced by feelings, which in turn produce thoughts and images which convey details about other people's experiences. Rarely does it happen that a psychic only sees, or only hears or only senses. Usually, input is by way of one or more faculty at the same time.

Development of clairsentience is a quiet thing. For the sensitive it's like rotating a psychic antenna in the direction of the object or person in question. Then, what comes comes. Period. Of course, it may not be factual, or some of the impressions may be fractured, but that gets back down to practice and refinement of the ability. There are numerous opportunities to develop clairsentient sensing. For example, before you open personal mail, hold each letter a moment and see what you get. Another way is to hold an object that has been on another person for some time, such as a wristwatch. Hair dressers, if they think about it, can go one better. The very act of holding their hands close to another person's head will greatly increase their ability to pick up what's going on inside. Actually, touching another person forms a tremendous link for the transmission of feelings, be it a handshake or a kiss, and it's a two-way street. Just as you get, so can you give; this is the secret behind a mother's touch or a healer's hand. And, remarkably, clairsentience is not limited by distance or time. It is entirely possible to pick up psychic impressions by injecting oneself into a former event. Tourists do it all the time, walking across old battlefields or ducking into castles.

On the downside, you may know when someone is firing at you. The "evil eye" doesn't have to be right in front of you to be effective. Is such a thing as the evil eye real? Of course it is. Malevolent thoughts are nothing new – but, then, self-protection isn't either. If someone is getting through to you and you want to block them, simply imagine yourself in a protective bubble, the surface of which is like a one-way mirror from which you can see out, but anything negative is reflected back to the sender. After all, it's theirs, not yours. If this sounds too simplistic, what makes you think it has to be complicated? Shields have been used ever since men and women started battling each other. Shields of all kinds.

CHAPTER TEN
MENTAL PHENOMENA

Apparitions

An apparition, as a spectral figure, may show itself subjectively as an internal experience, or objectively as something that impinges the physical senses from outside one's head. Many are the impression of ghosts, ghouls or other things that go bump in the night. A British "Census of Hallucinations," in 1889, reported that 32,000 persons claimed to have had evidence of paranormal activity, with the result that the Society for Psychical Research reaffirmed: "Between death and apparitions a connection exists not due to chance alone. This we hold a proved fact."

Mozart saw an apparition which warned of his death, whereupon he wrote his famous *Requiem*, which was played at his own funeral. In *Phantasms of the Living*, by Myers, Podmore and Gurney, there are more than 40 documented cases of apparitions involving victims of drowning. "Ghosts are, and have been throughout man's history, one of two things: a universal illusion or a universal truth." (*Exploring the Psychic World* by Fred Archer)

Frightful stories abound, but are ghosts real? For those who haven't had such a confrontation, ghosts will always remain a mere curiosity. For those who have experienced such things they are altogether too real, if not outright terrifying. The fact is, however, no one has ever really had the blood sucked out of them. Stories about vampires and demons are simply preposterous. Equally absurd is the fable that it is necessary to drive a wooden stake through a vampire's heart in order to kill him, or that ghouls rob graves to prey on corpses. Such notions are nothing more than superstitious absurdity.

An earthbound spirit is not a spirit at all, at least not in the strict sense of the word. It is simply a part that was left behind upon the death of the physical host. It is animated to a degree, but is essentially without power or mobility. Under certain circumstances it may wrap itself with power in order to make itself known, much in the way that a capacitor releases stored up energy. But, it's unlikely that you can sit down and have a rap session with it, though it may become visible at times, as evidenced by actual confrontations or photographs. It's nature is such that the manifestations are temporal at best. It has just enough power to affect physical vibration, either as sound, an image or a feeling, but very rarely does it have enough force to affect physical objects directly, including people. Curiously, and in spite of horror stories to the contrary, earthbound parts are not malevolent. They are not spirit ogres or beasts and they don't have fangs or whatever. Invariably, these wayward parts have been fragmented through trauma and they belong in the category of victims, not perpetrators.

These residual parts, sometimes called lost souls or such, are born in distress and remain so. Some may be passive, through resignation and sorrow, while others may be incessantly tormented, angry and frustrated. If there is such a thing as hell on earth, they're in it. Some, out of pure frustration, or not knowing what to do otherwise, throw tantrums or display various attention getting devices, as in the case of poltergeist activity (noisy spirits). And no wonder, they are out of sync with reality, but don't know what to do about it – and even if they did, they're still stuck. There are only two ways to handle the situation. One is through fear, in which case you empower the phenomenon without fixing anything; the other is through calm assertiveness and prayer – for them, not you. If qualified, you may intervene through the equivalent of parts integration; and, if you are sufficiently aware you may help by simply sending them your thoughts. In any case, it can be a tricky business and should not be undertaken by the faint-hearted or uninformed. A more practical route is to make an appeal to higher authority, then leave the remedy up to them, without fretting about it.

You do, however, have the right and the means to afford yourself all the protection you will ever need. But there is no point in assuming such armor if you're going to persist in ducking and running from every shadow. Although it may seem presumptuous at first, the very act of denying your fear gives you the upper hand. But, you can't fake it. That's where knowledge and unshakable faith come in.

You really don't have to be a wizard to assist those who seem to be in torment. Love really does conquer all – which doesn't mean inviting spooks for tea. You have your life and they have theirs, or at least what's left of it. If a fragmented part is in distress, then to that degree so is the owner of that part. To the extent of your abilities, you may set in motion forces which will remedy the situation. All you have to do is "call in the boys" and, without fear, let them handle things. It is your fearless assertion that empowers you. Remember, only fear empowers that which makes you afraid.

Then there is the stuff we put there ourselves, without realizing it. A true account from when I was a young man: Upon hearing rattling, I awoke in the middle of the night to discover, at the foot of my bed, a skeleton in a top hat and cloak, grinning evilly. Not knowing better, I immediately went through some supposedly protective mumbo-jumbo while holding up an imaginary cross. Believe me, I was scared out of my wits, especially when "Mr. Bones" informed me that he could come and go as he pleased and there wasn't anything I could do about it. After three nights of terror I could tolerate it no more and sought the help of a very fine medium. Ordinary "clearing" did no good. It turned out that Mr. Bones was a part of me! – some kind of projection from my own unconsciousness, with sufficient strength to give the impression of acting at a distance, as a seemingly separate and quite belligerent entity. Although subjective in origin, the part had actualized itself objectively. Had I died, the fragmented part may have remained. As it was, things were eventually brought under control and everybody lived happily ever after. But it took a professional to put things right, one who could discern what was of spirit and what was not.

Fragmented parts do not have happy beginnings – only happy endings, sooner or later. They arise out of extreme shock, inability to cope, heightened negative emotion and insanity. At worst they are a nuisance, just a fact of life, like the noisy kids up the block or the nit-picker across the street. They are not, however, life threatening.

So how come, some people will say, that the thing I see keeps coming at me with an axe? In answer: What you see is a part that couldn't get beyond the victim's trauma. In short, in self-defense, the victim simply left that part behind as being too traumatic to live with. The fragmented part, now on its own, is trapped to endlessly relive that moment of horror. Horror is what created it and that is all it knows, and, minds communicating as they do, enable you to see what it sees, in this case a man with an axe. But never in the history of mankind was an actual wound inflicted upon the viewer. It is entirely a mental thing, something like a dream or picking up bad-vibes. All you have to do is say: "Take it away, please. It's not mine." At the same time, you must have unshakable faith in the intervention that is made on your behalf. Anything less won't work, at least, not gracefully.

Astral projection

The Egyptians called the physical body *Kat*, and portrayed it as a curled-up fish. The holder of the body is *Ka*, the astral or auric body. It is shown as a breast with upstretched arms. Behind that is *Ba*, the soul, depicted as a bird with a human head, a creature that could fly in another dimension. According to Theosophy, founded in New York in 1875 by Helena Petrovna Blavatsky, there are seven bodies, one for each of the seven planes of reality. Well, maybe. In Theosophy, the terms astral and etheric have specific meanings, but in general use they are often interchanged. Max Freedom Long, in *The Secret Science Behind Miracles*, describes the auric body as a shadow body, an astral duplication of the physical body on the auric level, which survives death and, in the meantime, is capable of acting at a distance from the physical body.

The theory is that while the astral body may be projected unlimited distances, it is always connected to the body by the equivalent of an umbilical cord, variously called the silver cord, Ariadne's thread, or the paracord in the Bible. It is said to be attached to the head or solar plexus, is whitish gray and capable of infinite elasticity, being anywhere from 1" in thickness to that of a single strand of cobweb, with an aura up to 6". Normally the astral body is tethered within a few feet of the physical body, but under certain conditions, such as sleep, trance or anesthesia, it may travel great distances. There are numerous reports of near-death experiences in which the astral body hovered above the physical body, the patient later recounting to astonished medical personal all that was heard while in a coma.

Dr. J. Bjorken, of Sweden, based upon the evidence of 3000 case studies, declared that astral travel is a proven fact. Dr. Eugene Bernard, Professor of Psychology at North Carolina State University, estimates that at least 1% of people have experienced astral travel at one time or another. Dr. J.B. Rhine, of Duke University, is reported to have 10,000 documented cases of astral projection.

According to many, the astral body is not only the blueprint for the physical body, it is responsible for healing and maintenance of the system and is the reservoir for one's feelings. This may account for remote sensing that occurs under hypnosis when, for example, if a person is told their feelings are in a glass of water, they feel a pinprick sensation even when the glass is out of sight in the next room.

It is also possible that experiential dreams are the result of a type of astral travel, in which neither distance or time is an obstacle. A form of astral travel may also account for the many times people have been informed, by distant loved ones, of eminent demise.

Here is one account, by a person who frequently embarked upon astral trips as part of a developmental exercise: "When I am abed, I begin by relaxing the body and putting my mind in what I will call a transient state. In this condition I am awake and aware, but detached, with only the slightest mental preoccupation. Having stated my intention and an appeal for guidance, I wait. After a short time, if it's going to happen, I start to feel a slight rocking sensation, not side to side, but head to foot, like a banana. At this point I must keep myself calm, because the anticipation of what is coming can interfere. As the rocking increases – it is not an unpleasant feeling at all – I gradually become aware that I am several feet above my bed, still on my back, my hands at my sides, my fingers fluttering slightly. In this condition I have scaled the highest trees, sometimes sitting on the branches like an owl, quite bemused. Sometimes I pay friends a visit, traveling at great speed and often in the company of spirit friends. The mountains flash underneath until, landing as if on tip-toe, I check things out. One time I landed in an acquaintance's home, 300 miles away. The next day, much to her astonishment, on the telephone I described the unique and colorful dressing gown she was wearing, as well as the book she was reading in bed."

Auras
From ancient times, in literature and art, the Nimbus or Halo is portrayed as an aura around the head; while the Aureola or the Glory appears as an emanation around the entire body. The Bible makes mention of Jesus "appearing in Glory," while, in

the East, Buddha is said to have "descended upon a stairway of diamonds."

In 1911, Dr. Walter J. Kilner, of St. Thomas' Hospital in London, described in his book, *The Human Atmosphere,* a process whereby anyone can see the aura by using a special lens made from two glass plates separated by dicyanin dye mixed with alcohol. One would first look through the lens in daylight, then turn the eyes to focus on a person in dim light before a dark background. A similar lens has been manufactured with pinacyanole bromide filters under the trade name *Auraspecs*. By this process, three distinct radiations are observed, the first surrounds the body to a depth of ¼ to ½", like a colorless shadow. The next extends to 3" and the outer aura up to 12". Kilner reported that the thickness of the aura can be influenced by a magnet or electricity, dissipating under a negative charge then becoming half again as large afterward. The aura, it is claimed, also reacts to chemical influence and becomes less brilliant under hypnosis.

While some people say they can see an aura around inanimate objects, Kilner stated that his system could not detect an aura around a corpse. Certainly, plants and wee beasties have auras, cats can see them, and so can many people, with or without special goggles. It is easily done by simply observing an outline against a neutral background. The trick is to let the eyes look into the distance. Not surprisingly, the skeptics put it all down to eye strain, after-images and an overactive imagination. On the other hand, many psychics claim to be able to see specific colors and patterns which reflect one's state of mind and health.

> "The aura is the weathervane of the soul;
> it shows what way the winds of destiny are blowing,
> be it sickness, dejection, love or fulfillment."
> (*Edgar Cayce on ESP* by Doris Agee)

In general, the colors of the aura are said to reveal the following: Red indicates vigor and energy; dark red shows anger and turmoil; light red nervousness and impulsiveness;

scarlet indicates egotism; pink or coral shows immaturity. Orange shows a happy disposition, friendliness and helpfulness, or timidity if reddish. Yellow is the color of vibrant health or, if muddied, fear. Emerald-green with a dash of blue indicates healing ability. Forest green shows strength, balance, an outgoing nature, although dark shades portray envy. Lemon green shot with yellow shows deceit. Green with tinges of blue indicate honesty and trustworthiness. Deeper shades of blue show spirituality. Pale blue is a sign of immaturity. Indigo and violet are the colors of seekers, but tinges of pink indicate an overbearing nature. Having stated this, it must be added that it seems that different people perceive things in different ways, therefore making it necessary to sufficiently observe both the color and shape of an aura in order to build up a personal catalogue of interpretations.

Automatic writing

Inspirational writing, or automatic writing, is very much like inspirational speech. The words and sentences stream through the mind already formulated as to structure and content. The sensitive's job is simply to let it flow, as stated in the Old testament: "And there came a writing to him from Elijah the prophet saying…" (2 Chron. 21:12).

Mrs. H. B. Stowe, the author of *Uncle Tom's Cabin*, said that she did not write it: "it was given to her; it passed before her." In preface to his famous poem *Jerusalem*, Blake said: (It is) "the grandest poem that this world contains; I may praise it, since I dare not pretend to be other than the secretary; the authors are in eternity." Geraldine Cummins produced several very substantial books by automatic writing, such as *Paul in Athens* and *The Chronicle of Ephesus*, supposedly dictated to her by Philip the Evangelist, in longhand at the incredible rate of 2,000 words an hour. Her most noted work, *The Scripts of Cleophas*, in 6 volumes, is said to have come from President Roosevelt. Of another historical work, *Hafed, Prince of Persia* by David Duguid, Harry Edwards said: "The words were outside his knowledge. Furthermore, the legibility of the writing and the tremendous speed with which the book was written lifts his gifts out of the ordinary." (*A Guide for the Development of Mediumship*).

Here is a brief example, by J.H.Curran, in which thousands of pages were given at a rate that precluded normal processes of composition:

> "Oh, night is a hunter,
> with silver trumpet to his lips,
> the curving moon calling the stars;
> when the first note is sounded,
> behold, one star comes forth
> and leaps the hurdle of the west."

Mrs. Hester Dowden Travers-Smith, a British medium, wrote in Oscar Wilde's own handwriting: "Pity Oscar Wilde, one who in the world was king of life. Bound to Ixion's wheel of thought, I must complete forever the circle of my experience. Long ago I wrote that there was twilight in my cell and twilight in my heart, but this is the twilight of the soul..." At times Wilde lightened up with remarks about the Society for Psychical Research, whose members he referred to as "the most magnificent doubters in the world." On another occasion he proposed to form a similar group in spirit, under the title: "The Society of Superannuated Shades."

Some automatic writing has been produced in languages that are unknown to the medium, including dead languages. Sometimes, as verification, the writing will be produced upside down and backward, being legible only in a mirror. At other times it will be in the handwriting, and under the exact signature, of the one doing the dictating. As an indication of how far removed the writer may be from what is taking place, some people have been known to write with both hands at the same time, on entirely different subjects, which is quite a feat when one considers that it all starts with doodling.

To begin, sit at the same time for each session and in the same place. Make yourself comfortable, with pen and paper ready. Do not grip the pen firmly. Just relax, and when you feel ready then let yourself go. Doodles and circles and unintelligible scribbles may come for weeks on end, but don't despair. Alternately, you may feel something else right away. It is usually preceded by tingling in the writing arm or the fingers, together with the impulse to do something, even if not clear. During certain instances of control the writing arm has been seen to change complexion. Wiggly lines often come next, one after another, sometimes running off the page or in arcs. The pen never leaves the paper, however, and the words are written without a break and one line is connected to the next. Later, hours will be spent going over "what you got" and inserting slashes between the words in order to make sense of it. Do not be surprised if the letters are poorly formed: that is not uncommon. Also, never stop to dot the "I's", cross the "T's" or to punctuate. Remember, the pen never leaves the paper. Something else that often happens is that the writing curves down on one side of the page. Let it. Or, the writing may be huge or tiny. But, in time, everything will sort itself out. Finally, when necessary, slide the top sheet away without lifting the pen from the paper. Keep everything flowing. The trick, in the meantime, is to, as much as possible, keep your conscious mind out of the act.

In *Spirit Teachings* by W.S.Moses, he put it this way: "At first the writing was slow and it was necessary to follow it with my eye, but even then the thoughts were not my thoughts, and sometimes were opposed to my own. After a time I was able to read a book or engage in conversation at the same time."

Automatic writing may be produced in a waking state or in a light trance. The writing may be minute, extraordinarily slow (not usually) or extremely rapid, such that a stack of sheets are required. In time, those on the other side will become more adept at working through you. In the meantime, remain patient.

A lot of good work has been produced on the typewriter or, lately, on the computer. If it works, use it. To begin, only gibberish may appear, but persistence rules the day.

Deja vu

Deja vu is the feeling of experiencing something for the second time, even if you cannot remember doing it before. Emile Boirac (1851-1917) coined the term after the French word which means "already seen."

Some people have suggested that deja vu is caused by some kind of neurological trigger, as it sometimes precedes certain types of epileptic attacks. Wilder Penfield went further when, in 1955, he induced memory flashbacks in 8% of his subjects by electrically stimulating their temporal lobes. Others pass it off as unconscious memory or, as in the case of Bridey Murphy, the possible recall of stories or pictures long since forgotten. For the metaphysical types, it remains a past-life thing or the spontaneous ability to clairvoyantly look-back.

ESP

In 1935 J.B. Rhine, head of the first American Parapsychology Laboratory at Duke University in North Carolina, coined the term ESP for extra-sensory perception. He created a set of Zener cards with the symbols of a star, circle, square, three wavy lines and a plus sign. As the cards were turned up, a sender in one room would try to communicate the symbol to a person in another room. After thousands of tries, the best result was 588 hits out of 1,850 guesses, about 60% better than chance alone. More recent experiments use random bursts of energy to switch on one of four lights, while a person intuits which bulb will come on next. On another front, I've read that Princeton Engineering Anomalies Research claims to have statistical evidence in support of ESP, as a result of remote viewing experiments done on behalf of the CIA.

One of the great difficulties is that ESP, like hunches, is a spontaneous thing and not easily subjected to testing, although it was found that higher scores were achieved when the subject was informed of his results and maintained a positive attitude.

Premonitions

Precognition and premonitions are an aspect of clairvoyance, that of looking ahead. Premonitions may be vague feelings of disquiet, or a sense that something is about to happen, perhaps without knowing exactly what or why. Hunches and "women's intuition" are types of premonitions. At the other end of the scale, full-blown premonitions may be explicit and convey great detail. Many premonitions are given through dreams. Then, there is speculation about autosuggestion and the subconscious at work, drawing conclusions from a host of subtle congruencies that escape conscious attention.

Psychometry

Psychometry, or "soul measurement," refers to the picking up of impressions from an object, usually either by holding it in the hand or against the forehead. Professor William Denton claimed to have found the ability in 10% of men and 40% of women. The theory is that objects soak up auric and etheric radiations, which can be discerned later. Another theory is that objects may serve as a focal point whereby their past environment may be revealed clairvoyantly. The more intense the previous thought-field or emotions, the more readily the details can be ferreted out.

The best objects for practice are something that has been close to a person for a long time, such as a watch or a ring. Working with letters often reveals the feelings of the person at the time of writing, as well as particulars about their surroundings. Although most mediums have psychometric ability, all of them have developed it through practice and patience, and one good "hit" is encouragement enough to wade through a hundred misses.

Some people can hold another person's hand and get information as to their health and what not, but this is more an act of clairsentience than psychometry. The impressions gained by this means are not necessarily limited to small objects, and the impressions received can be quite overwhelming at times.

Remote viewing

Remote viewing is the ability to get psychic impressions about distant places and persons. Remote viewing captured public attention when it was announced that the C.I.A. and U.S. Army were funding a project called Stargate. According to Robert

Todd Carroll, in *The Skeptic's Dictionary*, there were up to 16 psychics working for the government and the Defense Intelligence Agency. One of them, David Morehouse, in his book entitled *Psychic Warrior*, recounts how he was recruited as a result of getting visions after being shot in the head while in Jordan.

According to Dr. Jessica Utts, a statistics professor at the University of California, who has a considerable background in psychic research, said that Joe McMoneagle produced accurate drawings of windmills from a *sender* at a windmill farm at Altamont Pass. She reported that "psychic functioning has been well established."

Finally, according to Mark Mansfield, a CIA spokesman, "The CIA is reviewing available programs regarding parapsychological phenomena, mostly remote viewing, to determine their usefulness to the intelligence community."

Telepathy

The term telepathy was originated by F.W.H. Myers in 1882, to describe thought transference between minds.

While telepathy may happen spontaneously, there is ample proof that the ability may be refined through practice. A simple exercise is for two people, in different locations, to sit at the same time every other day and "link up" mentally, writing down all of their impressions, then later comparing notes.

"The unconscious mind is more easily accessible to other unconscious minds than is the conscious mind...It is generally easier to travel between two points in New York City by subway than by surface travel."
(Gina Cerminara in *Many Mansions*)

Trance

Trance is an altered state of perception which covers various pathologic states including hypnosis, somnambulism, ecstasy, catalepsy, hysteria and even, perhaps, sleepwalking. As far as mental mediumship is concerned, the medium is usually fully conscious, although in a passive state. In effect, during inspirational speech, the medium is listening to himself talk, but exercises little control over the words that stream through his consciousness. In deep trance, however, the medium is unaware of what is going on.

Trance, it would seem, may well be a form of self-induced hypnosis, in which the mind of the medium becomes amenable to the influences of spirit. In any case, spirit must still use the mind of the medium to convey the message. There is a great weight of evidence in support of trance messages that have included information otherwise unknown to the medium, which was later independently verified.

Some medium's make a great display of going into and coming out of trance. There is much rolling of the eyes, pathetic groans and obvious distress. While such things may be convincing, at least to the medium, it is pure theatrics. If spirit has enough control to exercise a degree of dominion over the mind of the medium, it is fair to presume they have enough control to obviate the necessity for dramatics. Anything less is suspect.

In deep trance the medium simply nods off, possibly coming somewhat more erect, and then begins speaking in a voice that may have tonal inflection that varies from the medium's normal state – but not necessarily. Deep trance, unfortunately, is easy to fake, and it is equally easy for the medium to be a victim of his own desire. As evidence of the ego getting in the act, a surprising number of British mediums have adopted American Indian names for their "controls," not because it is necessarily so, but because it was vogue and supposedly added something to one's credibility. On second look, it is a moot point. At other times, trance mediums have done quite a job of mimicking what they think passes for a high-pitched Chinese accent in pidgin English, while squinting and screwing up the face in the most remarkable fashion. I suppose the bottom line is "whatever works." That being the case, the only valid test is the result.

In 1862, a 16 year old medium by the name of Miss Nettie Colburn, later Mrs. Maynard, gave Abraham Lincoln a trance address in the White House, having to do with his pending Anti-Slavery Proclamation. Most trance addresses, however, are very philosophic in nature. As a rule, very little hard evidence is given, such as specific names or dates. The reason, apparently, is that names and dates do not embody a visual or emotional concept, which is what spirit relies on when impressing the medium's mind. For example, while it wouldn't be unusual to hear that somebody had drowned, it would be very unusual if a specific river was named and, even more startling if a date was given beyond, say, in the springtime. Nevertheless, it certainly has happened, arousing considerable attention from the scientific community in the process.

Xenoglossis (glossolalia)

There was a time, perhaps before time itself, when man communicated with other than words, yet he was understood perfectly. He communicated in the language of spirit – let's call it original speech. Original speech, rather than being an intellectual abstraction, is the language of ideas in which that which is uttered empowers the thing that is spoken of. In spirit, to speak of a thing is to vivify it. (In the beginning was the word.) To hold something in thought is to actualize it. For those returning to the hereafter, there is no language barrier once one learns to think right. Does that make sense?

Look at it this way: we began life in spirit; that is our parent state, unbound by the constraints of 3rd dimensional reality and physical matter. The immersion into matter – the fall, if you will – fragments the ability to create by impulse alone. In its place, original thought has become intellectualized through self-consciousness, as symbolized in the Bible account of the Garden of Eden, man's temptation, carnal preoccupation and the Tower of Babel. In this lesser state, the process of creating was no longer an automatic outcome of being. The old rules didn't apply any more. Instead, creating became a cumbersome processes of thought, then action and then deed.

Xenoglossis, speaking in tongues, is the ability for spirit to make itself understood in any dialect. It is truly remarkable, especially when the dialect is otherwise unknown to the medium. At the other end of the scale, there is incoherent gibberish, called "speaking in tongues," a form of hysteria, which was considered a hallmark of the devil in medieval times. Only recently have some religious groups popularized it and attached inspirational value to it, although one is hard pressed to know why.

CHAPTER ELEVEN

PHYSICAL PHENOMENON
Materialization

Materialization is the quest to actualize things of spirit on the physical level. The want of proof is the reason, material proof, something of spirit that can be touched and measured and felt as real without having to be psychic to do it. To accomplish this, spirit must take on the garment of physical being or, at least, a part of it. Is it possible? What follows is one of the most notable accounts in the Bible:

"Now Samuel was dead and all Israel had lamented him." Saul said unto his servants: "Seek me a woman who hath a familiar spirit, that I may go to her and inquire of her." And his servants replied: "Behold, there is a woman at Endor who hath a familiar spirit." And they came to the woman by night and Saul asked: "I pray thee, divine unto me by the familiar spirit, and bring me him up whom I shall name unto thee." Then the woman asked: "Whom shall I bring up unto thee?" And Saul said: "Bring me up Samuel." And when the woman saw Samuel, she cried out with a loud voice, whereupon Saul said unto her: "Be not afraid; for what sawest thou?" And the woman said unto Saul: "I saw gods ascending out of the earth." And he said unto her: "What form is he of?" And she said: "An old man cometh up and he is covered with a mantle." And Saul perceived that it was Samuel and he stooped with his face to the ground and bowed himself. (1 Samuel, 28, 3-14)

If this doesn't give you willies nothing will. The mantle, that covered the old man as he "cometh up" was ectoplasm, from the Greek word *ektos* meaning exteriorised substance. The term was coined by Professor Charles Richet, a Nobel prize winner and Professor of Physiology at the Sorbonne in Paris.

In his book, *The Phenomena of Materialization*, Dr. Shrenck Notzing (1862-1922) described ectoplasm as a white substance, gossamer-like, extending from the several orifices of the medium's body, in this case Usseppa Paladino. He also stated that ectoplasm is formed of leucocytes and epithelial cells from the medium's body.

In other accounts, ectoplasm, by scientific examination, is said to be gray to luminescent, is sometimes transparent, has an odor similar to ozone and may appear as a vapor, a liquid or somewhat solid. In other accounts: The texture is like thin seaweed. It is moist, sensitive to light and warm, averaging 40 degrees F. It is a living extension of the medium's body. In some cases it is described as being gossamer-like, with pinhead openings that compare to cell tissue, or like spider webs with 13 to 15 strands interwoven four times around the sides of the cell pattern. "Within it we find conglomerates of bodies resembling epithelium, real plate epithelium with nuclei, veil-like filmy structures, coherent lammellar bodies without structure, as well as flat globules and mucus." (Ibid) Dr. Dombroski, in 1916 said: "The substance to be analyzed is albuminoid matter accompanied by fatty matter and cells found in the human organism. Starch and sugar discoverable by Fehling's test are absent."

Dr. Gustave Geley, in *Clairvoyance and Materialization* reported: "The primary condition of ectoplasmic phenomena is an anatomo-biologic decentralization in the medium's body and an externalization of the decentralized factors in an amorphous state, solid, liquid or vaporous. This decentralization is accomplished by a considerable expenditure of vital energy. The vital energy thus released may take the form of …amorphous ectoplasm. It then creates objective but ephemeral beings or parts of beings."

Dr. Duncan McDougall, when head of the Massachusetts General Hospital in Haverhill, put dying patients on scales and discovered, at the moment of death, a weight loss averaging 2 to 2 ½ ounces, more than could be accounted for by the loss of air from the lungs. Dr. H. Durville, Aksakof and Colonel Rochas, in Paris, working with Mme. D'Esperance, claimed to have determined the specific weight of an ectoplasmic "double" to be a similar 2 ¼ ounces. Whether or not there is a corollary, is speculative, since other researchers claim weight losses of up to 54 pounds. (Prof. W.J. Crawford, Queen's University in Belfast, the author of several books including *Experiments in Psychic Science – 1919*).

In the words of Mme. D'Esperance: "My first impression is of being covered with spider webs. Then I feel that the air is filled with substance, and a kind of white and vaporous mass, quasi luminous, like the steam from a locomotive, is formed in front of the abdomen. After this mass has been tossed and agitated in every way for some minutes, sometimes even for half an hour, it suddenly stops, and then out of it is born a living being close to me."

Those who claim to have witnessed physical phenomena state that ectoplasm, being alive, is capable of manipulation by spirit. In full or partial materialization, ectoplasm is draped around the spirit body, like a diver in a wet suit, rendering it visible to normal eyesight, while being capable of manipulation and movement within a limited distance. Ectoplasm is said to be so sensitive that it can only be touched under special circumstances without risking the very life of the medium. It is also extremely light sensitive, retracting instantly like deep sea fauna. It is produced in darkness, or in the presence of a faint red light, and, until stabilized to the point of withstanding ordinary light, is made visible between 18" discs coated with luminescent paint, much like a huge watch dial. In *The Mediumship of Jack Webber,* Harry Edwards reported taking photographs using a 100W infrared bulb in a light-proof cabinet, exposing the infrared film for $1/50^{th}$ to $1/75^{th}$ of a second, during which time only a dull red emission could be seen by the eye.

In the same book, Harry Edwards explains what happened when the medium was tied to a chair to rule out the use of props or assistants. "From the mouth there commences to emerge a substance that to the eye looks like heavy vapor. As it emerges it 'unrolls' and pours down in front of the medium's body to the floor...spreading for several feet each way. The emergence is rapid and the process of emission only occupies a few seconds. There is no noise from the medium's throat during this time. It is moist, though not very wet, and possesses a peculiar odor. The return of the ectoplasm is instantaneous. The author has had gentle hold of the material one moment, and within the second that followed, the material has been whisked away with a sound like the twang of a piece of elastic and it has disappeared."

Another accomplished physical medium was Carmine Mirabelli (1889-1950) of Brazil who produced phenomena in broad daylight. In a 1927 book entitled *O Medium Mirabelli* there are materialization testimonials by about 500 witnesses, including the President of Brazil and the Secretary of State, 74 medical people, 12 engineers, 36 lawyers, plus hundreds of professionals including people from religious orders.
(Prodígios da Biopsíquica obtidos com o médium Mirabelli 1937, by Eurico Dario de Araújo Goes (1878 - 1938).

Now a final example: "(Jesus) took Peter and John and James, and went up into the mountain to pray. And as he prayed, the fashion of his countenance was altered, and his raiment was white and glistening. And, behold, there talked with him two men, which were Moses and Elias who appeared in glory." (Luke 9:28-31). This account only comes into focus when it is borne in mind that, at the time, both Moses and Elias were long since dead.

Upon examining dozens of primitive photographs purporting to be evidence of materialization, it can only be said that there remains a great deal to be desired. The photographs, while interesting, for the most part are not very convincing. Sometimes the images look like no more than crumpled newspaper, others portray what appears to be cheap gossamer. For all that, the supposed experts at the time claim to have been as thorough in their examination as circumstances would permit. In fairness, there are many photographs and testimonies that are difficult to explain away. It may well be a true thing, in spite of some certain fraudulence, but until demonstrated to better satisfaction – after all, that's what it's for – it might be a good idea to hedge one's bets.

Currently, the problem is that practically nobody is doing it. Few dare to. Physical mediumship is hairy-scary and, from what little information is available, it appears that the medium is taking his life in his hands every time out. Some mediums, by account, have died during materialization, as in the case of Helen Duncan, while others have suffered extreme physical trauma including prolonged nausea, massive bruising, profuse bleeding from all the orifices and from the soft tissue under the fingernails, and "psychic burns" which ring the abdomen and upper arms. If that isn't enough, the development of physical mediumship involves the most arduous training regimen, far exceeding that of any form of mental phenomenon, over a period of many years. It's not exactly a slam-dunk.

During the course of development, the phenomena produced is realized in stages with, purportedly, the help of a host of spirit workers, during which time the medium's rate of breathing doubles and the heartbeat jumps to 90 to 100, which, under normal circumstances could be fatal when sustained for hours at a time. During the sit the medium may lose as much as 25% of his body weight, while at the same time his body may be seen to contract or expand.

Materialization, in some accounts, is an externalization of the medium's own body. Haraldur Neilsson, and other professors of the University of Reykjavik, three times witnessed the disappearance of the left arm of the medium Indride Indridson. The medium was examined in normal light and the absence of the arm in the sleeve was plainly felt. It reappeared a half hour later.

One of the early stages in physical mediumship may involve psychokinesis, or telekinesis, in which small objects are moved about by invisible ribbons of ectoplasm. Similarly, raps, taps and levitation may be accomplished by fashioning ectoplasm into rod-like levers, complete with knuckles, that can lift hundreds of pounds or flick a wisp of hair with equal dexterity. Then there is direct voice, in which a "trumpet" is used like a megaphone, or in which communication is effected through an ectoplasmic voice-mask. In the final stage of development, partial or full materializations are produced in which the body of spirit is able to move, speak and interact much as any other person, except that they remain tethered to the medium by an ectoplasmic (umbilical) cord.

Without exaggeration, physical phenomena is the most rigorous form of mediumship there is. Although it does afford tangible proof of life after death, the dedication and perseverance that is required is awesome, certainly not an undertaking for the faint hearted. Why, one wonders, would anyone bother? – unless, of course, he or she has a penchant for a short life. There are no old physical mediums on record. According to those involved, the medium's motivation is the oldest that ever was, namely, loving service to God and fellow man.

The physical circle
Most of the phenomenon produced in a mental circle is a prelude to what happens in a physical circle. During the long course of physical development, there is lots to see and do on the mental level. There are times when the proceedings in a physical circle are viewed by many in spirit as well: "As the haze lifted, around the circle could be seen hundreds of spirit children, as if sitting on an embankment, intent on what was taking place."

A physical circle usually comprises five to seven sitters, with extra chairs placed outside the circle for visitors, which usually are not invited until after the phenomena has stabilized. Most of the sitters are chosen not so much for their psychic ability or spiritual nature, but because they are able to provide certain ingredients which are drawn from them by a "spirit chemist," which is then combined with whatever is provided by spirit in order to make the ectoplasm. Dr. W.J. Crawford, a lecturer in mechanical engineering at Queens University, Belfast, in his book *Experiments in Psychic Science* (1919), reported that during a session each sitter experienced a 5 to 10 ounce weight loss.

The physical medium sits in a small cabinet, usually made of drapery, which is supposed to serve as a condenser for the "power" used in the production of ectoplasm. Oftentimes, the cabinet consists of curtains on either side of the medium's chair, with the front open. The cabinet also serves to shield the medium as he becomes increasingly sensitive to white light. On either side of the cabinet are the medium's most trusted associates, the circle leaders who watch over him closely. Reportedly, one serves as an *earth link*, sometimes called a ground rod, while the other acts as a generator for the power. Make of it what you will.

If a circle member is absent, his vacant chair remains in the circle and is occupied by spirit. From spirit, in addition to the chemist, there is a gate keeper who looks after those attending from the other side, and several others who look after the medium. All in all it's quite a production. Between sits, according to some sources, there are hundreds of spirit entities who coordinate and perfect their efforts in anticipation of the next sit. Their activity, it is said, is much as if in a factory, where they create and refine various ectoplasmic instruments, such as an artificial larynx, which is used in the production of voice phenomenon.

Circle requirements vary from a mental circle. Some persons claim that it is necessary to have only wooden chairs, no carpet or drapery, nor any soft goods that can soak up the power. All jewelry and metal objects are removed from the medium and the cabinet, including buttons, zippers, curtain rods and electrical wires; the theory being that metal causes some kind of short-circuit in the power. As strange as any of this may seem, and while one might wish the jargon sounded a little more scientific, there are things at work here that deserve a second glance. For example, during the sit, the temperature in the room may drop as much 10 degrees F., even though the temperature outside the room remains constant. All of this, of course, sounds a bit far-out. But, in the absence of more up-to-date information and modern scientific evaluation, one can only accede to those who have "been there and done that."

"And ye shall see the Son of man
sitting on the right hand of power,
and coming in the clouds of heaven."
(Mark 14:62)

Apports

An apport is an object, usually small, that has been dematerialized by spirit and then reconstituted on the physical level. It may pass through walls to land in the middle of a circle, or it may appear out of an ectoplasmic rod or trumpet. In any case, apports are a product of physical mediumship alone. Apports are often keep-sakes, supposedly lost to their original owners. Apports have included some small Egyptian statues of value, as well as colorful pebbles. In one case two wooden rings were produced which were seamlessly interlocked as if part of a chain. What makes them significant is that each ring was a different specie of wood, the linking being supposedly impossible to replicate except by dematerialization. At the other end of the spectrum, there have been a few circles in the U.S. that kicked out apports as if from a vending machine, at $5.00 a pop.

Here is an account, slightly paraphrased, from *The Mediumship of Jack Webber*, by Harry Edwards: "In its dematerialized state it passed through the mediums body, along the ectoplasmic arm, into the mouth of the trumpet where it materialized, the trumpet acting as a conserver or retainer of the ectoplasmic force."

Sometimes, it is said, when apports are first received they are too hot too hold in one's hand. On one occasion a flashy diamond ring was produced, astonishing the medium equally. Other apports have included a 22" plant, a jar of ointment, fresh eggs, numerous living birds and butterflies, flowers galore and once a 7 foot lily complete with vase. Sometimes, to their dismay, the sitters do not get to keep their souvenirs – they disappear as mysteriously as they appeared.

Much has been touted about sleight-of-hand artists being able to replicate apports and what have you, in an effort to debunk physical mediumship. To give credence to such undertakings is the equivalent of denying the Wright brothers after folding a paper airplane.

Direct voice

This is the voice of spirit, speaking directly to those present. Although a physical medium is essential for this phenomena, it is not the entranced medium who is speaking. To accomplish this, a spirit chemist takes certain ingredients from those in the circle and adds it to something from the other side to produce ectoplasm. The ectoplasm conglomerates beside the medium's throat where an artificial larynx is constructed, which is connected by an ectoplasmic tube to a mask, into which the communicating spirit presses his face. The mask adheres to the mouth and coats the spirit's tongue and throat. The medium's breathing activates the artificial larynx to produce vibration, which passes through an ectoplasmic tube to the mask where the words are articulated by spirit. Speaking in this manner is said to be difficult at first, because the material is heavier than what spirit is accustomed to. With a little practice, however, spirit is able to speak on the physical level once more. (*On the Edge of the Etheric* by J.Arthur Findlay)

"The *voice box* of Walter, Mrs. Margery Crandon's control, has been photographed as a white mass on the medium's shoulder, connected to her left ear and nostril with ectoplasmic tubes." (Rev. Stainton Moses)

Another variation employs a megaphone, going by the name of a trumpet. An ectoplasmic voice box and larynx are attached by a tube to the trumpet, where the vibrations are magnified. The trumpet is made of cone shaped, lightweight cardboard or, contrary to other instructions, aluminum. It is about 12" long by 5" at the wide end and ¾" at the small end. Only the medium is ever allowed to handle the trumpet, which is rinsed with clear water before each sit. The trumpet is wrapped with bands of phosphorescent tape, which glow in the dark and render it visible when flying about the room, supposedly still connected to an ectoplasmic rod, while it whispers a hushed secret in the ear of one sitter, then bounces around to address someone else in full voice. All the while, the medium never leaves his chair. Indeed, being in deep trance, the medium is the only one who misses out on everything.

I well remember the 13 years I spent, with some very wonderful people, in the course of developing direct voice phenomenon. According to spirit, the ectoplasmic apparatus is built and added to a little at each sitting. When it first started to work, only hissing and rushing sounds were heard after years of effort. Then came whistles. Then one night, just after sit number 2,000, we got the hoarse whisper of two words on tape, clear, distinct and unmistakable. I still have that that tape in my little box of treasures.

"I was in the Spirit on the Lord's day,
and heard behind me a great voice,
as of a trumpet."
(Rev. 1:10)

Direct writing
This type of writing is produced by the partial materialization of a spirit's hand, although, in this case, the ectoplasm is invariably invisible.

"A sheet of paper was lying on the edge of the table next to the window, on which a pencil was placed. We presently saw the pencil moving about on the pane. Mr. Home saw the fingers holding it. Adare noticed it also more than once, but of undefined form." (*Experiences in Spiritualism with D.D.Home*, in which Lord Adare's father is quoted.) Daniel Dunglas Home (1833-1866) is purportedly one of the greatest physical mediums of the past 200 years.

In another account, Sir William Crookes said: "A luminous hand came down from the upper part of the room, and after hovering near me for a few seconds, took the pencil from my hand, rapidly wrote on a sheet of paper, (put) the pencil down, and then rose up over our heads, gradually fading into darkness."

And, again: "In the same hour came forth fingers of a man's hand, and wrote over against the candlestick upon the plaster of the wall of the king's palace: and the king saw the part of the hand that wrote." (Daniel 5:5)

Direct writing has been tested in numerous ways. One hundred and fifty years ago, writing slates were bound together with a small piece of chalk in between. Later, upon examination, the slates were covered with writing. Writing has even appeared on paper that is placed in an unopened book, in a locked box, or in a sealed envelop. In one test a piece of paper was sandwiched between two sheets of bound glass, with the same result. Curiously, in at least some of the tests, the writing was made without causing an indentation in the paper. Thomas Everitt, in a report to the Marylebone Association of Inquirers into Spiritualism, said that he had first-hand knowledge of as many as 936 words having been written in a single second.

Levitation

As strange as it might seem, reports of levitation are not nearly as rare as one might expect. J.J. von Gorres, in *Die Christliche Mystik*, writes about 72 different saints that are supposed to have levitated. St. Joseph of Copertino at one time spent 2 hours floating above the tree tops and, while in the Acta Sanctorum, is said to have levitated 70 separate times, having been witnessed by entire congregations as well as Pope Urban VIII. Closer to home, Abraham Lincoln, in the company of Colonel Kase and Judge Wattles, watched a grand piano lift 4" off the floor, even though two soldiers where sitting on it, trying to hold it down.

Daniel Dunglas Home is possibly the most famous levitation medium. While in trance, and before unimpeachable witnesses, he floated feet first out a third story window and then returned by way of another window in an adjacent room – all of which was confirmed by the British Society of Psychical Research. A report in the Hartford Times reads: "There are at least a hundred instances of Mr. Home's rising from the ground, in the presence of many separate persons... To reject the recorded evidence is to reject all human testimony whatever; for no fact in sacred or profane history is supported by a stronger array of proofs."

Although not a true example of levitation, there is a parlor game that is sure to draw some comments. The subject is seated in a chair with two persons on either side, with their index fingers placed under the arms and knees of the subject. Breathing is coordinated, the lifters inhaling as the subject exhales. Then, with eyes closed, the lifters count to five. On each of the first four counts the lifters apply slight upward pressure, then on the fifth count they lift in unison, whereupon the subject will be lifted into the air with surprising ease. Please don't drop him. I was only in grade nine when I first tried this. My dad, a 220 pound science teacher was the subject. My assistant was another student, a slightly built grade 9 girl. When my dad rose out of the chair, with very little effort, no one was more surprised than I.

Dr. Hereward Carrington, while performing a number of tests on the same game, with everyone on scales, found that, during lifting, there was a 60 lb. weight anomaly. Meantime, D.D. Home said that mere intent staring from witness was enough to impede the effort. According to accounts, most levitations last for only a few minutes, with an average height reached of 20 inches.

A final account comes from Harry Edwards in *The mediumship of Jack Webber:* "The medium was seen to be in the air some distance from the floor. A major calamity was feared. Then the sitters saw the medium descend in slow motion, turning a complete somersault as he descended, arriving on the floor on his head…"

Psychokinesis
Psychokinesis is abbreviated to PK, or TK for telekinesis. This is the moving of objects by other than apparent physical means. During tests, it appears as if a great deal of energy is expended by the medium, even to make the smallest objects move, afterwhich the medium is exhausted. In *Psychic Discoveries Behind the Iron Curtain,* by Sheila Ostrander and Lynn Schroeder, it was reported that the Soviet Union has done extensive research on psychokinesis, including PK tests which prove the mind can effect the fall of dice beyond chance.

One time, about 30 years ago, when playing Yahtzee, my wife rolled the die to produce five sixes, a perfect throw. After whooping it up a bit I challenged her to do it again. With a gleam in her eye, she threw again. Another perfect throw. It was unbelievable, at which time I jokingly accused her of getting help from "the boys," meaning spirit. "Of course," she replied, whereupon I said: "Okay if it's really spirit, let's see you do it again." She did, and so help me it was another perfect throw. We were too spooked to try again. Shortly thereafter we took up Mexican Rummy.

In PK tests involving physical mediumship, the medium sits at a table with her hands about 6" away from a central object, which is said to be moved by invisible threads of ectoplasm that are strung between the mediums hands like a hammock. I do not recall, however, having seen any photographs as evidence, although I did once see a film clip which was pretty convincing. Be that as it may, considerable success has been documented, such as when a medium caused the white of an egg to separate from its yoke, without any apparent physical contact, which defies the debunkers who claim it is all done with invisible threads of nylon or such.

A simple exercise, which may involve other than PK, is to turn a small tumbler upside down on a very stable surface which is first covered by a vibration dampening foam mat. Then, place a cork on the upturned bottom of the tumbler and bury the eye of a needle in the cork, so that the needle sticks straight up. Now take a 3" square of light vellum paper and fold it corner to corner, to form a kind of umbrella. Place the umbrella on the tip of the needle and cover the apparatus with a heavy, transparent vase in order to eliminate air currents. The object is to focus on the umbrella and will it to rotate by force of mind. The first time I saw this done was in our living room. I was just a kid at the time. My dad was in one corner of the room and the apparatus in an opposite corner, covered over with a bell jar he had borrowed from the school lab. I had no idea what the gismo was for. After about a month, during which time he practiced every day, he called me in to witness the umbrella slowly turning. "So?" I queried, unimpressed. "I did it with my mind," my dad replied. I guess the look on my face told all. "Since you don't believe me, now I'll make it stop and rotate in the opposite direction." Which he did.

CHAPTER TWELVE

THE ARTOF HEALING
Miracles

In ancient days, having invoked the help of God, people would sleep in the temples or at the healing shrines of Aesculapium, Isis and Seraphis. Twenty-two archbishops and bishops of Lenguedoc wrote to Pope Clement XI: "We are witnesses that before the tomb of Father John Francis Regis the blind see; the lame walk, the deaf hear, (and) the dumb speak."

Inscriptions on the temples of Aesculapius, from about 1200 BC, record medical practice at the time as including rest, exercise, proper diet and magic. In the 5th century BC the Hippocratic school established scientific medical practice, but over the centuries the church has taken the position that disease is a religious matter, visited upon sinners. The patient lived if he had faith and died otherwise. Of those fortunate enough to get medical help, it was said that patients treated by homeopaths died of the disease, while those treated by allopaths died of the remedy. In 1860, Oliver Wendell Holmes said: "If the whole material medica were to be sunk to the bottom of the sea, it would be better for mankind and worse for the fishes."

Healing by faith alone is a well attested fact. Lourdes, for example, formerly a medieval stronghold in southwestern France, has become a pilgrimage ever since 1858 when a 14 year old girl, Bernadette Soubirous, saw visions of the Virgin Mary in a nearby grotto, which was substantiated four years later by Pope Pius IX. Now a shrine, the grotto is visited by 3 million pilgrims a year. From 1858 to 1914, not fewer that 6,000 people have been healed. Between 1914 and 1955, of thousands of attested cures 161 have been verified by ecclesiastical authorities as complete miracles. That works out to 4 confirmed miracles a year, about a 1% success rate. For the disappointed 99%, the question as Jesus put it is: "Dost thou believe? Then take up they bed and walk."

The French surgeon Ambroise Pare, a 16th century founder of modern surgery said: "I dressed his wound and God healed him." But, the best doctors, according to Jonathan Swift, are still Dr. Diet, Dr. Quiet and Dr. Merryman.

There is no doubt that faith, expectancy and a positive attitude contribute greatly to the healing process. There are, however, many instances of the miraculous taking place. In modern medical jargon it is called spontaneous remission. Well, maybe so, but something made it spontaneous.

The most noted psychic healer in America was Edgar Cayce, the sleeping prophet, who did 15,000 diagnosis at a distance, over the course of 40 years. The Association for Research and Enlightenment, ARE, now operates as a university at Virginia Beach and focuses on his *readings* and well documented remedies. In England, Harry Edwards is the most famous for laying-on-hands healing at his magnificent sanctuary in Shere. Even 25 years ago psychic healing was practiced in most English hospitals; the theory being that while it didn't appear to do any harm, it just might do some good. Today, in America, the idea of laying-on-hands is being popularized under the name therapeutic touch.

> "The smallest hurts sometimes increases and rage
> More than all art of physic can assuage;
> Sometimes the fury of the worst disease
> The hand by gentle stroking can appease."
> (Solon of Ancient Greece)

Psychic surgery
During the 1970's there was a great hoopla about psychic surgery being performed in the Philippines and Brazil. People like Tony Agpoa were credited with doing dozens of such healings a day, drawing out affected tissue amid pools of blood, without a trace of the wound minutes after. The hopefuls made appointments by the planeload. Documentary films of various

psychic surgeons were very convincing, with middle-aged women down to their scanties, waiting in lines all about. After one such operation, a TV crew managed to talk a woman out of her underwear, which had bloodstains on it. It turned out to be other than human blood, and in another instance the removed tissue was from a chicken. Was it all a sham? It's hard to say, however there are many cases where cures did seem to take place. Until more evidence is in, we'll call it mind over matter, which, while responsible for some remarkable cures, is equally at the root of a lot of hocus-pocus.

Secondary gain

There was a woman sufficiently debilitated that her husband had to quit work in order to look after her full-time. He did everything: the cleaning, cooking, the shopping too, and still found time to take her to a succession of doctors and therapists. Tad James, an NLP practitioner (*Neuro-Linguistic Programming*) reportedly got to the bottom of the issue by discovering that the woman had no intention of getting well because the fringe benefits were too great. That is what is meant by secondary gain. Some people don't want to get well; they'd sooner ride it out and enjoy the fringe benefits, which sometimes may be as simple as getting special attention. There are also those who resist getting well because, unfortunately, they think they are being punished.

Attitude

Attitude plays a significant role in wellness. Some people are so depressed, disillusioned and distraught that they'd just as soon get life over with as to try to fix anything. Seeming inability to cope is a breeding ground for dysfunction. Some psychosomatic ailments can be dealt with by parts integration, but, very often, the part first needs to be unhooked from the trauma that brought it into being in the first place. Unhooking is not a slam-dunk affair. Getting at the root-cause of dis-ease takes persistence and oftentimes great skill by the practitioner.

Fortunately, the body is organized to heal itself in spite of the most devastating points-of-view. Often, a change of heart seemingly leads to a new one. All said and done, there are people coping with all forms of aggravated conditions and deformity. Unlike salamanders, we cannot always grow new parts for missing ones, and in some cases illness has caused irreparable damage. Every time I see a person hobbling down the street, or in a wheelchair, the thought goes out to them that they'll be "flying" in the next life. In my opinion, a new word needs to be invented for the heroism such people maintain through their adversity. They are all dear.

Spiritual healing

Healing goes by many names, such as aura cleansing and group prayer. Then there is the chiropractor in Vernon, British Columbia, who sprinkled talcum powder on a large magnifying glass, which he then rubbed in circles as he passed the lens over my back. Astonished, upon asking him what he was doing, he replied: "I am balancing the power." I suspect it wasn't the power that was unbalanced.

As far as healing is concerned, perhaps the phrase "mind over matter" should be changed to "mind in matter." That is the agency at work: the thoughts of both the healer and the patient. Matter does not exist independent of mind, any more than individual mind is removed from the sea of consciousness. We all swim in an ocean of being, some to set personal distance records, others to save those who might succumb otherwise. That spiritual or psychic healing works is amply attested to, whether it be the outcome of positive thoughts or other interventions. But relief is not conditional upon penance or a particular belief system. Babies and dogs benefit equally, be they at hand or on the other side of the world. Absent healing, as it is called, is nothing new. But, in an age steeped in materialism, the practice of it often is. Faith and expectance are the horsepower behind the healing engine, regardless of the method used, be it magnetic healing, Indian sucking doctors or a caring touch.

Prayer and Visualization

Cleve Backster, a polygraph expert, noticed the needle jump excitedly when a plant was physically mutilated or even threatened. Rev. Franklin Loehr, of Princeton, did 900 tests on 27,000 seeds and made 80,000 measurements while 150 people prayed in test groups. Prayed-over plants grew demonstrably better. "In our research," Loehr said, "we found that prayer had the ability to regress or negate growth. This suggests that there is a force available in prayer for regressing unwanted growths – tumors and cancers – in the human body." (Margaret Waite. *The Mystic Sciences*)

Dr. Bernard Grad, of McGill University, working with plants and wounded lab rats, said: "I know of no conventional force that will act both on plant and animal growth as this prayer force apparently does."

Before pushing on, I must touch upon another aspect of healing, one that is often overlooked. A friend of mine, a very caring and capable nurse of 25 years, was virtually at war with her no-good son-in-law, a wannabe tough guy, an habitual liar who had the manners and mouth of a mercenary. If he had a broken back she would have cared for him without reservation. Does the fact that he has a broken mind mean she should care less?

Acupuncture

For 4,000 years the Chinese have been restoring harmony to the body by manipulating the energy called *Chi*, which supposedly flows through the body via 12 different channels, or meridians, on each side of the body. When one's *yin* and *yang* are balanced, the flow of chi is supposedly unobstructed and the body is healthy.

Balance, through acupuncture, is restored by inserting needles into several of the 500 critical locations on the body, sometimes twirling or heating them, or stimulating them with weak electrical currents. Another method of treatment, called auriculotherapy, uses the ear to treat all other parts of the body, much in the way that reflexology works with the foot. Another variation uses staples in the ear. Oh, goody – more body piercing.

In spite of the many successes claimed, especially in the area of pain control, acupuncture has practically no basis in modern medicine – which may only be an indictment against modern practice. Acupuncture was developed at a time when such things as the nervous system and molecular biology were unknown, and there appears to be no relationship between the traditional chi meridians and the actual location of organs and nerves. A nonprofit group called The National Council Against Health Fraud, Inc. noted that of 46 publications put out by the Chinese Medical Association, there were no endorsements of their own traditional healing arts. The position of the NCAHF is, simply: "Research during the past twenty years has failed to demonstrate that acupuncture is effective against any disease."

Of late, research suggests that the acupuncture points have more nerve endings than in surrounding tissue, which accounts for the release of endorphins, enkephalins and serotonin, the body's natural pain killers. Practitioners may also inject various solutions at these sites or use ultrasonic probes instead of needles. After about 20 minutes, surgery is possible without pain or the side effects from drugs. As a consequence, in 1996, the U.S. Federal Drug Administration gave acupuncture a huge leap of credibility when it approved acupuncture needles as medical devices in the hands of trained practitioners, thus fueling the half-billion dollars a year that Americans spend on this type of treatment.

Hypnotherapy
One's passive consciousness is amenable to suggestion, without rationalization, thereby inducing simple somnambulism or, in extreme cases, a hibernative state near death. The unconscious mind willingly does things that consciously one wouldn't think of doing. There is the presumption that a hypnotized person cannot be made to do anything that is contrary to their deep moral nature. That's comforting, but if a hypnotist told you that your clothes were on fire, guess how long it would take before you were standing naked before 2000 fans – or maybe just one.

Hypnosis, in the hands of a trained therapist, is a wondrous thing – if not for the fact that most of them get less than a week of training. Unfortunately, there is no professional organization to which hypnotherapists are held accountable. Anyone can do it, but few do it well. Some critics complain that hypnotherapists are leading their clients by planting suggestive cues as to what to expect. Big surprise, that's what hypnosis is all about. Such arguments are banal. That hypnosis is so popular is at least in part due to its effectiveness. Sure, there are lots of half-baked types out there, so what else is new? The shrinks are no different. The obvious remedy is to chose a hypnotherapist according to reputed ability – not what he says about himself, but what others say. You owe it to yourself to check it out.

Hypnosis may have had its roots in India, in connection with meditative techniques. In the Elber papyrus found in Egypt, there is a description of methods of fixation that parallel hypnotic induction. Around 1600, in Ireland, Valentine Braithwaite, known as "the great Irish stroker," applied laying-on-hands healing in a way that was popularized around 1750 by his famed student Franz Anton Mesmer. Mesmer got his MD following a dissertation on how the magnetic fields of planets affected the human body. For a time, he had people sitting in tubs of water with iron rods and filings, but then he decided that his cures were the result of the animal magnetism in his hands. Miraculous cures then abounded. In preparation for surgery, he put people into a trance by making passes with his hands for up to 24 hours at a time, presumably infusing the patient's aura with mesmeric fluid from his hands.

Dr. Paul Joire, in 1892, was the first to call attention to a subject's ability to sense things at a distance from the body. For example: If, during hypnosis, the subject is told that his ability to feel pain was transferred to a glass of water, if the water was pricked with a pin it caused various sensations and bruises on the subject's body, even if the subject was in one room and the glass of water in another. In yet another demonstration, the subject's senses were transmitted to his shadow.

Meanwhile, it was discovered that mesmerism helped patients heal more quickly while, at the same time, reduced the mortality rate. See James Esdaile's landmark book, *Mesmerism in India*, now published under the title *Hypnosis in Medicine and Surgery*. James Braid, M.D. (1796-1860), a Scott, becoming convinced after setting out to debunk mesmerism, coined the terms hypnotism and hypnosis in his book entitled *Neuripnology*. In the upshot, the medical fraternity forced both men out of Britain. Not long after that, Emil Gray, who claimed that self-suggestion was possible without hypnosis, came up with the phrase: "Every day in every way I am getting better and better." Apparently, it's all in the mind.

Psychoanalysis

Sigmund Freud (1856-1939), born in Czechoslovakia, spent most of his life in Vienna as a therapeutic hypnotist. In 1886, in order to support his new wife, he devoted himself to clinical neurology, studying with the noted Jean Martin Charcot, in Paris. Then, some cynics say, because of poorly fitting false teeth and a resulting speech impediment, he invented modern psychoanalysis in which the patient did all the talking. In 1895 he co-authored *Studies in Hysteria,* in which he advanced his idea of a "talking cure." Unfortunately, however, his cures were only for the rich since, in his own words: "It takes 100 to 300 hours."

> "It is possible that the most important decision
> in the history of therapy was the idea that
> it should be paid for by the hour."
> (Jay Haley)

Nonetheless, patients have been kept in a recumbent position of free-association ever since, trying to unravel their overactive or repressed sex drives, called libido, and their guilt and aggressions as a result of frustrated childhood sexual passions, called the Oedipus Complex. When, in 1900, Freud published *The Interpretation of Dreams*, we were introduced to the *id*, the superego, intrapsychic conflicts of anxiety and depression, together with narcissistic personality disorders and neurosis of all sorts. Apparently we're a lot worse off than we thought. But, if you want to unload on a stranger for, typically,

45 minutes a day, several times a week for the next two years, you'll be fine –notwithstanding that shrinks have the highest suicide rate of all medical professionals. Maybe they're bored to death.

In 1890, William James, who is credited with being the father of modern psychology, rejected German elementalism and wrote his *Principals of Psychology,* in which he laid out current practice based on the way a person thinks and feels. This, together with Freudian psychology, forms the basis of modern practice.

NLP

Neuro Linguistic Programming deals with how language and perception affect behavior. Neuro refers to the nervous system and the mind; linguistics refers to language and non-verbal communication; and programming is based on the way we process neurological data.

In the 1980's, NLP came to the fore as the means to model another person's excellence. Richard Bandler, with a background in linguistics and psychology, and John Grinder, a professor in linguistics at Santa Cruz university, are the founders of NLP, whose work has been furthered by a host of contributors: *Behaviorism*, the study of consciousness and physical acts, is the inspiration of Ivan Pavlov in his work on anchoring conditioned reflexes, such as causing a dog to salivate at the ringing of a dinner bell. This led to what is known as stimulus response. Andrew Salter, the author of *Conditioned Reflex Therapy*, went so far as to say that everything was a conditioned response. Fritz Pearls, a cognitive psychologist, an offshoot of behaviorism, wrote *Gestalt Therapy Verbatim*. Clark Hall, a professor of psychology at Yale, contributed his *Hypnosis and Suggestibility* in 1933. Dr. Milton Erickson, who supplied NLP with the idea of ambiguous metaphors, was single handedly responsible for having hypnosis recognized as a legitimate treatment for certain types of diseases. Ernest Rossi has written several books which were co-authored by Milton Erickson. Virginia Satir, credited with being the mother of family therapy in California, originated the idea of *specificity* as used in NLP *metamodels*, and also contributed to the development of personality modeling. Carl Prebrum, of Stanford University, added to the theory of stimulus response. Patslovic and Erickson advanced the idea of *reframing*. Ross Stewart and Roger Bailey launched *meta-programs*. In 1985, in his book entitled *Using Your Brain for a Change*, Richard Bandler introduced ideas about *submodalities*. Out of the profusion of NLP books, mention must be made of Tad James and Wyatt Woodsmall, whose book *Timeline Therapy and the Basis of Personality* unifies Freudian psychoanalysis, behaviorism and hypnosis under the NLP umbrella.

While there are many who criticize NLP as nothing more than pop-psychology, in many cases it seems to work quite exquisitely and quickly too. As far as traditional psychotherapy is concerned, perhaps the greatest threat NLP poses is to the incomes of the already established.

Reiki

In reiki, *Ki* is the Japanese equivalent of the Chinese Chi. Ki means spirit, in which reiki is the equivalent of a spiritual life force. Similar to acupuncture, reiki is based upon balancing the life forces through the channeling of universal energy, which is supposed to be stored in the practitioner's abdomen. Reiki was founded by Mikao Usui (1802-1883) as a religious movement in which, today, practitioners of reiki, pay about $10,000 to become masters of "attunements, harmonies and balances," as well as learning about certain Sanskrit symbols. A reiki master is entitled to charge each of his students a similar fee. According to The Reiki Handbook (1992) by Larry Arnold and Sandra Nevins, reiki can treat just about anything, from cancer to VD.

Therapeutic touch

This is an adaptation of what, for thousands of years, has been known as laying on of hands. The name therapeutic touch was invented in the early 1970's by Dalores Krieger, Ph.D., RN., and Dora Kunz. As a measure of TT's widespread acceptance, courses are now being offered at some 80 universities and hospitals, and it has even been adopted by the Ontario College of Nurses in their *1990 Implementation Standards of Practice.*

The idea behind TT is balancing the body's natural healing energies, much in the way that Chi or Ki is manipulated in acupuncture or Reiki. The practitioner focuses on passing energy from his hands to the subject's body, so as to stimulate the natural healing process, during which time the practitioner's hands may or may not actually come in contact with the patient. Some practitioners rely on focused prayer, while others simply concentrate with healing intent. Either way the results are often dramatic.

Prior to TT, laying on of hands was primarily the subject of religious or spiritual endeavor, ranging from the bizarre to the miraculous. Sometimes a great to-do was made about clearing the aura and then shaking off the negative "stuff" with exaggerated distress. Phooey. Even then, however, it often worked, no doubt in part due to the suggestibility of patients, their desperation and the occasional fluke. All that aside, there are countless cases in which suffering and disease have been ameliorated. It seems that imagined wellness and certainty of purpose have their own efficacy.

An example, which I can personally attest to, involved a pretty, single mom in her early 30's. She had a tumor surgically removed from the middle of her breastbone, only to have it grow back again even larger than before. After four years of such operations she was informed that the tumor was now inoperable, having grown to the size of a rolled up sock on the inside as well as the outside, and that she had, perhaps, only a year to live. As tragic as this is, the worst was yet to come. Although I would have not thought it possible, when as a last resort she went for spiritual healing, there was a similar tumor, the size of a pea, on the chest of her five year old son.

And so it began, three sessions a week, her mind tortured by the realization that she wouldn't be around to help her son through the same inevitability. But, after a month, it was the child who showed the way. As his tumor shrank and then disappeared entirely, something new was kindled in her eyes –

something more than mere gratitude to the Big Guy. Now she believed!

The last time I saw her, several years later on a downtown street, the tumor had not returned, neither had her son's, and she was happily remarried. This is a true story. In conclusion, there is no amount of skepticism that could possibly deter my conviction that therapeutic touch, by any name, is a godsend.

PART 5
ALPHABETICAL REFERENCE

CHAPTER THIRTEEN

THE WEIRD AND WONDERFUL
Akashic records
In ancient Sanskrit, the term Akashic refers to the etheric duplication of all things. In moral philosophy the Akashic record is also called The Book of Life, or God's Book of Remembrance.

"The sum total of the experiences of (a) soul is 'written,' so to speak, in the subconscious of that individual as well in what is known as the Akashic records. Anyone may read these records if he can attune himself properly." (Edgar Cayce)

Alchemy
Alchemy originated in Egypt and China. Later practices were based on Aristotle's (384-322 BC) conviction that the four basic elements are fire, air, earth and water. To this, Arab alchemists added salt, sulfur and mercury. The idea was that everything in nature contained these elements, thereby by transmutation and magic (called the philosopher's stone) base metals, like lead, could be turned into gold. Gold was considered to be a pure healing agent, as well as the elixir of life that granted immortality.

Throughout the middle ages, in medieval Europe and the near East, alchemy flourished, based upon translations from Syriac, Arabic and Greek into Latin. Alchemy wound its way into the works of such notables as Roger Bacon (1220-1292), the English scholastic philosopher and early advocate of modern scientific methods, and Saint Albertus Magnus (1193-1280), noted for his work in philosophy and natural science. A 14th century Spaniard named Jabir ibn Hayyan, codified 8th and 9th century Arabic and Greek into what has became the alchemists bible, preserving many of the mystical recipes and magical incantations. This was followed, in 1455, by *Corpus Hermeticum*, a compendium attributed to the sacred writings of the Egyptian god Thoth and Hermes Trismegistus.

Throughout, the alchemist have relied on the metaphysical rather than the scientific, and have never accomplished any of their goals. Although the fountain of youth eluded them, they did, however, lay the foundation for what has become modern chemistry.

Aromatherapy

In the 1920's, a French chemist, René Maurice Gattefossé, used the word aromatherapy to describe healing that is derived from the essence of various oils. The oils are sometimes inhaled as vapors or, more often, rubbed on the skin or taken as a tea. Although the supposed benefits are greatly lauded by practitioners of aromatherapy, there is little empirical scientific evidence in support of the claims made.

Astrology

If the earth was the size of a marble, the moon would be a pea 14" away, and the backdrop of constellations would be a mile distant. Yet, almost from the beginning of time, the Druids, Aztecs, Persians, Chaldeans, Babylonians and others have been gazing intently at the heavens, divining meaning from the nighttime sky. It was in 450 BC that the Babylonians developed the 12-sign zodiac, but it was the Greeks who formulated the elements of modern astrology and the interpretation of planetary and stellar influences at the time of a person's birth. A horoscope is a mathematical computation of the earth's position in relation to the other planets and stars. Today, astrological forecasts are in practically every newspaper, a far cry from when the church condemned Rabbi Bachai for "placing the Son of God under the influence of stars." Although some people take astrology very seriously, it is more speculative than fact.

The 12 signs of the Zodiac roughly correspond to the months of the year, and have been identified with certain cell salts or chemicals that are supposed to play a role in one's health. One theory is that a person, through successive life states, must experience each of the Zodiacal influences in order to attain completeness.

Planetary and stellar influences wax and wane according to the varying position of the earth at any given time. Everything is in motion, wheels within wheels, a cosmic machine. The earth spins once every 24 hours, the moon rotates around us once a month and we rotate about the sun once a year. But, behind all this is the backdrop of enormous constellations through which our galaxy passes in 2500 year cycles, called a Great or Platonic Year. The ancient Egyptians believed that every 2500 years Iusa, or Horus, the Ever-coming One, would appear as a new Messiah under each great sign of the Zodiac. About 12,000 years ago he was worshipped as Scarabaeus (scarab) under the Cancer sign, which was symbolized by a crib, a manger star and an ass. Then, under the influence of Leo, he appeared as the lion in the great sphinx. In another Platonic year, approximately 5,000 years ago, we were in the Age of Taurus, characterized by the winged-bull of the mighty Babylonians and the Golden Calf. Then came the Jewish Dispensation as the earth passed through the influence of Aries, symbolized by the Ram, in which the Messiah was reborn as the sacrificial lamb of God - it took 900 years before blood sacrifices were banned by the Emperor Theodosius in 391. Ancient blood baptism, being washed in lambs blood, began as an Aryan and Greek pagan practice, while the sprinkling of water and the marking of the cross on the forehead is a distinctly Mithraic rite. Then, about 2000 years ago, the fish of Pisces ruled the day as fishers of men sought converts to Christianity. Even now, the Pope wears a ring bearing the symbol of a fish from the time of the Pisculli, the early Christians. We are now entering the age of Aquarius (2200AD), which is symbolized by the water-carrier. This is the age of enlightenment in which the waters of life will be poured out to mankind. We are now at the dawning of a New Age, one that will eclipse the next millennium and the next.

It takes 34,000 years for the earth to pass through all of the 12 Platonic ages. The last Age of Aquarius was in the time of Atlantis. Some people claim that Christ will reappear in the next Aquarian Age, not as Jesus, the lamb of the Christian era, but as the Christ spirit, the way-shower.

A generalization of the monthly astrological signs of the Zodiac begins with March, simply because that is the start of the year as established by Julius Caesar when systematizing what later came to be known as the Gregorian calendar. In this system, the tenth month became December, deca meaning 10 in Latin. Until 1752, some English colonies still used March 25 as the last day of the year, thereby making taxes due before 1 April.

People born close to the start of a sign are said to be born on the cusp and may partake of both signs until the 7th of the month. Each sign of the Zodiac is ruled by a different planetary influence, while the latitude of the place of birth determines the "house" of ones character and destiny. To cast an accurate horoscope, it is necessary to know the place of birth as well as the time of birth, within 5 minutes.

Aries
March 21 to April 21. The fiery Ram rules the brain which is nourished by potassium-phosphate, depletion of which results in sluggishness and lack of comprehension. The Arien individual is ruled by Mars, the planet of war which inflicts the hazards of poor judgment and susceptibility to deception. Under the stimulating influence of Mars, the Arien beginner is involved in feverish activity as the red planet imparts vitalization. Ariens must guard against overwork. Mars, the planet first seen in the evening sky, further influences the iron in heated red blood. Tonics for the Arien include iron, red peppers, musk and other red foods such as cayenne. Their gems are the vibrant red ruby and the diamond, and their flowers are the persistent daisy and the sweet pea.

Taurus

April 21 to May 21. This earth sign is symbolized by the strong, quiet bull which plunges to his goal when aroused. Venus is the ruling planet and love is part of the second lesson. Taurians are often courageous, devoted, and lovers of nature. Their cell-salt is sulfate of sodium which rules the liver and aids in the elimination of fluid; deficiency leading to diabetes and quincy. Taurians are strong, but easily over nourished. Their colors are green or light blue like their stones, the emerald and the agate. Their flower is the Lily of the Valley. Green, being in the middle of the spectrum, is the Taurians best color, reflecting their need for endurance, stability and quietude.

Gemini

May 21 to June 22. Gemini is the airy sign of the twins, indicating duality. Geminis are changeable, ambitious, difficult to govern, quick-minded and often two-faced. Their third lesson is in logic under the influence of the yellow planet, Mercury, stimulating them intellectually, coupled with brilliance and a fast pace. Although active, Geminis tend to be high-strung and are subject to ailments related to thickening of fibrin in the blood, which is dependent on the cell-salt potassium-chloride, which also regenerates the nervous system. Consequently, Geminis are of nervous disposition and may suffer from ailments such as bronchitis and asthma. Their gem is the pearl and their flower is the rose. Yellow is their best color, as found in numerous purgatives, such as sulfur and tartar, which stimulate the nervous system. Their lesson, because of their dual nature and the ability to see both sides of a situation, is to become wise like Buddha who dressed his priests in yellow robes.

Cancer

June 22 to July 22. This water sign is symbolized by the crab who carries his house on his back and moves through life in a zig-zag fashion, suddenly going backwards when least expected. Cancerians, like the crab, have great patience and tenacity, coupled with a genius for organization and family life. These are complex people, restless and inclined to travel. These charming people are ruled by the magnetic moon and are inclined to be sensitive and passionate, however they do need discipline and order. Their cell-salt is fluoride of lime, which controls the spleen and builds the elastic fibers of the body; deficiencies cause various stomach problems as well as dropsy and depression. Their stone is the ruby. Their color is the silver of the moon and their flowers are the mysterious water lily and larkspur.

Leo

July 22 to August 23. The fiery lion is the symbol of the lion-hearted. Leo people are powerful, proud leaders who are ambitious and strong, both mentally and physically. Ruled by the orange sun, the heart of the solar system, Leos may suffer heart problems as well as high blood pressure and circulatory disorders because of a deficiency in phosphate of magnesia, the regulator of muscle spasms and heart beat. Their color is the golden orange of the sun, symbolized in the Sardonyx and the Gladiola; their gem is the peridot. Leos have risen to the heights through forcefulness, dedication and a talent for self-expression; now they must learn discrimination under the sign of Virgo.

Virgo

Aug 23 to September 23. Ruled by intellectual mercury, the earthly Virgo is fastidious and critical in nature, whose lesson is discrimination rather than dynamic thought. These adaptable people are often found in the fields of journalism, art and analytic pursuits. They are, however, inclined to be over-sensitive and imaginative, which causes anxiety and insecurity when they try to surround themselves with material compensations. Potassium sulfate rules the solar plexus and stomach through lubricating oils which, if thickened through deficiency, may cause clogging of the pores, skin disorders and other forms of stagnation. Their narcotic color is blue, as found in the sapphire and the aster. Virgos have gone half-way around the wheel and must now learn to live in two worlds at the same time, under the balancing aspects of Libra.

Libra

September 23 to October 23. Those under airy Libra, symbolized by the scales, constantly seek balance as evidenced by their plodding over-evaluations which frequently result in a missed opportunity because of indecision. Man's intuitive faculties are now emerging under the influence of Venus, drawing Librans to the mental side, rather than abstract expression. Librans are often involved with judicial matters and must endure enforced loneliness and isolation in order to bring their new abilities to bear on the problems confronting them. Librans often overwork themselves, causing a depletion in the cell-salt carbonate of sodium, which rules the kidneys and the balance of acids and alkalis in the system; an imbalance causing excess acidity, headache, lumbago and psychosomatic ailments arising out of jealousy, hate and depression. Greens and blues are their colors; their stone is the opal, their flowers are the dahlia calendula.

Scorpio

October 23 to November 22. The scorpion, ruled by mars and Pluto, is the sign of magnetic personality in persons of unique character and depth. The water sign of the Scorpio has produced more notable saints and sinners than any other; they are capable of the best and the worst, as indicated by the scorpion's ability to sting itself with its own tail. The Scorpio is his own worst enemy and must learn to overcome self and every aspect of sexual adjustment. His energies compel him, through a versatile nature filled with ideas, to become a proud, ambitious but sensitive, leader. He is a mental fighter, capable of intense and enduring feelings. The scorpion rules the sex organs through the birth-salt sulfate of lime which, when transmuted by water, forms plaster of paris which, in turn, strengthens the entire system and gives tone to the gray matter of the brain; deficiency results in demoralization, perversion, preoccupation with sex and limited ability for elevated thought, together with nose and throat disorders. His flower is the chrysanthemum and his gem the topaz.

Sagittarius

November 22 to December 22. Fiery Sagittarius is symbolized by the archer shooting straight into the sky; the Sagittarian mind, like the arrow, leaps out to its target, seeking truth and the realization of beauty and harmony. These are lovers of live, full of humor, continually absorbed and, at times, stubborn and egotistical. The archer rules the thighs through silica (quartz) which is formed in minute arrow shaped particles, which stiffen the walls of hair, nails, nerve sheaths and cell linings, and may pierce their way to the surface making eruptions. Deficiency in the cell-salt results in various forms of self-poisoning such as rheumatism or inflammations. Higher vibrations of the violet-indigo Jupiter influence the Sagittarian love of ritual and music, however they are prone to self-indulgence. Because they are very excitable and tense, Sagittarians need intervals of complete rest. Their stones are the turquoise and zircon; their flowers are the holly and the narcissus.

Capricorn

December 22 to January 20. Earthly Capricorns are ruled by the crushing influences of Saturn – Satan, the tester – whose metal is heavy lead, pushing one down as he tries to rise until the dross is eliminated. No longer a sheep, his symbol is the ram, able to stand on his own, independent, proud and domineering. At the same time he is thoughtful, practical, and frequently pursues the mysterious and matters of intellect. Calcium phosphate is the ruler of the bones, as symbolized by the massive horns of the ram, which uses albumin to make the cement of the bones. Deficiencies cause eye diseases resulting from the overflow of albumin, and imbalance of the gastric juices show up as Bright's Disease and digestive problems. In old age the Capricorn may suffer from arthritis and, in any event, is a frequent visitor to the dentist. His stone is the garnet.

His colors are black and brown which are brightened by his flower, the carnation.

Aquarius

January 20 to February 21. Although their element is air, this is the sign of the water-carrier for all mankind. Aquarians have now lost much of their crudity and are less egocentric. They are visionary, inventive, selfless and honest. They are often found in gatherings and their understanding of nature allows them to see through people. Sodium-chloride rules the water-carrying white corpuscles; deficiency results in frailty and diseases such as jaundice, although the Aquarian has great reserves of strength. His color is purple, as found in the amethyst and his flower, the violet.

Pisces

February 21 to March 21. Pisces, denoted by the fishes of the water element, are two-fold in nature. Under this sign are born both the strongest and weakest, who are constantly faced with two paths, one leading to excesses and the other to spirituality. The Piscean is ruled by Jupiter which imparts love of ceremony, as evidenced in the purple gowns in religious rites. He has identified himself with the universe, loves to travel and is often involved in public service. The fishes rule the feet, the foundation of the body in which red corpuscles are dependent upon phosphate, or iron. Deficiency causes circulatory problems, chills, fever and anemia. The gem is the brilliant giver of light, the diamond, although aquamarine and bloodstone are frequently used as well. Their flowers are the radiant daffodil and jonquil.

After all the hoopla, as far as astology is concerned is there any real celestial correlation between what happens up there and down here? Is a woman's menstrual cycle really affected by phases of the moon? If tides are, then why not us, especially since the human body is 70% water? The statistical evidence swings both ways, however, and more than metaphysical proof leaves much to desired.

Bilocation
Bilocation is the ability to be physically in two places at the
same time – something that only teenagers are good at.
Bilocation has little to do with astral travel or the like. It is not
the astral body that appears in two places at the same time, but
the actual physical body. In 17 September 1774, for example,
Alphonse de Ligouri, while still in prison in Arezzo, claimed
that he had been at the death-bed of Pope Clement XIV, which
was confirmed by those present at the time.

An older account is that of St. Anthony of Padua, who
was preaching at the Church of St. Pierre du Queyroix at
Limoges in 1226. Apparently, upon remembering that he was
simultaneously to speak at another monastery, "…he drew his
hood over his head and knelt down for some minutes while the
congregation reverently waited. At that moment the Saint was
seen by the assembled monks to step forth from his stall in the
monastery chapel, read the appointed passage in the office and
immediately disappeared." (*Encyclopedia of Psychic Science,*
Dr. Nandor Fodor, 1934.)

Although the next account may be more of an out-of-
body thing, I once had the following experience: I was driving
home on a familiar road in bright sunshine when I noticed the
scenery looked somehow different from what I was accustomed
to. I was looking miles beyond my normal range of vision. I
could even see over the hills on either side of the road, with the
countryside undulating into the distance. The thought of driving
caused me to feel the steering wheel in my hands, whereupon I
looked down, only to be astonished to see my car speeding
along sixty feet below me! This lasted for several minutes and
was quite a shock. For the moment it was a marvelous
sensation and I continued to look around and enjoy the ride.
Then, at one point, I wondered if I really had control of my car
at all, whereupon, suddenly, in the next instant I was back in
my car, blinking furiously.

Breathing

In old Sanskrit there is a type of rhythmic breathing called *Pranayama*. It begins with breathing through the left nostril (*Ida*) for 8 seconds, then holding the breath (*Kumbakas*) for 32 seconds, and then slowly exhaling through the right nostril (*Pingala*) for 16 seconds. Each cycle begins with an alternating nostril. Twenty cycles, four times a day, are said to cleanse the body of impurities, increase vitality, improve appetite and digestion, and enable the voice, although softer, to carry further. It is also said that it imparts greater strength, personal magnetism and freedom from pain and illusion.

The average person has a lung capacity of 250 cubic inches, but we only empty 150 cu in. at a time. This is why deep breathing refreshes the system, causing us to relax with a deep sigh. In normal breathing at 16 to 18 cycles per minute, we take in 30 cubic inches of air with each breath, pause, and then exhale over the span of four heartbeats. But, surprisingly, the vast majority of people breathe incorrectly. Instead of causing the lungs to expand upwards, most people breathe in a downward fashion, putting pressure on vital organs and distending the belly. The simplest remedy, and the way to instill deep breathing is to put one's shoulders back, which is why erect posture plays such an important role in yoga, martial arts and meditation.

Breathing quickly, at 26 short breaths per minute, overcomes pain. Excessive alcohol, which increases respirations, has much the same effect. On the other hand, a person automatically calms down when breathing in 6 second cycles, and after five minutes the brain is focused and ready for work. At 3 respirations per minute, body activities are subdued and the mind becomes psychically attuned. At 1 respiration per minute, concentration peaks and, with training, hibernative activity becomes possible.
Breathing exercises should be done through the nose, with the mouth closed. Maintain regular cycles, breathing without strain and avoid practicing just after meals or when torpid.

Divination

Reading the message in a fortune cookie sure beats *haruspicy*, sorting through the entrails of a sacrificial goat. Ancient civilizations to the present have a predilection toward omens and portents, signs and wonders, all in the hope of a better future because of advance warning and the ability to duck the heavies. The Greeks consulted oracles at Delphi, the Egyptians had priests do it for them, while the Romans had official augurers on state payroll.

Divination has been done by just about every method one can imagine, from dropping the bible to an open page (bilbliomancy), throwing knuckles with letters on them (astragalomancy), casting pebbles, sticks and dice (sortilege), and more familiar means such as turbaned fortune tellers with crystal balls (necromancy), astrology, teacup reading (tasseography) and palmistry (chiromancy). All the while, the Chinese used I Ching since 4,000 years ago, referring to mystical hexagrams in the *Book of Changes*.

Exorcism

In classical terms, possession is the invasion of a body by a malevolent spirit. Better stated, it is the attachment of a transient part to an unwilling host.

The litany of most exorcisms is pathetic, particularly the mumbo-jumbo of priests who quote from the *Rituale Romanum*: "Hear therefore and fear, O Satan, enemy of the faith, foe to the human race, producer of death, thief of life, destroyer of justice, root of evils, kindler of vices, seducer of men, betrayer of nations, inciter of envy, origin of avarice, cause of discord, procurer of sorrows..." etcetera.

Parts aren't bad per se, even though their effect may be, and name-calling and diatribe is hardly a remedy, impressive as it may be to some people. Moreover, a caring attitude may modify the delivery, but not likely the lack of results; exorcism works only if the itinerant part believes it will and if the part knows how to back off. If the purpose of exorcism is to remove unwanted parts, the solution, therefore, is the equivalent of parts integration, nothing more or less. It ought to be easy, now that you understand it, but fear of the unknown oftentimes creeps in and adds fuel to the fire. To be effective, exorcism requires an act of love or, in the very least, sureness, and ought to be left to those persons who have proven ability in such matters.

On the subject of proven ability, years ago, when I was in England, I met an Englishman who was touted to be "the king of exorcists." He was a wiry man with the disposition of a bull terrier. The truth is he was sufficiently obnoxious so as to cause everyone to back off. I have also been present when mediums intervened. Some went to great lengths and exhortations, while others went about their business quietly and effectively, without the need for showmanship.

A lot has been written about spiritual mediums and so-called rescue circles, in which a transient part is "led to the light" by spirit helpers or guides. This is an act of integration, pure and simple. An exorcist may make a great to-do about inviting the part into himself, then making out like a great battle is taking place. Frankly, the only battle taking place is in the interloper's mind. Nevertheless, even this can work with the help of assisting forces that are "pulled-in" by the helper's intention. Exorcism is accomplished by integration, or by adoption of the part, preferably by helpers from the other side. Additionally, intervention without integration may be accomplished by reinforcing the victim's defenses. This is done through heightened suggestibility coupled with a reinforcing physical gesture to hook the determination into the material level, a natural consequence of thought-action-deed. This is why waving the cross about is sometimes effective, if evn once in a blue moon.

A forced remedy, as presumed in traditional exorcism, is a contest of wills in which one seeks to overwhelm the transient part. This is the least desirable approach, if for no other reason than it is the least effective. Sometimes, it may seem to be the only way, but it's not likely. Will-power and strength of mind can be put to better purposes. If you want a war, however, the choice is yours.

On the subject of exorcism, there is the matter of what is called clearing. Religious ceremonies and dedications, attended by invocations and the sprinkling of holy water, are precautions before the fact, because parts do hang around, particularly in the vicinity of traumatic events. But, curiously, these parts aren't the bad guys as it were, they are the victims. So, I ask you, what's all the fuss about? The answer is morbid imagination, that's what. Superstition and ignorance have more sway that then gentle realizations. And, besides, movies sell better if they scare you. The pity is that so much nonsense is made believable. A fertile, non-discretionary mind is a great place to instill fear, even if it is groundless and the terrifying outcome is self-generated.

It may be surprising, but many transient parts have no idea how they came to be in the state they're in. For them, the moment of abandonment is swept with trauma and recall may be partial or not at all. They simply are – they know that much – but what to do about it is another matter. For all intents and purposes while they may be wayward, they most certainly are not lost souls. There is no such thing, even though appearances are deceiving. The deception, however, is purely unintentional. A part sees itself as it always has. Such a thought, of itself, creates a spectral image by which the transient part may be seen or sensed on the physical level. But, more than that, some transient parts know they can change their appearance by merely focusing on it. It is possible, therefore, for the same part to appear one time as a boy and then as a man – or, less likely, as a bird. The transient part creates its image on the level of the mind. It shouldn't be surprising, therefore, that such images may be perceived by yet other minds, whether sporadically or through attunement.

It would be improper to leave the suggestion that transient parts play Halloween all the time, jumping into whatever costume strikes their fancy. It can happen, but rarely. Most transient parts simply haven't that much power, that much presence of mind or the desire to do so. Indeed, some transient parts appear to be almost mindless, which gives rise to the Friday night spook shows about ghouls and zombies and other gross sensationalism. But, it sells. Then, if that's not enough, there's vampires, a totally outlandish feat of imagination. But, that sells too. Some people get a kick out of having the wits scared out of them. That is unfortunate for the innocent, for even if there is no rationale behind it, it can lead to nightmares while other parts wrestle with the incongruency until it is abated. Remember, even children empower what they fear, justified or otherwise.

Dowsing

Dowsing, or radiasthesia, dates to Roman times. In the Bible: "Moses lifted up his hand, and with his rod he smote the rock twice; and the water came out abundantly." (Num. 20:11). This ancient divining technique was noted by Georgius Agricola in his 1556 treatise on mining entitled *De Re Metallica,* in which he describes using a forked hazelwood stick, called the *virgula divina*, or divining rod, to locate silver ore in medieval German mines. A dowsing rod has also been used to find underground water, lost metal objects and even underground pipes and cables. In Vietnam, some soldiers used wire dowsing rods to find mines or unspent ammunition. Until 1954, the government of British Columbia retained an official diviner, E.M. Penrose, who worked from maps alone, sometimes using a cork or metal pendulum on a thread, with a sample of whatever was being sought in his other hand. Some people, using this method, claim to be able to tell the sex of eggs or unborn children.

Throughout history, dowsing has changed little. The operator grasps the ends of a Y-shaped stick up to 18" long, made of hazel wood or wire, palms down, then twists until his forearms are in a vertical position, thereby tensioning the main part of the rod parallel to the ground. As the operator moves about, the end of the rod dips when something is found. While some say it is all somehow the result of unconscious muscular control, there are films in which the end of the dowsing rod has been recorded bending through 90 degrees.

Fakirs

A dervish or *fakir*, which in Arabic means poor, refers to a Hindu or Muslim holy man who lives by begging alms in exchange for feats of apparent miracles. In his book *Powers That Be*, Alexander Canon recounts the feats of a fakir named Tahra Bey, in which he was stabbed in the chest with a knife, following which he was able to make the wound bleed at will, and only minutes later the wound was healed without a scar. Then, controlling his heart beat so as to induce a cataleptic state, he allowed himself to be buried for some time, without any observable aftereffects.

When asked about the absence of scars, in spite of numerous cuts and punctures, he explained that it was the result of being able to increase his pulse rate to 135 beats a minute, as well as controlling his body temperature and the bacteria and cell tissue associated with the wound. Neat trick if its true.

Feng Shui

Feng Shui, pronounced fong shway, translates literally as wind-water. It is an ancient form of Chinese divination in which harmony is sought between man and nature. The philosophy is that one is inescapably influenced by the environment, be it unbalanced and negative or beautiful and ennobling.

Masters of feng shui are allegedly capable of discerning the flow of positive and negative forces, thereby suggesting changes in architecture and decor in order to enhance the flow of *chi*, and to retard its opposite, *sha* or hard energy.

In countries like Indonesia, feng shui is a part of the university curriculum, and influences everything from the placement of potted plants to city planning. As far as the skeptics are concerned it is simply New Age metaphysics with a fortune-cookie approach.

Kabbalarian Philosophy

Kabbalarianism, much like numerology, is the metaphysical interpretation of one's name according to values attached to each of the letters. Kabbalarianists make broad claims as to its efficacy with respect to understanding one's path and spiritual relationships. Of other New Age systems which make similar claims, Kabbalarianists say those systems lack the tangible reality of their analysis. In the Kabbalarianists supposedly foolproof system, each letter of the alphabet is supposed to have an impact on one's personality, strengths and weaknesses, and success or lack of it. According to this system, one's destiny is created the moment one is given a first name. Peculiarly, middle and last names don't count for much. Anyway, they say you can change your destiny by changing your name, from Tom to Thom for example.

Karma

Karma is the law of "come back" in Sanskrit. The idea of karma is a part of all East Indian religions. In Hinduism, *samsara* is the transmigration of souls, in which one's reincarnation is dependent on previous deeds. For the Buddhists, the cycles of rebirth are a maze of suffering (*duhka*), the result of desire (*pratityasamutpada*), which leads to an unbroken chain of causation until, through meditation, discipline and enlightenment, one takes the Eightfold Path to *Nirvana*.

Karma embraces more than cause and effect or the idea of opposing and equal actions. Every act, no matter how trivial, brings its own reward, good being returned with goodness, evil with evil. For the reincarnationists, everybody is getting exactly what they deserve, if not in this life then from a previous one. Although this invites resignation in the face of misery, it might explain the irrational way that some good people are overcome by misfortune and some apparently evil people come out smiling.

In some Western pursuits, such as Theosophy, karma and reincarnation are accepted as a fact of life. Some people go so far as to believe that karma, not free will, is behind the untenable way in which people harm each another. It's not exactly like "the devil made me do it," it's more a matter of "you had it coming."

Near-death experiences

Near-death experience (NDE) refers to the stories told by people after nearly dying, or having been pronounced clinically dead for a short time. While the accounts vary, there are common instances of mystical experience, confrontation with loved ones, life-review phenomena and peacefulness during the "light at the end of the tunnel" experience.

As far as Elizabeth Kübler-Ross is concerned, a noted writer and lecturer on death and dying, NDE's are proof of life after death. Raymond Moody, M.D., Ph.D., in his books on life after life, wholeheartedly agrees. But, as far as the skeptics are concerned, it is simply a matter of the neurochemistry in a dying brain, in which neural noise and retino-cortical mapping produce the tunnel effect of moving out of darkness into light. On another level, NDEs can be replicated using ketamine, an anesthetic with hallucinogenic properties that is related to phencyclidine (PCP). Simulations with drugs do not, however, take away from the NDE hypothesis.

One day there will be a new twist to the age-old marvel when the brain will be sufficiently mapped and wired so that computers will be able to translate near-death experiences into a video. That ought to be interesting.

Numerology

The practice of numerology, dating back thousands of years, assigns numbers to each letter in the alphabet. By adding the numbers that correspond to the letters in a person's name, and by studying the numbers in the birth date, numerologists are able to come up with an interpretation of characteristics based on key numbers, repeating numbers and various totals. Out of this they produce information regarding personality and a "reading" of life influences.

In many respects there is little difference between numerology and other forms of divination, nor is it more or less reliable. Some people, naturally, are amazed at how accurate the readings are, while others are just as enthused by reading between the lines and picking out the stuff that strikes their fancy.

There are couple of different ways of attaching numerical values to letters, some omit vowels and the letter Y. The easiest systems assigns numbers in simple rotation, as follows:

1	2	3	4	5	6	7	8	9
A	B	C	D	E	F	G	H	I
J	K	L	M	N	O	P	Q	R
S	T	U	V	W	X	Y	Z	

Bill Smith then becomes 2,9,3,3 1,4,9,2,8, the totals being 16 and 24. These are added together to get 7 and 6, equaling 13 which then becomes 4. Of course the numerologists have a method of analyzing each letter in relation to the other letters, and have complicated formulas for arriving at all kinds of results. Birth dates work much the same way; the numbers are added together to produce an end result, loosely interpreted as:

1 is a pioneer with fighting spirit, a forceful leader.

2 indicates a sociable person, affection, diplomacy, a home-maker.

3 is for self-expression, but the person may not necessarily be orderly or reliable.

4 is for foundation types, the backbone of the country, patient, reliable, plodders.

5 are seekers of experience, interested in travel, variety and drama.

6 is drawn to family life, guardianship and higher destiny.

7 denotes an inward spiritual life, the sciences, truths, discipline, organization, loneliness.

8 is the organizer with leadership backed by spiritual inspiration.

9 is the complete person of sacrifice, service, humanitarian pursuits and the arts.

Ouija Board

The name Ouija comes from the French and German words meaning yes. Today's Ouija board is similar to that which was used in the days of Pythathagorus, 2500 years ago. The board has a large alphabet, numerals and the words yes and no. To use it, two people face each other with the board on their knees. The fingers of both hands are lightly placed on a planchette, often heart shaped, that points to the letters or numbers. One person acts as a control, usually having his eyes shut, while the other person is the reader. At the start, it helps to let the planchette move around a bit, to get the feel of things. Sometimes the planchette moves so fast that it's all the reader can do to call out the letters, while a third person jots them down to be analyzed later.

Of course, the planchette doesn't move the hands of the operators. It's the other way around: unconscious muscular action produces the results. The mind, in turn, may or may not be amenable to psychic influence and the results, more than likely, are ego-based regurgitations. For beginners, however, it can be a fascinating way to explore things. A word of caution, though, although the Ouija is not really a game at all, resist the temptation to take it too seriously. Remember, part of the mechanism at work is your own mind and attendant ego.

Photography
It is always fascinating to look at photographs, such as family portraits, in which extras show up. Some of the photographs are very convincing, some are not, and very often resemble nothing more than a double exposure. One time, in Vancouver during the early 1970's, when I attended a group that was investigating poltergeist activity in a private home, we discovered that one of the residents had an open box of pet snakes. One of the group took a Polaroid photograph of the snakes, in which – to our great surprise – there appeared several faces about the size of a dime, or smaller, all perfect in every detail, of both men and women. Maybe there's a way of faking that, but not that I am aware of. The same cannot be said for all. Sir Oliver Lodge made a sensation with his book entitled *Fairies*, in which a couple of girls were photographed in a garden setting with 8" fairies. It was only after the book became a best seller that the girls revealed the fairies were merely paper cut-outs.

The object of this type of photography is to film spirit images which people claim to see or, alternatively, to capture what escapes the naked eye, such as was claimed by Dr. H. Baraduc, who caught on photographic plate, at the moment of death, a luminous, cloud-like mass that appeared over a person's body. There are some reports that even phantom limbs have been seen on the screen of a spectroscope, being visible only during the period that the patient felt they were still attached. Semyon and Valentina Kerlian, a Russian husband and wife team with a background in high-frequency electronics, went further by developing a simple way of photographing phantom parts. They began by photographing detached leaves in a high-frequency photographic field, and were amazed to discover a galaxy of sparks and strings of pulsating lights, like headlights on a freeway, flashes, twinkling dots and auric-like emanations that slowly subsided to half their intensity after the first 10 hours and then diminished entirely after about 20 hours. One day they photographed a torn leaf, only about $2/3^{rd}$ intact, when, to their utter astonishment, the image produced was that of the entire leaf. The immediate question is, if what they photographed wasn't produced by a physical body, what was it? Is it proof of an etheric or spirit double?

There is yet another form of psychic photography that is, to say the least, remarkable. Peter Hurkos seems to have been able to capture mental images on film. Under controlled test conditions, a camera is aimed at his forehead, then exposed at the instant of peak thought intensity, thereby producing the photograph. In another case, when hypnotized, Ted Serios was told his thoughts could be photographed and, apparently, he's been doing it ever since.

Psychic readings

Dora Lindsay, one of the finest British medium's of my acquaintance, would say: "I'm the seventh child of a seventh child, so I'm very fey." And she meant it, but I doubt that it really had anything to do with her psychic ability. It's just a part of the mystique, the hype if you will, which instills a certain awe and expectancy.

They all do it to a degree, oiling the works, so to speak. Sometimes the best performance is had only after the stage is set. The problem is that, all too often, one's enthusiasm is such that he plays into the hands of a less gifted psychic – I call it priming the pump. The psychics on TV are certainly "prime" examples: "I sense there is another man in your life." No matter what the response is, the supposed psychic then says: "I thought so." Or, the psychic says: "Are you thinking of taking a trip?" Well, no. "Then, have you recently taken a trip?" Well, no. "Then watch for this, will you? because I see you taking a trip sometime in the future." Well, golly gee.

And so it goes, a grand fishing trip for which the subject pays good money and invariably comes away saying; "Wasn't that wonderful? She was right on." Being right on generally means that the psychic pinned down sufficient facts to be convincing, notwithstanding that nearly anybody can do the same thing, but maybe without the same flair. Then there are those readers who can say absolutely anything and get away with it, such as when talking about one's guides or past lives. This doesn't mean that what is said isn't true, it just means that you have no way of proving that it is. It comes down to gullibility and credibility. Yours and theirs.

So, what do you do about it? The first rule is offer nothing. This doesn't mean being obstructive or negative, it simply means letting the medium do what she's being paid for. She's the one who is supposed to be giving the information, not you. As a rule, when a psychic asks a question it is either to confirm that they are properly "linked," or to get enough information to fudge it if they are not. If you are going to put any credence in what you hear, you owe it to yourself to stay out of the process. Let them do the work. In most readings it is surprising how little information is conveyed by the medium, even though it is greatly impressive. As a rule, the generalities are such that it's like throwing the byproduct of bulls against the wall to see how much sticks.

Then there is the real thing, rare though it is. Uncle Joe really did say something and it's comforting to know that Grandma is watching over you. Be that as it may, the only real evidence is hard evidence, that you know is true or can be verified later, without you having contributed to what was given. Part of the problem is that even a good reading usually contains a bunch of misses or information that you cannot pin down. Invariably, however, one glosses over the unsupported in favor of that which captures the imagination.

The best readings are had when the seeker has prepared his questions beforehand. On the premise that spirit is real, it's fair to give them a chance to check things out before the medium gets put in the hot-seat. For your own interest, always tape record the reading, so that you can play it back later and objectively sort out the hits and the misses and the stuff in between.

Finally, going to a medium isn't like going to a therapist. It isn't supposed to be a once-a-week or once-a-month affair. The unwary can easily be led into a state of dependency, and there are many so-called mediums who thrive on that kind of opportunity. The next step comes with the invitation to join a select group because you're so special. That being the case, just hand over everything you've got and get the agony over with.

Reincarnation

"And man became a living soul." (Gen. 2:7) That seems like a pretty important event. In the original Hebrew part of the Bible the word soul *(neph'esh)* is found 800 times. In the Christian-Greek part of the Bible the word soul *(psyche)* appears 102 times. Whether the interpretation is Hindu or Judeo-Christian, the idea of a soul is that which, while imparted to man, transcends his physical nature. That being the case, it stands that we really are spiritual beings both here and hereafter. In any case, on face value, it seems reasonable that if we got here once, we just might be able to do it again.

When Jesus and his disciples, Peter, John and James, came down from Mount Tabor, after the transfiguration, Jesus said: "Speak to no one about what you have seen until the son be risen again from the dead." The disciples asked why? Adding: "Don't the scribes say that Elias must come first?" Jesus replied: "It is true that Elias must come, and that he will reestablish all things. But I declare to you that Elias has already come and they knew him not." Then the disciples understood that he spoke to them of John the Baptist. (Matthew 17: 9-13).

Lots of people believe that when you die you're eternally zapped. Game over. As far as they are concerned mind is a state of matter, not a state of being. Does that make sense? I hope not, because if that's true then who cares what you do here, just so long as you get away with it. Surely, life is more than that and the soul expands with every experience.

On the subject of souls, there is a lot of banter about old souls as compared to young souls. Maybe there is such a thing, but if we are immortal and if our souls transcend time, what has age got to do with anything? Perhaps it is a measure of how many times a person has had a chance to kick the can on this level. We'll see. In the meantime, I'm comfortable with the notion that we're all soul mates.

"Life not only provides us with the opportunity to learn who we are and what we are, but provides different avenues on our road to becoming. These roads are as multiple and varied as the sands of the sea, and each person must find his own. The way, the path in itself, is not important as long as we are headed in the right direction. Nor is it important while we are in the process of traveling, whether we say our beads, memorize passages from the Bible, recite the Koran, read from the Torah, meditate on the Bhagavad-Gita or quote from the Vedas. The thing that is important is that we understand that the life of the spirit transcends the human span and that this is the only true reality; and that no matter by what road we travel, when we reach the top of the hill we join as one in a mighty 'Gloria in Excelsis Deo'." (Unknown)

Synchronicity

How often has it happened that you and a friend dialed each other's phone number at the same time? Or, how about two people on opposite sides of the globe coming up with the same invention at the same time? Is it coincidence, or is something else at work? Carl Jung (1875-1961) thought so. He called it synchronicity. He is also responsible for coming up with the idea of the collective unconscious.

Jung's idea was that there is a causal principle that links events and that "the premise of probability simultaneously postulates the existence of the improbable." Stating it differently, the law of probability is such that whatever can be, must be.

Tarot cards

Tarot cards are the oldest playing cards in common use. Possibly based on the Hebrew alphabet, or Egyptian or Hindu mythology, they were introduced into Italy in the 14th century, likely by fortune-telling gypsies or returning Crusaders. Further redesigned, the tarot deck portrays medieval society; the wands (farmers with clubs) correspond to the modern clubs suit; cups, the heart suit, symbolizes the church; swords, the military, is represented by spades, and the pentacles, the 5-pointed stars, are merchants in the suit of diamonds.

The tarot deck consists of 78 cards which are divided into two distinct groups, the Major and Minor Arcana. The Major Arcana consists of 22 cards with pictures such as the Hanged Man and the Wheel of Fortune. The Fool was first introduced in America in 1865, to correspond with the jokers in a regular deck of cards. The Minor Arcana consists of 56 cards divided into four suits, each having numbered cards from ace to ten plus royal cards.

At first Tarot cards were hand-made, but with the 15th century printing press they quickly spread worldwide. For popular usage, the French dropped the Major Arcana and combined the Knight and Page, thereby creating the 52 card deck of today. In France, the royal cards were supposed to represent Charlemagne as the king of hearts, Julius Caesar as the king of diamonds, King David the king of spades and Alexander the Great as the king of clubs.

Either the full pack or the Major Arcana alone is used in fortune-telling. The cards are shuffled, a question asked, then the cards are laid out in a specific formation and interpreted according to the classical meaning attributed to them, as well, hopefully, a little intuition on the part of the reader.

CHAPTER FOURTEEN

NEW AGE REVELATIONS

Cults

A cult can be anything you want to make it. More than just a set of beliefs or rituals, a cult can be anything from phallic preoccupation to hero worship. The original word in Latin means, simply, cultivation. But, nowadays, it is often used to decry anything that exists outside of the establishment – unless, of course, it's an Elvis Presley cult.

Every religion began as a cult and then became a sect before formalizing its dogma. Then as now, the size of its following is not the measure of its truth. Indeed, were it otherwise, fewer people would be so motivated to keep searching. Unfortunately, for those who are searching, there are lots of dead-ends and entanglements. I doubt that any cult or sect or religion has all the answers, but, collectively, maybe they come close. Christianity has some of the answers, so does Zen Buddhism, the Charismatics, the followers of the Reverend Sun Myung Moon and even gurus like Bhagwan Shree Rajineesh, who is supposed to be a living embodiment of God – but, then, aren't we all?

Isis, the mythological Egyptian goddess of fertility, death and resurrection, took on Greek divinity as Aphrodite before becoming the most significant Roman deity in competition with the early Christians. It was not until the 1170's that the Virgin Mary made her first appearance on a church portal, the Cathedral of Senlis in France. About 50 years later, in the Cathedral of Notre Dame, she finally made her appearance with the Christ Child. Following this, the Mary cult blossomed to send her image worldwide. The reason for stating it in this way is to underscore the fact that, contrary to some opinions, cult is not a nasty word.

And, yet, there is the incident at Jonestown, Guyana, where, in 1978, 900 beautiful people of the Christian Assembly of God committed mass suicide at the behest of James Warren Jones. That is a cult too. As terrible as that is, what about the heroic early Christians who marched into an arena of lions rather than disavow their faith?

All said and done, as far as any cult is concerned, it behooves us to use our common sense. Consider, for example, some of the cults listed by Margaret Thaler Singer and Janja Lalich in their book *Crazy Therapies:* There is *Reparenting* by Marguerite Sechehaye and John Rosen, in which the therapist becomes a pseudo-parent to overcome the botches made by the real parents. Jacqui Shiff's approach is to have the patient wear diapers and suck his thumb to get well. Other therapists use hypnosis to cure the trauma of alien abduction. Arthur Janov's *Primal Therapy* and Daniel Casriel's *New Identity Process* are based on learning the correct way to scream, while Nolan Saltzman advocates his *Bio Scream Psychotherapy* because there is more love involved when he screams.

One thing for sure, what a person gets out of a cult need not necessarily be proportional to what he puts into it. Sucking a person in is how they make their money.

Dianetics

In 1950, Lafayette Ronald Hubbard came out with his book entitled *Dianetics: The Modern Science of Mental Health,* the bible for *Scientology*. Contrary to a total disclaimer at the front of the book, Hubbard goes on to say that dianetics "...contains a therapeutic technique with which can be treated all inorganic mental ills and all organic psycho-somatic ills, with assurance of complete cure...."

Hubbard puts forward the idea that the mind has three distinct parts: the analytical mind of differences and similarities; the reactive mind which reacts to pain; and the somatic mind which, directed by the analytical or reactive mind, tries to effect solutions on the physical level. Further, the reactive mind is said to contain *engrams* (memory) of physical or emotional trauma which override the somatic mind, and that the most harmful engrams arise when still in the womb, caused by, for example, hysterics by the mother or overly passionate sex.

Treatment, as one might expect, is by a Dianetic therapist, called an *auditor*, who uses *dianetic reverie* to fix things by removing content from the reactive engram bank. Although there is a lot of supporting data in the form of anecdotes and testimonials, in spite of Hubbard's wide-ranging claims practically nothing about Scientology or Dianetics is very scientific.

Est

In 1960 John Rosenberg, a Christianized Jew, left Philadelphia to sell cars in St. Louis, where he Germanized his name to that of Werner Erhard. The term Est is a combination of Erhard's seminar training and the Latin word for "it is." From 1971 through 1986, an estimated 700,000 people took Est training, after which time Werner Erhard left the country and subsequently sold Est technology to a group known as the Landmark Forum. In its wake, Harry Rosenberg, Erhard's brother, is running the Landmark Education Corp. (LEC) out of San Francisco, and doing a whale of a business out of 42 offices in 11 countries.

Est teaches people to "get it", a concept gleaned from Alan Watts, who taught small groups on his houseboat in Sausalito. Recognizing a good thing, Erhard rented hotel ballrooms and started packing 'em in. Using the Zen master approach, sudden enlightenment *(satori)* was taught through a combination of master-disciple authoritarianism and meditation *(dhyana)*. In addition, Est unabashedly draws on a host of other sources in the burgeoning human potential market, such as Maxwell Maltz's *Psycho-cybernetics*, Napoleon Hill's *Think and Grow Rich*, existentialism and motivational psychology. Est promises to "blow your mind" by rewiring the consciousness, overcoming negativity and personal empowerment.

Parapsychology

It is surprising how many psychologists take a dim view of the majority of New Age therapies, passing them off, at best, as pseudoscience or psychobabble, while at the same time endorsing the classical psychoanalytical approach put forward by Sigmund Freud, 110 years ago, a known cocaine addict.

While the bulk of New Age therapies are indeed controversial, it is also true that modern psychology is anything but an exact science. Were it otherwise, perhaps there wouldn't be so many people drawn to the metaphysical and cult fringes. Either way, people are not merely derailed sex machines and it is human nature to inquire beyond established paradigms.

Psi, or psy, is the 23rd letter of the Greek alphabet (*psykhe*) which means soul, hence, psychology is knowledge of the soul. Nevertheless, many psychologists do not believe that psi even exists and that parapsychology, meaning transcendent knowledge of the soul, is pure bunk. Nevertheless, in a 1979 study of 1,100 American university professors, Wagner and Monnet found that 34% did believe that ESP is real or, at least, likely. About 70% of other academics agreed. (Attitudes of College Professors toward Extra-sensory perception. *Zetetic Scholar*)

As to the scientific validity of an inner child, reactive mind, parts, time-lines and such, in fairness there is not greater proof of an id or superego either. It is merely a case of semantics. But it is not the jargon that's important, it's the results. For psychiatrists and psychologists to turn their collective backs on what appears to be far out stuff, is like biologists and chemists refusing to use microscopes. The future may be conditioned by the past, but it is not confined by it. No single discipline holds the patent on truth: everybody does.

Psychotherapy

Psychotherapy is the treatment of psychological disorders, such as phobias or depression, as well as behavioral difficulties such as drug abuse. Psychotherapy falls into four main categories: psychodynamic, phenomenological, cognitive and behavioral.

Psychodynamic therapy assumes that emotional disorders are the result of repressed childhood conflicts that surface in adult situations. Treatment is usually Freudian in approach, sometimes combined with dream interpretation and word association. Some of the variations include *analytic psychology* (Carl Jung), *holistic therapy* (Karen Horney) and *transactional analysis* (Eric Berne).

Phenomenological therapy resolves false values and emotional disorders resulting from distortions relating to society. The focus is on current happenings, rather than childhood experiences. Variations include *client-centered therapy* (Carl Rogers), *gestalt therapy* (Fritz Perl) and *existential* approaches (Abraham Maslow and Rollo May).

Cognitive therapy treats emotional disorders as being the result of irrational beliefs or perceptions. For example: Loss of self esteem because of unemployment. The approach is to reinstate more realistic personal evaluations. Variations include the *personal construct theory* (George Kelly), *rational-emotive therapy* (Albert Ellis) and *cognitive therapy* (Aaron T. Beck).

Behavioral therapy, popularized by Joseph Wolpe, is based on the assumption that conditioned responses or habits can be modified as a learned behavior. Treatment of phobias, for example, involves learning how to relax instead of reacting fearfully. Role playing is also used in overcoming specific social situations.

Aside from the traditional methods of psychotherapy, there are several New Age approaches, most of which are dimly viewed. This doesn't mean they don't work, but, rather, that they haven't yet gained acceptance by the majority of mental health specialists. In general, those immersed in standard practice don't give much credibility to any New Age system involving repressed memory, aliens, reincarnation or any other aspect of metaphysics. Indeed, some go so far as to disclaim anything that involves religion or a belief in God. Invariably, the establishment takes the position that any system of treatment is invalid without scientific proof that it works. But, if that yardstick was universally applied, most of them would end up shucking corn.

"To society's loss, there is an alarming laxity within the mental health professions when it comes to monitoring, commenting on, and educating the public about what is good therapy, what is negligent behavior by trained professionals, and what is or borders on quackery." (Margaret Thaler Singer and Janja Lalich. *Crazy Therapies*)

Scrying

Scrying has its roots in antiquity, such as staring into the flashing blade of a sword or scrying pools, into which one gazes intently in search of visions. In olden days a saucer of dark oil was used. In recent times the crystal ball has taken over, but the mechanics of it all are the same. There is nothing mystical about glass globes or supposedly sacred oil. There is, however, something extraordinary that happens when one's attention is sufficiently arrested that he becomes amenable to that which, otherwise, would escape attention.

Just about anything will work, a doorknob even, just so long as strain upon the eyes is avoided, such as happens when looking into a flame. The trick isn't to stare at the object, but to let your mind focus beyond it, or through it if you will. The object itself is only a lens of sorts.

In classical definitions, scrying is a form of automatism in which the unconscious mind sends images to the conscious mind. Some research suggests that at least 1 person in 20 have the ability, which may be refined by practice. An easy way to get started, let's say with a cup of dark coffee, is to gently concentrate until the surface absorbs your attention. When you've got that much, the trick is to "go into it" by focusing deeper. You'll know when it happens. Now you're ready to ask what you will, but you must do it without jarring your mind-state. Just go with the flow, as it were, and don't charge too much.

Spiritualism

Dr. A. Russel Wallace (1823-1903), the co-discoverer of the Theory of Evolution, with Darwin, openly declared the "science of Spiritualism" to rank with all of the other sciences. Sir William F. Barret (1848-1926) many years Professor of Experimental Physics at the University of Ireland, publicly advanced the statement of survival and spirit intercourse. Noted British physicist, Sir William Crookes (1832-1919), the discoverer of thallium and inventor of the radiometer, among many other devices, set out to debunk Spiritualism. But, after many years research with such mediums as D.D.Home and Florence Cook, who repeatedly produced full figure materializations under rigorous scientific test conditions, he said: "Thirty years have passed since I published an account of experiments tending to show that outside our scientific knowledge there exists a force exercised by intelligence differing from the ordinary intelligence common to mortals. I have nothing to retract. I adhere to my already published statements." (Presidential address to the British Association at Bristol 1898).

Lord Raleigh (1842-1919) an eminent British physicist, an authority on sound vibration and the co-discoverer of Argon, contributed greatly to the 1882 Society for Psychical Research, becoming its president in 1919. The Society for Psychical Research was founded in 1882 by Sir William Barret. Notable contributions have been made to the Society by F.W.Myers (1834-1901), whose classic *Human Personality and its Survival of Bodily Death* established psychical research as an organized science.

Alan Kardek of France (1804-1869) wrote several books, such as *The Medium's Book*, that outlined the bases of spiritual mediumship and had a profound influence in Brazil in what came to be known as *spiritism*, now a widespread religion. William Stanton Moses (1839-1892), an Oxford M.A. and clergyman of the Church of England, produced automatic spirit-writing which was published as *Spirit Teachings*. William T. Stead (1849-1912), did spirit writing and formed *Julia's Bureau*, a newspaper column to which thousands of people wrote. Lord Dowding, who commanded the Royal Air Force during the Battle of Britain, became an indefatigable champion of spiritualism after obtaining messages from dead airmen who were able to give evidence of their survival. Sir Oliver Lodge wrote *Raymond* after communicating with his son by that name, and in 1908 and 1913 he stated before the British Association of Physicists that he was convinced of survival beyond death.

I could add another hundred prominent names, but you get the idea. Dr. Cornel Hart of Duke University, in 1952 said: "The brain is an instrument by which the consciousness expresses itself, rather than being a generator which produces consciousness." He went on to say that the essential aspect of individualized consciousness is that of being able to act at a distance from the brain. Meanwhile, the U.S. military has recently spent a million dollars on distance viewing.

In any case, psychic phenomena and the pursuit of one's spirituality is running swiftly with the times. No longer is it a freak of nature, or necessarily an imbalance brought on by hypnosis, anesthesia or aberration. It is the birthright of a new generation, the result of meditation, education and, above all, the natural progression of man.

"The day must come when all men will appraise themselves as instruments only, will place their proper identification in a world of spiritual beings. They will be what they are because they exist, but they will always know their true existence is infinite, eternal, and changeless." (U.S.Anderson in *The Secret of Secrets*)

We are physical-spiritual beings. From the list of nebulae that shapes the auric moment of conception, the elements of our genetic past combine in embryonic growth, like the stalk of a plant, then as a fish, then as an amphibious creature and, finally, as a human being, whose earliest recollections are climbing trees and eating raw carrots. In the fullness of time, like a butterfly emerging from a cocoon, man is reborn in the world of spirit, caressed by mother nature as she severs the ties to the dark womb of before. All things considered, it would be a wonder if we could not communicate with our loved ones, those who are ever only a thought away.

The world of spirit is like a hot stove:
even a blind man can feel its heat.

Theosophy

The term Theosophy combines *theos*, which is Greek for God, with *sophia*, wisdom. The principal founder, Madame Helena Petrovna Blavatsky (1831-1891), was born in Russia of German parents. Blavatsky, both well-read and well-traveled, claimed that she had been trained by mahatmas and adepts in Tibet, India and Egypt, who instilled her with the secrets of ancient wisdom and the charge to unite the world under the *Great White Brotherhood.*

After becoming a United States citizen and championing the spiritualist's cause, in 1875 she founded the Theosophical Society in New York, together with Henry Steele Olcott, (1832-1907) a lawyer and writer, and W.Q. Judge (1851-96). According to Blavatsky, the objective was "to reconcile all religions, sects and nations under a common system of ethics, based on eternal verities."

Theosophy attracted huge followings in Europe and America, including Rudulf Steiner, who later founded the Anthroposophical Society, and Annie Besant who, while leading the movement in Europe and Asia, founded the Order of the Star of India and promoted Jiddu Krishnamurti as world mentor.

Theosophical mysticism draws upon a host of sources, the philosophies of Plato (427-347 BC) and Plotinus (204-270) and Jakob Boehme (1575-1624), together with some of the teachings found in Zoroastrianism, Manichaeism, Hinduism and Gnosticism, to name but a few.

Plotinus elevated Plato's philosophy to that of a religious point of view, arguing that humans have the ability to acquire transcelestial knowledge of the One ultimate principle, and that souls could indeed return as a result of ascetic morality, contemplation and self-surrender. Gnosticism professes secret knowledge based upon ancient Egyptian and Greek mystery cults, Zoroastrianism and the Jewish Kabbalah. Manichaeism, from 3rd century Babylonia, is based on the endeavors of Mani who, following divine revelations in which he was declared the "Messenger of Truth," set about to combine the teachings of Jesus, Zoroaster and Buddha into a single Gnostic dualist religion.

Putting all this together, and more, Madame Blavatsky proclaimed that the tenets of Theosophy were grounded in secret knowledge of an immutable principle that transcends human understanding; she upheld reincarnation and karma, and the revelation of one's identity within the Over-Soul. In her book, *The Key to Theosophy*, Blavatsky said that one must renounce self in favor of strict morality and "must be either a philanthropist, or a scholar, a searcher into Aryan and other old literature, or a psychic student."

Blavatsky's major works are *Isis Unveiled*, 2 vols. (1877); *The Secret Doctrine*, 2 vols. (1888); *The Key to Theosophy* (1889) and *The Voice of Silence* (1889).

Transcendental Meditation
Transcendental Meditation is the 1956 brainchild of Maharishi Mahesh Yogi, who teaches 4,000 year old Hindu meditation techniques throughout the world. According to some of the alleged 4 million followers, *TM* will elevate one's consciousness to a state of enlightened bliss, in which one experiences *dharma*, the ideal way of life. Part of the secret is repeating a personal mantra, often the name of a Hindu deity.

In spite of the fact that all meditation is to a degree transcendental, TM goes a giant step further: "Over 500 scientific studies conducted at more than 200 universities and research institutions in 33 countries have documented the benefits of Transcendental Meditation for mind, body, behavior, and environment." In spite of the plethora of supposedly hard scientific evidence, there are skeptics who equate TM's evaluations with the fox guarding the hen house.

The Maharishi University of Management in Fairfield, Iowa, offers "a full range of academic disciplines for successful management of all fields of life." And, "As a student at Maharishi University of Management you discover that when you experience transcendental consciousness, you are experiencing the ocean of consciousness or intelligence, which is at the basis of the life and evolution of the universe."

Well and good, but anyone who has seen TV documentaries of TMers bouncing around in the lotus position, trying to levitate, have cause for pause. In fairness, with so many followers, if one listens long enough anything can be heard, including their claims to invisibility, and the so-called *Maharishi effect* in which: "collective meditation causes changes in a fundamental, unified physical field, and that those changes radiate into society and affect all aspects of society for the better."

Cutting through the hype, does TM, or any form of meditation for that matter, really induce relaxation and, possibly, elevated awareness? Of course it does. So does prayer, quietude, serene music and rolling surf.

Trance messages

Trance is one of the easiest things to fake and one of the most difficult to do well. It does happen, however. Andrew Jackson Davies, the Poughkeepsie seer, dictated *Nature's Divine Revelations* while in trance. David Duguid's historic romance *Hafed, Prince of Persia* and its sequel *Hermes, a Disciple of Jesus* was given the same way. *Telka*, Patience Worth's poem of about 65,000 words, took only 35 hours to dictate, while wide awake, answering the phone and smoking. So much for fluttering eyelids and weird voices.

Light trance is akin to inspirational speech, in that the medium puts his mouth in gear and his mind in neutral. It is like listening to yourself talk, without knowing what comes next. The words simply stream out of you; you're aware of them, but not consciously involved in the content. In deep trance, the stream of words becomes inaudible to you and you aren't even a spectator any more.

"Take no thought how or what ye shall speak:
for it shall be given you in that same hour what ye shall speak.
For it is not ye that speak,

but the Spirit of your Father which speaketh in you."
(Matthew 10:19,20)

Many people are capable of speaking while in trance, of course not everyone dictates books in the process and very few indeed are founts of wisdom. Being in trance is absolutely no guarantee that one is inspired, although most presume otherwise. The ego, the subconscious, and spirit, all work on the same wavelength.

Perhaps, one gets only what he deserves. I wish it were otherwise for those who come to a medium with overriding earnestness. The fact is: "You pays your money and you takes your chances." It is said that "by their works ye shall know them." Fair and good. If someone starts bantering something about "many moons ago," or labors with a pitiful Chinese accent, or starts talking about a hand maiden of Cleopatra, grab your checkbook and scoot.

For the beginner, going into trance isn't too hard, but having sufficient faith to get on with the job is. No amount of earnestness for the work of spirit will overcome the initial fear of making a fool of oneself. There comes a point, however, when you have to pee or get off the pot. No doubt, by this time you have been hearing stuff as it streams through your mind; now you have to have the courage to will your voice to the words, without getting further into the act. Don't edit, just let it flow. So what if you end up feeling foolish? Aren't we all?

For those receiving a trance address, it is important to remember that the instrument at work is the mind of the medium. Invariably, the words used to express the message are limited to the medium's vocabulary. During deep trance, however, anything is possible, language unknown to the medium to language unknown to anybody - which is not to be confused with the gobbledygook that passes for speaking in tongues. After all, if the whole idea is for spirit to communicate, why would they bother with anything that doesn't make sense?

In closing this section it is worth mentioning that there is a tendency for people to exaggerate the worth of what they are "getting" and their own importance in the scheme of things. Guide worship is appalling. Undue homage to a medium is no better. Presuming too much is the rope we hang by, and, very often, being needy is the same as being greedy; only the medium of exchange is different. Finally, in the name of common sense, never ever presume spirit. It's too easy to do and too hard to get out of.

The words that I speak unto you,
they are spirit and they are life."
(John 6:63)

Voodoo

Voodoo is a religious system found in Haiti and the West Indies. It was brought from Africa on slave ships of the 17th to 19th centuries. It combines African and native West Indian religion with French Catholic liturgy and sacraments. Vodu is an African word relating to spirits and god. Voodoo deities, called loa, are spirits of nature or ancestors, which are supposed to make themselves known during special ceremonies presided over by Voodoo priests, called houngans. The loa are divided into two groups: the rada, which is generally helpful, and the petro, which is malevolent. The petro priest, or bocor, is feared for his supposed ability to turn an entranced person into a zombie, then to be animated by whatever elemental spirits are under the bocor's control. But what passes for black magic is really the outcome of hypnotic frenzy or temporarily immobilizing poisons.

Where zombies are concerned, everything is based on heightened suggestibility, the effects of which can be profound. In order to be rendered into an apparent mindless state, one must believe firstly that it is possible and, secondly, that he is defenseless against it. In certain hypnotic experiments in exteriorization of the senses, when hair was removed from a sleeping subject, then glued to a ball, when awake the subject reacted when the hair was pulled away from the ball. One can imagine the extent to which voodoo dolls and pins might similarly impale the mind of a believer.

CHAPTER FIFTEEN

SANCTITY

Fraudulence

The term occult comes from the Latin word *occultus*, which means hidden. It generally refers to any spiritual or magical powers, including psychic discernment, which, until recent times, incurred the wrath of the Catholic Church. In 1483, Pope Sixtus IV endorsed the Spanish Inquisition which, up until 175 years ago, tortured and killed 32,000 people. Not to be outdone, in the Netherlands, Charles V murdered another 100,000. In 1955, in Ojinaga, Mexico, with the sanction of the town priest and mayor, rumor has it that there was a public witch burning.

The British Witchcraft Act of 1735, the Vagrancy Act of 1824 and Section 308 of the Criminal Code relegated any form of mediumship to that of fortune-telling, for which no amount of evidence was admissible as a defense. Those so impugned got a fine or 3 months in jail which, in that day and age, effectively ruined many people, most of them being ladies. The Witchcraft Act was repealed in 1951 and replaced by the Fraudulent Mediums Act.

A 1988 study by the National Research Council summed things up by declaring that over the past 130 years there has been no scientific proof in support of parapsychological phenomena. They did admit, however, to finding "probabilistic anomalies" that defied explanation. Geesh. According to The Committee for Scientific Investigation of Claims of the Paranormal, based in Buffalo, N.Y., even an amateur magician can deceive a psychic investigator.

"One occult hoaxer had astonishing success. And he so bemused those that he met that two daily newspapers, when taken together, pictured him as being 'tall, short, slim, bald, dark haired, and clean-shaven with a beard." If this bemused Cyril Hoskins, he must have laughed all the way to the bank when *The Third Eye*, a book he had written in the guise of a Tibetan Lama, Lobsang Rampa, became a best seller. He claimed that on the morning of his eighth birthday three lamas bored a hole in his forehead and that this operation was performed while he was fully awake, and from then on he had psychic vision. Tibetan scholars hired a detective who discovered that he was a plumber's son from Devon and not the son of a nobleman who had entered a lamasery as a child. His publisher summed it up with: "It is no mean feat to have hoodwinked the world for fifteen months." (Fred Archer. *Exploring the Psychic World*)

Critics of spiritualism quickly point to the Hydesville incident, in which the Fox sisters cracked their toes to mimic messages from beyond. There are conjurers of all sorts who defraud the public, while others, like Houdini, was hell-bent on making a bigger name for himself by exposing his contemporaries, but, upon passing, said would relay the message "believe" through the noted medium Arthur Ford.

The way to catch someone prancing about in the dark of a séance room is to sprinkle cornstarch to capture their footprints. One way to read the message in sealed envelopes is to render them transparent with quick-drying lighter fluid. The tricks are endless and sometimes, as in the case of the Chesterfield conspiracy, to the profit of an entire town. Flammarion, in his book *Mysterious Psychic Forces*, said: "One may lay it down as a principal that all professional mediums cheat. But they do not always cheat; and they possess real, undeniable psychic powers."

In something of a defense, it is claimed that unconscious fraud by a medium can be induced by the sitters' thoughts. Well, maybe. Even if there is a connection between the medium and spirit, what's to stop him from helping out a little, or a lot?

Everyone knows there are hucksters out there, playing at every con game ever invented. Still, there is a deep yearning for closeness with the sublime, our maker and the truth such as we might perceive it. In the final analysis there is no substitute for either common sense or uncommon sense, the inexplicable and the inspirational. It is all part and parcel of what makes us and our quest so wonderful. But the best, invariably, demands the best of us, and there are no reliable short cuts that I know of, no matter how enthusiastic one might be or how much he can afford. So, we push on, sometimes getting a helping hand and the encouragement to believe yet one more time, if only in ourselves. But, try as we might, screw-ups are inevitable. That's human nature, and so are the excuses: either "the devil made me do it," or it was "the will of God."

> "You will never have it 'all together'
> that's like trying to eat 'once and for all.'"
> (Dr. Robert Anthony)

Breakthrough

Like the fable, there is mystical treasure at the end of a rainbow, whether it spans a thousand yards or a thousand lifetimes. The treasure is a transcendent state of realization, perhaps not an oracle of all time, but surely a revelation within one's capacity to embrace it. In the case of Mozart: "When all goes well with me... the thoughts come streaming in upon me most fluently; whence or how is more than I can tell." For Beethoven: "Inspiration is for me that mysterious state in which the entire world seems to form a vast harmony, when every sentiment, every thought re-echoes within me, when all the forces of nature become instruments for me."

It is this that compels us to seek by every means, the rational and irrational, the scientific and the metaphysical. If the answer could be found in logic alone, we would idolize

Plato; if in pure science then perhaps Thales of Miletus; if esoteric, then Spinoza. But no single person can provide a definitive answer. Nevertheless, whatever the truth of it, and however couched, the only redeeming solution is the one we find for ourselves, which momentary satisfaction is only a stepping stone unto the next reality.

Strike, Thou the Master, we Thy keys,
The anthem of the destinies!
The minor of Thy loftier strain,
Our hearts shall breathe the old refrain,
Thy will be done.
(John Greenleaf Whittier)

The End

Bibliography

Adams, James. Engines of War. 1990.

Agee, Doris. Edgar Cayce on ESP. Paperback Library 64-122.

Anthony, Dr. Robert. Sayings by… Berkley Books, NY. ASBN 0-425- 09572-X.

Alder, Vera Stanley. The Finding of the Third Eye. Alder, Rider & Co., London.

Anderson, U.S. The Secret of Secrets and Three Magic Words. Wilshire Book Company.

Archer, Fred. Exploring the Psychic World. Paperback Library. 53-648.

Asimov, Isaac. The Clock We Live On. 1963. Inside the Atom. 1974.

Atack, Jon. A Piece of Blue Sky : Scientology, Dianetics, and L. Ron Hubbard Exposed. New York, NY: Carol Publishing Group. 1990.

Bandler, Richard. Using Your Brain for a Change. 1985

Baum, Joseph L. The Beginner's Handbook of Dowsing. 1974.

Beyerstein, Barry. The Encyclopedia of the Paranormal.

Blackmore, Susan J. Dying to Live: Near-death Experiences. Prometheus Books, 1993.

Blavasky, Helen.P. The Secret Doctrine. 1888.

Bogue, Donald J. Principles of Demography.

Bradley, D.B. & R.A. Psychic Phenomena. Paperback Library 65-666.

Brandon, S.G. The Judgment of the Dead. 1967.

Bucke, Richard Maurice, MD. Cosmic Consciousness. E.P.Dutton & Co. Inc. 1966.

Calvin, W.H. and Ojemann, G.A. Inside the Brain. 1980.

Canon, Alexander. Powers That Be.

Carey, G.W. and Perry, I.E. Perry. The Zodiac and the Salts of Salvation.

Carrington, Herewood. MD. The Coming Science, and Phantasms of the Dead.

Charroux, Robert. One Hundred Thousand Years of Man's Unknown History.

Crawford, W.J. MD. The Reality of Psychic Phenomena.

Cummings, Geraldine. The Scripts of Cleophas.

Cunningham, C. Introduction to Asteroids. 1987.

Delfano, M.M.. The Living Prophets.

Ebon, Martin. Test Your ESP. Wilshire Book Company 58-13650

Edwards, Harry. The Mediumship of Jack Webber. The Healer Publishing Company Ltd.

Ehrlich, Dr. Paul R. The Population Bomb.

Findlay, J. Arthur. MBE, On the edge of the Etheric. The Rock of Truth. The Unfolding Universe. The Psychic Stream. The Curse of Ignorance. A Guide for the Development of Mediumship.

Fodor, Dr. Nandor. Encyclopedia of Psychic Science. 1934. 1966 University Books, Inc.

Freud, Sigmund. The Interpretation of Dreams. (Eng. trans. 1913).

Hubbard, L.Ronald. Dianetics. 1950. The American Saint Hill Organization, LA.

Hyslop, James Hervey. Borderland of Psychical Research. H.B.Turner; G.P. Putnam's Sons

Hyslop, James Hervey. Enigmas of Psychical Research. H.B.Turner; G.P. Putnam's Sons

Randi, James. Flim-Flam! Prometheus Books. 1982.

James, Tad and Woodsmall, Wyatt. Timeline Therapy and the Basis of Personality. 1986.

Kannan, A., Impact of Theosophy and Science. 1971.

Kardec, Allan. The Spirit's Book.

Kennedy, C. The Divination Handbook. 1990.

Kerboull, Jean. Voodoo and Magic Practices. 1978.

Kilduff, Marshall, and Javers, Ron, The Suicide Cult. 1978.

Kittler, Glenn D. Edgar Cayce on the Dead Sea Scrolls.

Korzipsky, Alfred. Science and Sanity. 1933.

Kramer, Edward L. Pathways to Power.

Leakey, Mary. Africa's Vanishing Art. Doubleday, 1983.

Lorrain, Paul. Electromagnetic Fields and Waves. 1988.

Lindsay, Hal. The Late Great Planet Earth.

Lodge, Sir Oliver. Phantom Walls. Hodder and Stoughton Ltd., London.

Long, Max Freedom. The Secret Science Behind Miracles.

Maltz, Maxwell. Psycho-cybernetics.

Meadows, DH & DL; Randers, J and Behrensill, W.W. The Limits to Growth. A report for the Club of Rome's project on the predicament of mankind.

Myers, Podmore & Gurney. Phantasms of the Living.

Melton, J.G. The Encyclopedic Handbook of Cults in America. 1986.

Miller, George. The Magic Number Seven, Plus or Minus Two. 1970.

Moses, W. Stainton. Spirit Teachings. London Spiritualist Alliance.

Neilhardt, John G. Black Elk Speaks. Pocket Books 671-7236.

Nordmann, Charles. The Metamorphosis of the Stars and Their Temperature.

Ostrander, Sheila and Schroeder, Lynn. Psychic Discoveries Behind the Iron Curtain.

Over, Raymond van. ESP and the Clairvoyants. Award Books. A672S.

Owen, Rev. G. Vale. Life Beyond the Veil (5 volumes).

Pressman, Steven. Outrageous Betrayal: The Dark Journey of Werner Erhard From est to Exile, St. Martin's Press, NY. 1993.

Schure, E. From Sphinx to Christ: an occult history.

Patterson, Stephen and Meyer, Marvin. Translation of The Gospel of Thomas.

Rainey, F. Archeological Investigations in Central Alaska. 1940.

Raso, Jack. Alternative Healthcare: A Comprehensive Guide. Prometheus Books, 1994.

Rossi, Earnest. The Psychobiology of Mind-Body Healing. 1986

Singer, Margaret Thaler and Lalich, Janja Lalich. Crazy Therapies.

Smith, Steven S. and Hallowell, Davis. Hearing. 1983.

Snell, Richard. Clinical Anatomy of the Eye. 1989.

Steiger, Brad. The Aquarian Revelations.

Thomas, Rev. C. Creighton. Beyond Life's Sunset. Precognition and Survival. From Life to Life. Life Beyond Death with Evidence.

Trimble, Russell. The Encyclopedia of the Paranormal. Prometheus Books, 1996.

Utts, Professor Jessica. University of California: An Assessment of the Evidence for Psychic Functioning.

Velikovsky, Immanuel. Earth in Upheaval. Dell 2303.

Waite, Margaret. The Mystic Sciences.

Wallace, William. Life of Arthur Schopenhauer. 1970.

Williams, Margery. The Velveteen Rabbit. Avon-0-380-00255-8. 1975.

Wise, S.P., Higher Brain Functions. 1987.

Wolf, Ernest. Treating the Self. 1988.

Wright, G.F. The Date of the Glacial Period

Zurer, Pamela S. The Chemistry of Vision.

ABOUT THE AUTHOR

Thirty years ago Kim Vincent was host and writer of a 33 week television series entitled "This Psychic World." About the same time, after coming across his lecture papers at U.B.C., a Doubleday representative asked Vincent to write an encyclopedia on parapsychology. Since then he has written eight books and has three more in the works, during which time he managed a construction and land development company, an architectural design practice, a vinyl window factory and a pewter foundry. In short: Things have not been dull. Kim Vincent says: "If I've got it figured right, I'm now on my third life, doing what I love most."

Tymly *Books*

www.ingramcontent.com/pod-product-compliance
Lightning Source LLC
Chambersburg PA
CBHW060244290526
45789CB00001B/191